The Dialogic Self

The Dialogic Self

Reconstructing Subjectivity in Woolf, Lessing, and Atwood

Roxanne J. Fand

SUP

Selinsgrove: Susquehanna University Press
London: Associated University Presses

Associated University Presses
440 Forsgate Drive
Cranbury, NJ 08512

Associated University Presses
16 Barter Street
London WC1A 2AH, England

Associated University Presses
P.O. Box 338, Port Credit
Mississauga, Ontario
Canada L5G 4L8

The paper used in this publication meets the requirements
of the American National Standard for Permanence of Paper
for Printed Library Materials Z39.48-1984.]

Library of Congress Cataloging-in-Publication Data

Fand, Roxanne J., 1937–
    The dialogic self : reconstructing subjectivity in Woolf, Lessing, and Atwood / Roxanne J. Fand.
        p.   cm.
    Includes bibliographical references and index.
    ISBN 1-57591-022-5 (alk. paper)
    1. English fiction—20th century—History and criticism.
    2. Woolf, Virginia, 1882–1941—Criticism and interpretation.
    3. Lessing, Doris May, 1919– —Criticism and interpretation.
    4. Atwood, Margaret Eleanor, 1939– —Criticism and interpretation.
    5. English fiction—Women authors—History and criticism. 6. Women and literature—England—History—20th century. 7. Women and literature—Canada—History—20th century. 8. Subjectivity in literature. 9. Self in literature. I. Title.
PR888.W6F36   1999
823'.91099287—dc21   98-16572
                                                                                    CIP

PRINTED IN THE UNITED STATES OF AMERICA

To the memory of my parents,

Hyman and Mary Gershuny

If I am not for myself, who will be?
But if I am for myself alone, what am I?
And if not now, then when?

—Rabbi Hillel

Acknowledgments

Writing this book has been a truly dialogic enterprise. I am most grateful to Jay Kastely, who was my closest reader from the earliest drafts, and whose integrity and attunement to my vision fostered the kind of critical dialogue called for. Jay's recommendation of my work resulted in a grant from the Research Corporation of the University of Hawaii, which enabled me to concentrate on writing for a year free of teaching duties. I thank him and RCUH for that boon. Another mentor and supportive reader has been Craig Howes, who, as a fellow Canadian knowledgeable about Margaret Atwood's work, contributed valuable insights. Craig's interests in satire and dialogism intersected fruitfully with my project. For years, both Jay and Craig generously offered their time and thought, from practical advice to stimulating discussion, which I shall always remember with gratitude.

I feel privileged to have worked with other colleagues in the Department of English at UH, a community of diverse scholars in touch with national and international currents of thought as well as the island spirit of Aloha in their collegiality. I note with thanks Valerie Wayne for her ideas on feminism and deconstruction, and Miriam Fuchs for hers on modernism. Both Val and Miriam led me to rethink Woolf's concept of androgyny. My personal and professional conversations with Judith Kellogg on feminism, selfhood, and even the Arthurian legend (relevant to the discussion of Percival) were supportive and very much appreciated. Gay Sibley asked probing questions and ratified some of my ideas in her own work, while Arnold Edelstein sharpened my focus on formal issues, and I am grateful to both. And I have to thank Kathy Ferguson, of the political science department, for contributing her idea of "mobile subjectivities" and for her perceptive comments on my work.

I fondly remember Alan MacGregor, sadly stricken with illness in his prime, who encouraged me to write while he was at UH, and also the late Joe Chadwick, who was always helpful and contributed insights on modernism and *The Waves* in particular. I miss both and shall always feel grateful to them.

Besides those I have known personally in our island community are the many I have encountered in print who have stimulated my thinking. Foremost are the authors themselves—Virginia Woolf, Doris Lessing, and Margaret Atwood—whose lives and work struck a responsive chord in me that continues to reverberate. All others cited, even if only mentioned in a note, have been importantly engaged in this dialogue, and I am very appreciative. I also thank Hans Feldmann and the Editorial Board of Susquehanna University Press for recognizing the worth of my manuscript, and their reviewer for giving helpful advice.

I am grateful to my long-suffering family, who stood behind my pursuit of this work when they might have wished me to be more attentive to them. My husband, Richard, was particularly encouraging. He and our three daughters—Raya, Daria, and Lani—enabled me to realize dialogue in action in our family life. And my sisters, Lee and Grace, who live too far away, but who are close to me in spirit, have provided the true sisterhood that is part of my own dialogic self. I am deeply indebted to all my sources.

Contents

CONTENTS

Abbreviations

The following abbreviations are used in the text for some frequently cited works. References to other works are given in the notes in short-title format.

Anton Chekhov:

"TD"   "The Darling," in *The Tales of Chekhov: "The Darling" and Other Stories*, trans. Constance Garnett (New York: Macmillan, 1928).

Virginia Woolf:

MB   *Moments of Being: Unpublished Autobiographical Writings*, ed. Jeanne Schulkind (London: Chatto and Windus for Sussex University Press, 1976).

MD   *Mrs. Dalloway* (New York: Harcourt Brace Jovanovich, 1953).

R   *A Room of One's Own* (New York: Harcourt Brace Jovanovich, 1957).

TTL   *To the Lighthouse* (New York: Harcourt Brace Jovanovich, 1955).

W   *The Waves*, in *"Jacob's Room" and "The Waves"* (New York: Harcourt, Brace & World, 1959).

WD   *A Writer's Diary: Being Extracts from the Diary of Virginia Woolf*, ed. Leonard Woolf (London: Hogarth, 1953).

Doris Lessing:

FGC   *The Four-Gated City*, vol. 5 of *Children of Violence* (New York: Bantam, 1970).

GH   *Going Home* (New York: Popular Library, 1957).

GN   *The Golden Notebook* (New York: Bantam, 1962).

LL   *Landlocked*, vol. 4 of *Children of Violence* (New York: Plume, 1958).

MQ   *Martha Quest*, vol. 1 of *Children of Violence* (New York: Plume, 1952).

P   *Prisons We Choose to Live Inside* (London: Cape, 1987).

PM   *A Proper Marriage*, vol. 2 of *Children of Violence* (New York: Plume, 1952).

RBS   *The Ripple Before the Storm*, vol. 3 of *Children of Violence* (New York: Plume, 1958).

"SPV"   "The Small Personal Voice," in *A Small Personal Voice: Essays, Reviews, Interviews,* ed. Paul Schlueter (New York: Knopf, 1974).

"STD"   "The Story of Two Dogs," in *The Sun Between Their Feet*, vol. 2 of *Doris Lessing's Collected African Stories* (London: Michael Joseph, 1954).

Margaret Atwood:

C   *Margaret Atwood: Conversations,* ed. Earl G. Ingersoll (Princeton, N.J.: Ontario Review Press, 1990).

LBM   *Life Before Man* (New York: Simon and Schuster, 1976).

LO   *Lady Oracle* (New York: Simon and Schuster, 1976).

"TP"   "The Page," in *Murder in the Dark: Short Fictions and Prose Poems* (Toronto: Coach House, 1983).

S   *Survival: A Thematic Guide to Canadian Literature* (Toronto: Anansi, 1972).

SW   *Second Words: Selected Critical Prose* (Toronto: Anansi, 1982).

Introduction:
Dialogism and the Female Self

IN THE WAKE OF THE POSTMODERN IDENTITY CRISIS: THE WAVE OF DIALOGISM

As the twentieth century draws to a close, the "New World Order" seems to be more of a disorder, with power centers shifting and the marginalized rising along new fronts, as if to fulfill Christ's prophecy that the meek shall inherit the earth. It was not until the advent of the modern era that the empowerment of the meek was made possible by the questioning of centralized authority. Once revolution took the high ground of the historical process in the West (e.g., the Reformation and the Scientific Revolution against the hegemony of the Catholic Church, the Industrial Revolution and the rise of the middle class against the aristocracy) the romanticizing of the individual became a powerful discourse, especially in the United States, where ideologies of freedom, equality, and democracy were poured on the newly anointed head of the Common Man, no longer a member of the faceless meek but now invested with the human dignity of an individual face and voice. No longer to be patronized as a child, he would assume the responsibility of determining his destiny democratically by negotiating with equals. Or so the myth went.

But if the playing field seemed leveled, the old power games continued, newly sanctified by the ruling discourse of rugged individualism. Those who have used their freedom of opportunity to get ahead economically have played a double game of consolidating their interests through the government while decrying that government whenever it seemed in danger of actually representing the interests of the meek, who, like the poor, somehow remain ever with us. For example, the old saying that money talks has been legitimized by U.S. courts in granting the right of freedom of speech

15

to the money that buys the media (and through it the government). Michel Foucault's work has traced the ways old power games continue by appropriating the newest discourses,[1] a recent example of which is that many former leaders of Communist regimes quickly changed their stripes and took charge of the new reformist governments. Capitalism, the system of individual economic competition that undermines equality, seems to have won out over Communism, the system of economic collectivity that undermines the individual. Either way the meek lose.

But the old labels and the confrontational rhetoric of the Cold War have lost their meaning in the ensuing New World Disorder, where a new movement is taking shape to diffuse (or defuse) the old centers of power—and even the way the old power games are played. Since no one knows what to expect, or where the boundaries are drawn, or how to define the entities one is dealing with anymore—such as whether a corporation is really American or Japanese, or whether, ironically, the winning superpower has the influence it once had—and since technology in this Information Age has cut across old boundaries bringing contacts through trade and cultural exchange rather than military conquest, the emphasis has been turning increasingly toward negotiation rather than confrontation on every level of human interaction from the personal to the political. We are witnessing peace breaking out in the Middle East and elsewhere between what seemed to be implacable opponents.

On the other hand, new power vacuums and confusion have increased fears and precipitated conflicts as people clutch at old ideologies or identities for empowerment, some newly taken out of mothballs and dusty history, as in Yugoslavia. For there are many dangers in this rapidly changing world where new contacts and conditions outpace the human ability to adapt, creating culture shock, disorientation, and identity crises worldwide. The impulse of "the modern" to overthrow the old has always provoked a counterrush to nostalgia, and both change and reaction against it have been intensifying with every generation to the point where, as Kenneth Gergen phrases it, the self is saturated with possibilities.[2] He cites numerous examples of how changes in ordinary life seem to bear out postmodern academic theories that disperse and destabilize individual identity in the pressure cooker of cultural pluralism exploding globally.

The global drama being played out at the level of the individual identity crisis is the focus of this inquiry, which seeks to explore a model of self-formulation that is in better keeping with the times than the old discourse of individualism. For those in the thick of conflicting values, the search for some kind of integrity and stability is most acute, notably in postcolonial contexts or highly pluralistic societies like the United States where the cult of individualism simply won't do anymore. "Doing your own thing" does not work if one does not know what one's thing is, due to overexposure to conflicting values. On the social level, the fragmentation that individualism promotes cries out for a new ethic of solidarity to stave off degeneration into chaos.[3] Attempting to create insulated communities of common values, as Alasdair MacIntyre advocates in *After Virtue*, can't work either, Gergen claims, because of the effects of technological change on social organization that tend to fracture communities as much as individuals.[4]

Gergen would prefer to mine for its riches the current state of fragmenting disorder, in spite of the danger of getting lost in the dark, crashing into something adamant, or caving in from fear of dissolution. Indeed, precisely because divergent values are mixing in the social stream more fluidly, rising from underground into the public light, they can be sources of creative local solutions and empowerment at the grass roots of society through dialogue and negotiation. To counteract the dissolution or gridlock of old centralized power structures, there is a new dialogic movement to disperse power from "win-lose" games to "win-win" outcomes and to flow around or through the old monoliths by "networking" or cross-fertilizing ideas for innovative solutions. While networking can also centralize power and spread disinformation, the growing number of people with access to the Information Superhighway will probably tend to decentralization, while the diversity of messages may promote greater skepticism toward any one, or at least a dilution of the power base of any one.

The diversity of messages includes recycling many old discourses and attitudes, so that side by side with the adolescent antiauthoritarian individual who is romantically or competitively independent of society there is still a childlike longing for dependence on authoritarian parent figures who monitor society. However, at the grass roots a new adult is beginning to emerge from older self-concepts, occupying a position alongside them, one who is ready to declare *inter*dependence, that is, one who neither assumes a position against authorities nor is meekly ruled by them, but who assumes an individual freedom and dignity that entails social responsibility.

This new individual[5] faces possibilities that at once seem to both empower and disempower the exercise of that responsibility. At the individual level, the skepticism against old authorities—now competing against new ones—brings skepticism about one's "true" self, in whose mind all these authorities are vying, endangering one's ability to take a position while opening up possibilities for new positions. At the social and political level, as the marginalized meek rise up to claim positions of power, they find that revolution no longer means installing themselves at the center in place of the old authorities, because they have to contend with each other as well—

group against group and individual against group where identities are split across groups, as in the feminist movement, which is split across other groups in the increasingly fractured game of identity politics. While none of them can gain the center of power, the "old boys' network" remains, but its eventual replacement may be a much broader network as late capitalism undermines itself with its own technology by empowering new constituencies of the meek.

As the Information Age advances from putting the individual person into greater contact with the world *passively* (e.g., via television) to greater contact *interactively* (e.g., via the modem), the technological means of power redistribution seem to be at hand. The question is, what will the individual person do with new technological possibilities for empowerment if the old model of an isolated self-concept is at odds with the perceived and theorized breakdown of individual identity? It now becomes necessary to see the individual less as a stable and seemingly independent entity and more as a dialogic switchboard dynamically plugged into a social network, re-routing messages within and without for interconnected purposes. The literary model that admirably lends itself to the purpose is Mikhail Bakhtin's currently prominent theory of the novel as a "dialogic" interplay of voices that resist unification by a single authorial voice.[6] In the comparison of writing a novel to writing oneself, subjectivity can be revisited and the self revised.

Of all the values of the self being negotiated, perhaps none is more fundamental than one's gender identity, which cuts across every other category of nationality, race, class, and ethnicity. Challenged by the feminist movement, women and men are uncertain of their culturally gendered identities. The questioning of gendered values arose from women first because wherever the modern idea of equality took root, women of every category were left out politically and economically, in contrast to their men. Furthermore, beginning with such consciousness-raising books as *The Second Sex* by Simone de Beauvoir,[7] women realized that they were oppressed by a self-defeating and disempowering identity imposed by patriarchy, a more pervasive, complex, and entrenched authoritarianism than the church and the aristocracy in that it underlay those institutions. Patriarchy is not a given set of institutions or ideologies, but a process of thinking that works toward the concentration and retention of power regardless of which ideology is current, to the detriment of both men and women kept too long at the margins, as well as to the detriment of those isolated at the center.[8] It is only called patriarchy because it is associated with a very broad masculine hegemony that is by no means monolithic in the diverse and even conflicting forms it may take. Even in the period of modern revolution the concentration of power in a masculine order has continued precisely because masculine power, relative to feminine power, is decentralized at the level of the individual's self-image, where every man is (ideologically, at least) the power center of his domestic domain, the king of his castle. Men's self-images, in contrast to that of the women of their own social group, have continued to be generally affirmed as superior to the women's, regardless of whatever other issues or self-concepts men might be oppressed by or rebelling against other men for (some of which, like "Orientalism," have been perceived as "feminized" and therefore demeaning).

To be confirmed or exalted as a woman under patriarchy has been a dubious distinction, as Anton Chekhov's short story "The Darling" illustrates. This story, together with Leo Tolstoy's commentary upon it, nicely focuses the central issue of concern for this study by illustrating the monologic plight of its female protagonist in comparison to the dialogic possibilities of self in the protagonists of the novels to be discussed here.[9] The following summary of "The Darling" will serve as a touchstone for analyzing the narratives of self by Virginia Woolf, Doris Lessing, and Margaret Atwood in the ensuing chapters.

"The Darling" tells the tale of Olenka, a woman who "was always fond of someone and could not exist without loving" ("TD," 4). She is so compassionate toward women as well as men that when she listens to them with her "kind, naive smile," women grasp her hand and call her a "darling" (5). She marries her first husband because she is sympathetic to his problems as a theater manager, even though he is a petty and unattractive man. While they are married, she becomes totally absorbed in his theatrical business and is convinced of all his opinions. The theater means as much to her as to him. When he dies, she is devastated.

However, she soon finds another man to love, and remarries. She gets along as well with her second husband as with her first, becoming totally occupied in his affairs as a timber merchant. Again, she assumes all his opinions, and now regards going to the theater as frivolous. In time, her second husband passes away, and she takes up with a veterinary surgeon who is separated from his wife, but no one condemns her because she is such a darling. When she assumes his opinions, manner, and discourse, just as she did with her late husbands', he sometimes gets annoyed by her seeming to put on airs in speaking of professional matters without any training. She can only reply in her bafflement, "But . . . what *am* I to talk about?," and beg him to forgive her (15). Then the veterinary surgeon leaves her and she is bereft again.

Chekhov describes her utter emptiness: "And what was worst of all, she had no opinions of any sort. She saw the objects about her and understood what she saw, but could not form any opinion about them, and did not know what to talk about. . . . now there was emptiness in her brain and in her heart. . . . And it was as harsh and as bitter as wormwood in the mouth" (16). Finally, the veterinary surgeon returns, reconciled with his wife, and Olenka offers them lodgings in her house. Now she becomes attached to his young son and her whole life—her thoughts and dreams and discourse— is filled with a schoolchild's.

Indeed, all that is available to darling Olenka is to remain in permanent childhood, more a caricature of a loving woman than a real person. Tolstoy defends Olenka (from Chekhov's obvious satirical intent) for her wonderful feminine quality, her ability to empathize and take on the life of her immediate love-object, which Tolstoy magnanimously concedes men cannot do as well, but which, however, serves their interests. Olenka does not have a modern feminist identity crisis because she, too, accepts herself in the category of the feminine, which unquestioned identity reduces her to childish helplessness because its essence is lack of any coherent, continuous self apart from her relationship to immediate others, particularly to the significant men in her life. Her narrative is a set of disjunctive experiences of happy, meaningful relationships alternating with bitter and meaningless episodes of existence. She can only achieve form and purpose when some significant other bestows upon her the terms of rendering the flux of events intelligible. She becomes a tabula rasa to be reinscribed anew, as if nothing had ever been inscribed in her singular history before, an ideal of plasticity of self that those in power would like to see in their Olenka-like subjects,[10] so that they can inscribe their opinions and ideologies upon them without resistance. She is exaggerated, of course, since most women have better memories of their prior relationships and of the discourses they have assimilated into their inner stream of identity to form some kind of coherent self-continuity.

Olenka highlights the patriarchal discourses that women have assimilated into their self-concept that promote their participation in a polarized monologue rather than a dialogue. Olenka's function is to validate the discourses of her partners by virtue of her passive "difference" as a seemingly independent other without voicing any actual difference. Thus, not only does she lack the continuity of a self across relationships, she also lacks legitimately different subject positions within any given relationship, being reduced to an object that only echoes the man, in spite of "[seeing] the objects around her and underst[anding] what she saw." That is, her conscious ability to apprehend objects, i.e., her subjectivity,[11] is diminished by the lack of a socially endowed authority to reflect independently and to articulate anything different from the man, who is authorized to exercise his subjectivity fully. Her polarization as an empty object relative to the man as a full subject not only obscures her subjectivity, but it diminishes his subjectivity as well, for Olenka can contribute nothing new to her partner, who stagnates instead of grows by hearing only his own monologue in her voice.

The first self-conceptual goal of feminists, therefore, has been to claim equal subjectivity to men, to liberate both sexes from stagnation and injustice. However, from the postmodern perspective, both men and women can be regarded as disempowered Olenkas. In Jacques Derrida's theory of deconstruction, for example, the "self," "subject," and "individual" are only signifiers, artifacts or constructs of language, full of sound and fury but signifying nothing in an endlessly reflexive system of linguistic signifiers whose meanings are ever deferred to each other rather than to any prior ontic referent (the signified) that can be apprehended outside the system of signification.[12] We can only behave as if our constructs had ontological or epistemological truth value, as if a signifier like the "self" referred to a reality or set of experiences to be known.

Yet it is precisely the pragmatic as if stance that renders all terms and positions negotiable and in keeping with a dialogic concept of self that goes beyond deconstruction, to where truth and authority are not claimed as essentially inhering in any one position but as being relatively and provisionally tenable relevant to a given situation. Thus, as in a game of musical chairs, all subject-positions may be occupied for a time locally and contingently when the music stops, only to be vacated in the deferred march of the meaning system when the free play of the music resumes. In the complexity and reflexivity of the linguistic system, disrupting (deconstructing) signifying constructs from their halted positions and putting them back into the free play of the game enables new meaning positions to be negotiated from the old when the music stops again. Gergen might put it in terms of the distinction between the "finite game" and the "infinite game" that he cites.[13] Deconstruction would be an infinite game where no final meaning is ever declared the winner (departing from the analogy to musical chairs), which does not prevent finite games with specific outcomes from taking place.

The game plan might seem to level the playing field so that signifiers can be played as if equally meaningless and disempowering or as if equally meaningful and empowering—except that available discourses are value-laden, as Barbara Herrnstein Smith points out to those who mistakenly assume relativism means an equality of value across discourses.[14] Her version of a dialogic self is that of a kind of marketplace where all subject-positions are invested with value that might be arbitrary rather than inherent, but that, as in the material economy, have an exchange rate of relative worth with respect to everything else. Foucault's works also emphasize the un-equal value-coding of discourse positions that are put into play by power games. Thus, traditional gendered discourse positions that men and women players occupy are still skewed in favor of men's self-enhancement what-ever seat they take.

That is why some feminists are resurrecting discourses that validate the feminine as essentially positive in value (e.g., as nurturing and cooperative). Other feminists counterclaim that this separate-but-equal position only plays back into the hands of subtle patriarchal discourses that grant women equal-ity and even superiority in those respects but keep them forever in their place, in the way Tolstoy pays homage to Olenka.[15] While essentialist femi-nists have promoted feminine qualities as virtues, they have failed to make them available to men or to claim masculine virtues for women. Further-more, it seems that fixed gendered identities, even if assigned equal values, are becoming increasingly untenable since "essential" traits of one gender or the other are readily observed in individual persons of both sexes, deconstructing any unified gender subject-positions in them. At every turn deconstruction seems to destroy the feminist agenda for empowering women as a real category. But as Toril Moi maintains, as long as women are treated as an essential category, they have to respond *as if* they were one, despite their understanding to the contrary. From that understanding, Moi defends Virginia Woolf's concept of androgyny (a precursor to the dialogic self) against feminists who fear that Woolf's deconstruction of a gendered self destroys her ability to take a stand for women as gendered beings.[16] The chapter on Woolf will elaborate upon this issue.

And yet, the dilemma of difference continues to collide with visions of equality. Carol Gilligan's study, for example, illustrates the difference be-tween women's and men's way of negotiating their moral positions.[17] Other feminists, like linguist Robin Lakoff, rail against the way women use lan-guage differently and are spoken of differently to their detriment, while linguist Deborah Tannen testifies (rather neutrally, it would appear) to the phenomena of men's and women's different cultural attitudes and language.[18] On the other hand, technology obscures old divisions of labor as petite women drive buses and big men type at computers like their female col-leagues. A dialogic approach would recognize differences across individuals who are equal only in their right to life, liberty, and the pursuit of happi-ness, not in their sameness. Their happiness might allow the interplay of similarities that unite same-sex members as well as differences that divide them, and differences between opposite-sex individuals as well as similari-ties that unite them.

Such a construct might seem too complex and confusing to be pragmatic, since it is easier for women as well as men to imagine the totalizing unity of a gendered identity that corresponds to biological differences deemed essential and inevitable. (More will be said about the prior-to-culture category of the biological.) Indeed, the major advantage of abstract, fixed identities is their simplicity, as Thoreau might remind us, even if they break down in practice. Or would he? Isn't he the one who marched to a different drummer and whose only fixed identity was oddball and unconventional curmudgeon who defied social categories? Perhaps in practice the specter of endless flexibility turns into simplicity itself based on one's limited perceptions and alternatives in a given situation, because only a small fraction of available discourses is ever called upon at one time.

Since Woolf's time, the battle has heated up, pitting the liberation and equality of the female individual against the postmodern dismantling of the subject—just when women are ready to declare their rugged self-reliant independence as their brothers before them did. Or as Eileen Schlee wittily puts it in the title of her survey article on the dilemma of feminism in search of subjectivity: "The Subject is Dead, Long Live the Female Subject!"[19] Any feminist may find herself in contradiction with her own values and goals. On one hand, if she advocates moving women into political and economic situations equal to those of men, she may find herself provisionally advocating patriarchal values of capitalism and competitiveness, rationality and reductiveness. On the other hand, if she affirms her difference by what seem to be essentialist "feminine" values of cooperation and intuition, she may find herself outside the power track where decisions are still made that affect her life.

Feminism in its later phases has had to deconstruct binary oppositions such as those that demarcate the public sphere as the rational domain and the private sphere as the emotional domain, a move symbolized by the slogan "The personal is political." But feminists still carry on the public-private split. For example, among academic poststructuralist feminists like Julia Kristeva, the radical indeterminacy of female identity makes radical political action seem impossible, so that their turning back to a kind of privatism or quietism contrasts with those who are trying to articulate public political resistance, even though their theoretical dilemmas remain unresolved. Rita Felski puts the public-private issue succinctly:

> It is in this context that the category of the subject occupies a central position in the feminist project; not in terms of an appeal to an essential female self, but in the recognition that women's positioning within existing social, familial, and ideological structures differs fundamentally from

that of men in distinct although often varied ways, and that the emanci-
pation of women requires an examination of the nature and implications
of such differences. . . . *[The] acknowledgment of the conditional and contingent
nature of knowledge does not invalidate the importance of any oppositional politics as a
process of critical self-reflection* which can test the assumptions of prevailing
ideologies against the specificity of women's changing interests and needs.[20]

Felski observes that the public-private split in feminism is only one variation of the general dichotomy between the impersonal structural forces of
society and the possibility for change originating in human agents. She claims
that while subjects are constituted by language and other social structures,
they still have a potential for resisting and changing those very structures,
so that women formed partly out of heterogeneous patriarchal influences
may nevertheless expose the contradictions within patriarchal discourses
and institutions and introduce a new dynamic interplay between power
"centers" and their "margins."

Thus she assumes responsibility for working out gender differences and
affinities in concrete contexts rather than resorting to either biological or
cultural essentialism. Her pragmatic approach holds the theoretical resolution of the female subject in abeyance. Instead, she prefers to examine self-
narratives of women, including those cast in the patriarchal literary mold
of realism, which presents a coherent, linear view of self. She claims that
patriarchy can be counteracted even through its own forms, while modernist
or postmodernist forms with fragmented self-narratives do not necessarily
undermine patriarchy but may even be appropriated by the very ideology
they aim to undermine. Although Felski does not wish to theorize the female subject, implicit in her approach is, indeed, a theory: that the female
self consists of a pragmatic dialogic process constructed into some form of
narrative of self-negotiation, like a Bakhtinian novel.[21]

The dialogic self, then, can be likened to a literary construct of narrative. This study will demonstrate that the dialogic process includes the formal properties of the narrative—its metaphors, symbols, narrative strategies, style, and generic structure—which are related to the content of the
discourses being negotiated.

In foregrounding the particulars of narrated experience as "foundational" to a dialogic self-concept, one cautionary note should be sounded.
Diana Fuss warns of the danger of turning experience into its own essentialist epistemology, as if one's experiences are a direct source of knowledge
that establish one's identity as a woman or any other category and therefore exclude those who are presumably outside the experiencer's circle. Fuss's
purpose is to deconstruct the binary opposition essentialist-constructionist

by showing how having multiple, even contradictory, positions may be no less essentialist than having some unitary identity, if those diverse positions are just as nonnegotiable. She argues that when the category of concrete historical specificity becomes a new foundational ground of knowledge, essentialism has crept back in. Experience itself is a cultural construct, she claims, an interpretation rather than a given fact transparent to some reality. Yet she endorses the taking of positions as empowering as long as they are held open to renegotiation, as Gayatari Spivak suggests by her idea of "strategic essentialism," i.e., the temporary assumption of positionality for some purpose.[22] As a spokesperson for deconstruction coming from a postcolonial context, Spivak recognizes that the music of the infinite game of musical chairs has to pause for finite games, as do Felski, Fuss, and Moi.

The discussion in the following chapters will draw upon a number of other contributing theories and issues underpinning the theory of the dialogic self as a narrative construct—from such diverse fields as psychology, social philosophy, sociolinguistics, and literary theory—which will now be sketched in.

SOURCES OF THE DIALOGIC SELF

In positing a schism between the conscious and the unconscious in the unified individual, Sigmund Freud's theory laid an early foundation for a dialogic self-narrative.[23] The importance of Freudian psychoanalysis for dialogism is its emphasis on a process of negotiating conscious meaning from clues to the unconscious that erupt in various forms, such as in dreams or free association. Moreover, his theory and practice are quite literary in the allusions to traditional literature (as in the Oedipus complex), the reliance on symbolism, metaphor, and wordplay in dream interpretation, and in the close reading of patients' narratives and other verbalizations. Even in non-Freudian approaches that focus more on present states and problems rather than on analysis of past childhood experience, such as in some types of Gestalt therapy, the play of imagination and articulation in language is crucial to the process.[24] While therapeutic methods and emphases may differ, most recognize that language, particularly the general human propensity to render experience figuratively and narratively, is a crucial shaper of self and that the inception of such discursive strategies in the primary stages of self-development has lifelong effects.

Freud's theory further advances toward a dialogic model by fracturing the intrapsychic structure of the self into the three subject-positions of id, superego, and ego, which elaborate on the mechanisms of the dialogue.

The id represents the organic drives or libido in conflict with the superego, which represents the interests of society in keeping the desires of the id from disrupting interpersonal relations. Mediating between those opposing subjectivities is the ego, which represents the individual's sense of self as undivided vis-à-vis other individuals and itself. The ego tries to maintain or defend that unified sense of self from others and from the disintegration of inner conflict, often by ignoring the conflict between the id and the super-ego in such a way that the self-narrative excludes the demonized id, suppressed in the unconscious in favor of a socially acceptable unified self. Antisocial or perverse acts and impulses can be rationalized into the seamless narrative by resorting to an alternative social discourse that justifies what would be unacceptable by other standards, conveniently ignoring or denying the contradictions among social discourses. Self-defense mechanisms like rationalization polarize the ego's self-concept as either morally good, or, in cases of perverse self-concepts, bad. In transpersonal relations the need for a unified self-image may impel the ego to split off from its own unconscious subjectivities (usually bad, but sometimes good) by denying them and projecting them imaginatively onto someone else, reserving the conscious subjectivities for its morally self-righteous monologue.

However, when the unifying impulse of the ego is disrupted by pressure from the suppressed subjectivities, causing problems, the ego must find a better solution than repression, i.e., conscious acknowledgment of desires hitherto kept unconscious, a negotiation of possible alternatives, and an assumption of responsibility for the transaction. In short, some dialogic process of psychotherapy has to break the monologic barrier. The paradox is that the unifying impulse of the ego is better served when it accounts for its disunity and conflict instead of denying it, so that a more comprehensive self-narrative can be constructed for pragmatic purposes of sustained action. Yet what psychoanalysis overlooks in its bias toward the "cure" of a socially acceptable new unified self is that every new unity will have to be deconstructed in turn as successive issues arise to be accounted for. Thus, varying with the context, one's self-narrative may be an alternation between phases of disunity and unity, which is dialogic in the turn-taking sense.

Jacques Lacan surpasses the limited structural model of Freud in a theory that allows for a more diverse play of voices.[25] This more "polyphonic" model (to use Bakhtin's term) is based on an account of how self-consciousness emerges from a putative unself-consciousness in earliest infancy. Although the development of a sense of self may be gradual, it seems to be clearly marked when one reaches the "mirror stage" of self-recognition, which is closely linked to the child's entry into the symbolic (language) order whereby distinctions are made, especially between "self" and "other."

Consciousness of selfhood—the sense of plenitude (a solid-seeming positive presence or fullness of being) marked by the ability to enunciate "I" as if a unified individual is speaking—is only one subjectivity in a complex, fragmented, and indeterminate process that could be narrated in various ways to construct any number of "selves" the "I" might assume. Indeed, according to Lacan, the "unconscious" aspect of self is precisely where the solid-seeming self encounters all that it *isn't*, that is, its "otherness"; by altering its boundaries to internalize that other, the concept of self can be expanded theoretically to infinity. The enunciatory component (the *ego* in Freudian terms) merely foregrounds (or has foregrounded in it) limited particulars, while vast amounts of material that impinge on it or influence it are either readily available (the Freudian *preconscious*) or are relatively inaccessible (in the *unconscious*) and are screened out at any given time. This material consists largely of prior stimuli and experiences as well as the immediate stimuli of encounters in the world (including subliminal impressions) that are always being assimilated into potential meaningful associations with prior content.

Both past and present material, conscious and unconscious, have simultaneous existence and effects, even if they cannot be at the forefront of conscious attention simultaneously without overwhelming or jamming one's ability to function. Indeed, this *screen* of consciousness can be thought of as acting in both senses of the word—as a screening-out or excluding mechanism as well as a "blank sheet" or "stage" upon which momentarily included elements "perform." Another way to conceive of consciousness is as a relatively linear stream in time against a timeless, global curtain or backdrop that is always feeding contents into it as previous contents recede back into an unarticulated or inchoate state, for possible recycling. What the screen excludes at any given time frame may make an entrance at another, while that which is featured on-screen goes back into the "wings" or memory bank.

Carl Jung extends the idea of the unconscious beyond the contemporary experiences that influence a particular person to a connection between that person and a racial memory of all humanity's experience throughout its evolution and history, genetically programmed in the *collective unconscious*.[26] This is self-as-other conceived on a grand scale. Such a concept cannot reduce the self to an isolated, separate, or irreducible individual, no matter how solidly distinct and exclusive the conscious component may appear to itself. If one conceives oneself to be linked not only with one's own society but with all humanity, and even beyond that with nature or the cosmos, one can derive some basis for an ever-widening conception of a morally constituted self such as the morally responsible collective self that Doris Lessing narrates for her protagonist Martha Quest. But the idea of *interconnectedness* (broadly or narrowly defined) is insufficient in itself for a moral rationale. An account of power distribution must be included.

Freudian theory has been expanded upon from its original emphasis on sexual repression to theories focusing on the power drive in the unifying ego that corresponds to the exercise of power in social relations. The ego's power-concentrating, polarizing, and splitting propensity is analogous to the patriarchal process, while the ego as mediator between conscious and unconscious subjectivities is analogous to a democratic process in which power is assigned by the voters for limited times and purposes as participants take turns leading or contributing according to what they offer to the situation. At both the interpersonal and the intrapsychic levels, dominance and subordination or relative positionality as to center and margin are at stake, but in the patriarchal or egocentric model such power positions remain fixed, whereas in the dialogic model of self and democracy the positions are mobile, or can be alternatively reconceived.

It is ironic that Freud's theory, with its insight into the patriarchal ego that suppresses its own otherness, should have itself become a patriarchal discourse, another male self-defense mechanism against women. From a supposedly "objective" scientific subject-position, Freud reduces women to lack, even physically, as in his notion of penis envy, while Lacan, for his part, also defines women as a lack contained within his phallocentric symbolic order. Both theorists speak as authorities on women, without considering women as authorities on their own self-narratives. The present book is part of a larger feminist project to correct that kind of oversight.

While Freud, Jung, and Lacan all draw upon language and social discourses, they remain preoccupied with the individual person's intrapsychic history and self-concept as a moral being in contrast to sociological analysts and philosophers who wish to account for or attend to society's mental and moral health. Wendy Hollway is one psychologist in a growing field whose concern is not only with the individual but with transpersonal relations and group dynamics.[27] She draws upon psychoanalysis as well as upon Foucault's theory of the formation of subjects through dominant social discourses, preferring his emphasis on current ideologies (however far back he may trace them genealogically) to Jung's emphasis on ancient archetypes (however current they may be). She combines intrapsychic and transpersonal dialogues by representing them in a diagram as the intersection of two axes: a horizontal axis of available social discourses that are value-coded, and a vertical axis of the individual's unique history. In this way she bridges the inadequacy of either approach alone, that is, Foucault's insufficient account for unique subjects in the dispersal of subjectivity in ideologies, and the insufficient account of psychoanalysis for the social context of the individual's problem. On one hand, she cites cases from her practice that show how individuals have formulated idiosyncratic meanings and values from the pool of available discourses that could not have been determined by those social discourses alone. On the other hand, she goes beyond early formative or racially programmed determiners in her analysis of subjectivity and ego issues. In her clinical practice she directs patients to the potential for change through a dialogue within *current relationships* (i.e., group or family therapy), drawing upon any relevant social discourses, rather than restricting the dialogue to old intrapsychic issues from childhood through a process in which the only interpersonal relationship is with the analyst.

In her emphasis upon the *current* dialogic process Hollway comes close in practice to the theory of Francis Jacques, a sociolinguist of the self who regards the ego-bound subject as a linguistic mirage and, in dispensing altogether with subjectivity, focuses on the *person* as a *relational* construct, not one of fixed individuality.[28] Even that interpersonal entity is not a fixed construct, but can only be discerned in distinct speech acts, every one of which is a process of negotiating meaning based on the language system and set of available ideologies, the individual's unique history intersecting with them, and also on the constraints of the situation. Each individual person contributes differences to the negotiation of that situation, which is just one site where the relationship can be located. Jacques emphasizes *difference* as being a positive contribution of the individual person to the relational entity, rather than a means to preserve the individual's ego boundaries negatively by relegating differences to the "not-self." Instead of self-other polarization there is a convolution of discourses, as in Bakhtin's revelation of the different voices involved in a character's utterance. By Jacques's lights, Olenka does not realize her personhood because she does not retain, for example, theatrical discourses from her first husband to contribute to any subsequent relationships or to her own intrapsychic dialogue between those relationships.

Jacques's purpose is to construct a moral self-concept that will transform society, as social philosopher George Herbert Mead attempted to do with his theory of a dialogic self.[29] Mead, like Lacan, attributes consciousness to the symbolic order and, like Jacques, to speech acts. As in their theories, Mead posits a self that first appears as the object of others, the "me," which becomes a "generalized other" in the self, the voice of society that judges the impulses of the unique individual, much as the superego is the observer-judge of the id, which Mead posits as creative and free of social convention. Mead, like Hollway and Jacques, subscribes to the intersection of the unique, creative individual axis with the social axis, but whereas their focus is at the level of interpersonal dynamics in primary groups, Mead's is at the level of society at large. He observes that the pool of discourses available to individuals and subgroups is in turn altered by their contributions to it, so that there is a continual flow of influence both ways. Mead supposes that a dialogic self incorporating the "generalized other" would have to be a moral one. However, the very conflicts that Mead recognizes to be part of the process prevent any single notion of what is moral to prevail.[30]

A variation on Mead's problem has been the preoccupation of post-Marxists such as Paul Smith who wrestle with the theoretical difficulty of locating resistance to the dominant ideology of capitalism in the individual determined by that ideology. He discusses other post-Marxists such as Althusser and Adorno who have acknowledged the importance of the subject's unconscious in accounting for the successful dominance of capitalist ideology, but who have reached an impasse in "interpellating" (Althusser's term for "calling" someone by a certain identity tag) subjects as "socialist."[31] Smith seeks to account for human responsibility *in spite of* and *because of* determining factors in self-formation by postulating that a concrete human agent may be empowered to act by the very contradictions within her/his own heterogeneity—of being neither totally dominated by any single strand of influence among the available cultural ideologies, nor paralyzed by an overdetermined multiplicity of factors.

By locating potential resistance at the places where one "falls through," so to speak, the network of various ideologically interpellated subject-positions, Smith does not maintain that one assumes a place of "no position" or "disinterested" neutrality; rather, one chooses among various positions or creates a new composite or compromise position. That is, one still takes a stance ideologically determined by prior experience and thus not strictly a matter of either free will or "autonomy." Yet one may give the appearance of being innovative or resistant and therefore seemingly independent-minded.

Clearly, Smith rejects the "meaninglessness" of postmodernism, which has no positive ideology or vision but only negativity, a neither-this-nor-that, nonessentialist claim of no-Truth that seems to wash its hands of moral involvement at the level of the self, since taking a firm position on anything would contradict its mission as *ironic* underminer of all positions. Ironically, that is a position in itself. It comes close to the one Socrates pursued in his challenge of fellow Athenians' self-definitions and values and in his own quest for self-knowledge through dialogue. Yet the moral implications of the ironist stance emerge from Socrates' case as his gadfly function toward society (and perhaps towards himself, if one assumes that he was seeking refutation in order to continually reexamine his own assumptions). But while

Socrates might have emphasized negativity as his style, even he argued for positions. Negativity cannot be a fixed stance, but must be undermined by the self's ability to act at least provisionally.

Smith, however, does not account for the taking of positions he would consider immoral or disabling rather than enabling. Neither does Charles Taylor, who relies upon a morally dialogic self that operates upon a "Best Account Principle." Such a Best Account may be derived through a dialogic inner and outer process of rational thinking or epiphanic experience as individuals come to insights and in turn help transform society by their vision if they can communicate it effectively.[32] He, too, rejects the negativity of the postmodern stance, but unlike Paul Smith, his agenda seems to be driving toward a foundational or substantive ground for values, even if he subscribes to a process of arriving at them dialogically. However, Taylor's arguments in favor of substantive values against philosophies of "proceduralism" (process orientation) or "instrumentalism" set up a binary opposition between ends and means without acknowledging what his substantive values owe to the process.

Herrnstein Smith's marketplace analogy seems to fill in what Mead, Smith, and Taylor omit. She resuscitates pragmatism and utility from narrow materialistic goals of "happiness" to include priorities for taking any position whatsoever, including the most spiritually conceived and altruistic. The inner-outer economy that accounts for personal character and behavior may also allow for perverse, ambivalent, and seemingly self-defeating behavior, as an outcome of relative strengths among conflicting urges, many of which may be unconscious, as Freud observed, operating like the "unseen hand" of the marketplace. She puts the play of power back into the process, instead of into some ideal and disinterested ego-mediator, as Taylor seems to imply.

Because positions must contend with one another, Herrnstein Smith asserts that some ideas are better than others from a contingent, pragmatic point of view, not because they are more true in any absolute sense but because they are more workable in a particular situation, or have more explanatory power for a given set of data, pending revision of the data. Thus a judgment about what is right or wrong, better or worse, is not verified by any appeal to general principles like Best Accounts, but by apparent success or failure with respect to specific goals and purposes, which are assumed to be provisional givens, themselves subject to reevaluation if necessary.[33] In this way she retains an ability to discriminate and create hierarchies of value as a basis for moral action or aesthetic preference at the same time that she enables flexibility and creativity.

However, since these provisional concepts are always in tension with the counterurge to dismantle them (destroy what is no longer viable) or to deconstruct them (reveal their simultaneous "otherness" within self and self within the other), the ability to act overtly may be inhibited because of uncertainty and disorder at the level where conceptualization takes place in thought. Which brings us back to the question of paralysis in the face of overdetermined alternatives or ironic doubt. While Herrnstein Smith accounts for economic decision making as if it keeps steadily churning, Spivak acknowledges that sometimes the computers of self *do* break down, calling a temporary halt or "interruption" to trading among subject-positions.[34] The dialogic paradigm does not offer any guarantees of moral outcomes in particular situations.

Yet there are some moral implications to a dialogic concept. One paradoxical advantage of not needing to claim truth in view of radical heterogeneity is that the self may be less threatened by the dismantling of any given concept and therefore capable of recovering from a blow or a change to any particular valued concept, since it has many resources or alternatives to fall back on and reassemble. There may be a greater capacity for resiliency and thus a long-range kind of stability if one has "faith" in the processes of heterogeneity to bring forth alternatives upon which to act in the positive mode. This is not faith in the sense of a belief in anything in particular, or in any preconceived outcome, but rather a willingness to meet situations by being alert to change and reevaluation when it seems necessary. This readiness to be resilient corresponds to the practice of that crucial Aristotelian virtue, *phronesis*, upon which all other virtues depend—the ability to exercise judgment in particular cases.[35]

Such an open-ended faith is in contrast to religious fundamentalists and believers in the truth-value of their concepts, who are vulnerable to radical destabilization in the face of evidence that contradicts their beliefs or notions. They may question their sanity, the very foundation upon which they have predicated a unified sense of self, and become disoriented, unable to act coherently or to respond adequately to the demands of a heterogeneous reality. It is out of this fear of chaos that the clinging to stable truth-values is so fixed and intense, inducing paranoia, as Paul Smith points out. In the need to fortify one's position, it becomes necessary to deny or suppress contradictions, the very rich resources from the "other" of the self, which shuts off creative potentialities.

It might be added that the asserter of truth is also arrogant in presuming to have a "handle" on reality in all its complexity, whereas a self that is freer to conceive of being subject to the unknowable must be more humble (in acknowledging a limited power to conceptualize) as well as more courageous in facing the unknown and the contingent. Ironically, some old-fashioned virtues seem to emerge—faith, humility and courage—in connection with any provisional self-definition in terms of radical heterogeneity. MacIntyre would add others, like honesty and even constancy, which might be justified from contingent points of view, but the Aristotelian value system he advocates as a worldview would be another totalizing move that could create the very simulacra of virtues he is rejecting under present systems.

Nevertheless, some very traditional positions come back to haunt us when readiness to respond to the particular becomes a conscious stance—albeit not a constant or automatic one, our ironic sense hastens to add. In privileging the historical specificity of the situation over any "universal" ideas or states, Herrnstein Smith can account for contingent agreement among communities of people, even to the point of unanimity, a pragmatic "objectivity," on certain points.[36] She recognizes that there are repetitions, patterns, and needs for stable forms, since ongoing change does not imply total chaos in human life and self, but rather element-by-element renewals, as the cells of the body are continuously dying and reproducing themselves in altered variations here and there, while the system to which they belong retains enough stability to maintain coherence on the whole.

Yet a dialogic system would not reach the homeostasis of a closed whole where the parts merely take turns and achieve a dynamic equilibrium. Destabilization is built into the dialogic paradigm because it is an open-ended process that takes place at the level of the speech act, where the always-new conditions of possibility intersect to forge new meanings from old. Thus, paradoxically, every local change makes the whole system different by altering the possibilities for constructing new meanings, while preserving enough sameness in the repetitions of pattern for continuity .[37]

The constant renewal of the whole system comes close to Bakhtin's theory of novelistic discourse, which he articulates as a tension between unifying tendencies and the unruly proliferation of a "heteroglossia" that keeps unification and systemization ever at bay. In *Problems of Dostoevsky's Poetics*, for example, Bakhtin discusses Dostoevsky's art as dialogic in that the author does not impose his own monologue upon the characters in order to unify the work, but allows them to speak—not in simplified monologic voices either, but in the multiple and conflicting voices they bring to their situations, negotiating with each other from their unique fund of subject-positions.[38] Bakhtin's analyses of the texts of a character's thoughts or speeches point out the interpenetration of influences from another's, so that moves to differentiate one's self from the other subtly incorporate that other, while moves toward solidarity are underscored by difference.

Well before Bakhtin's idea of a dialogic imagination, Keats made similar observations about what he called Shakespeare's "negative capability," which signifies a state of self that is so powerfully empathic that it is imaginatively bonded with its object, not as other but as if that other were its very self.[39] It can be conceived of as active, incorporating another into the self; or as passive, abandoning itself to be taken over by the other; or as transpositional, assuming the subject- or object-position of the other. This ability might be like Olenka's, except that in her case the effect is so total and disconnected that it is monologic, whereas Shakespeare's protean capability plays with subject-positions *within* characters as well as across them in what Keats felt was the highest state of artistic creativity. Woolf admired that same quality, which she put in terms of the androgyny of Shakespeare's "incandescent" mind. Translating models of artistic imagination to self-concepts, we are artists of ourselves, then, to the degree that we are negatively capable of being alert to the subjectivities of others.

Keats's own art is characterized by a tension between subject-positions, particularly between the centripetal tendency to formulate a positive vision and the centrifugal tendency to destabilize it, both chasing each other through every utterance. A literary theory of his time describing such a textual dynamic is "romantic irony." The term is attributed to the German philosopher Friedrich Schlegel, who posited a view of the universe as a perpetual "becoming" in an indeterminate flux, in which apparent forms both are and are not themselves.[40] Hence, consciousness is in constant play, entering into the illusions of created forms "romantically" and then dispelling them "ironically." Schlegel's emphasis on the cosmically purposeless chaos of life as a form of play, of delight in the endless passing spectacle, alarmed not only believers in absolute truths, but someone like Kierkegaard, who also saw nonbeing through being in his existential philosophy.[41] His position was that irony is not merely an aesthetic game, but a stern discipline by which an individual might carve a moral path out of the abyss.[42] Kierkegaard posited the creative individual who could freely choose to be responsible by progressing from ironic insight into faith.

Although various theories of dialogism show considerable overlap, they cannot be translated into each other's terms in any simple one-to-one correspondence. Every negotiation among discourses entails a loss that is unaccounted for, which does not permit any single neat formulation of how the dialogic process works or readily solves moral problems of equality and difference or free will and determinism in locating individual agency and responsibility in a dispersed network of interdetermining elements. Neither can such binary oppositions as subject-object, mind-body, or masculine-feminine be resolved at the theoretical level because of what is left out. Perhaps it is the very indeterminacy of dialogism as a paradigm of the self that might appeal to feminists, men as well as women.

THE RELATION OF DIALOGISM TO FEMINISM

While some of the foremost theorists and practitioners of dialogism are men, the paradigm itself would appear to correspond to an "essentially feminine" one, as defined by traditional patriarchal discourses. Perhaps that is why it might lend itself to empowering women more than the egocentric patriarchal model does. Meanwhile, those men attuned to a more dialogic self-concept than their fellows might experience more varied and enriched possibilities for power than in the patriarchal model, with the loss of masculine egotism offset by a gain in creativity. The features of dialogism that might appeal particularly to women feminists as a self-enhancing construct, and which will therefore figure importantly in the analysis of self-narratives in this study, can be summed up as follows.

First, dialogism emphasizes relating and negotiating rather than isolating and polarizing positions. Going back to ancient times of clan warfare, women have been expected to cultivate diplomatic skills as "peacemakers." They are supposed to understand the others' point of view or find some validation in each of the contending sides. Hence, their style tends to be consensus building rather than authoritarian. These qualities are gaining ascendancy as honorable for men, although there is a fear that having negotiating skill is tantamount to being unable to take a strong position. However, the point of peacemaking is to put provisional solutions into effect, to take a stand for something more advantageous to all concerned than war—not to sink into indecisiveness and chaos.

A second feature of dialogism is the emphasis on responding very precisely to concrete particulars rather than acting on abstract principles. For example, in Carol Gilligan's study, her sample of women use terms that reveal how they are guided in their moral judgments by concern for particular relationships, in contrast to her sample of men, who tend to rely on abstract principles to guide theirs. This reliance on an orientation to the particular rather than to the general might counteract any tendency to indecisiveness, since practicality requires action to be taken without too much weighing of discourses in the abstract. Of course, quick and decisive action is possible based on handy principles, but there is a risk of ignoring crucial details that make a difference in a given case.

The need to act in a timely way in practical situations requires a third feature of dialogism, namely a mode of thinking that does not use strictly linear ways of structuring meaning, but is capable of scanning multiple levels of association more rapidly than verbal syntax allows.[43] "Intuition," the intelligence associated traditionally with women's ways of thinking, or with poetic, visionary, or mystical experience, is more efficient in a dialogic model where complexity would boggle the analytical way of thinking. As efficient as the computer may be, the human mind has creative and synthesizing capabilities far beyond it. Indeed, in powerful mystical experiences the human mind seems to be able to transcend normal consciousness of time and space, and can access multiple dimensions at once. These, too, will figure in the texts under study.

The ability to access experience and ascribe meaning to it beyond verbal linearity indicates that a larger sign system or range of "discourse" is available to us, as the study of cultural semiotics has made us aware. Moreover, as socially based as his dialogism was, Mead realized that there was a semiotic system beyond even human society, although he did not theorize it. Julia Kristeva has gone further than cultural semiotics to the biological, preoedipal "signs" that are still implicated in the thetic or propositional symbol systems of verbal languages.[44] Her theory of the semiotic as both preceding and coextensive with the symbolic is a recognition of the importance of the body's signal system in which women have been traditionally more "immanent" (to use de Beauvoir's term) than men. Bodily knowledge is related to that sense of the concrete and the multidimensional that verbal language can only "translate" with difficulty. For indeed, while the biological may also be a verbal, cultural, or ideological construct, as Judith Butler would maintain, it could be regarded as another kind of language system, as Ralph Waldo Emerson intuited in his claim in his essay "Nature" that nature itself is symbolic.[45]

Kristeva uses her thetic propositions to point to an intersection between two symbolic systems in which much is lost because they have incompatible dimensions. That intersection might extend deconstruction's claim that a verbal signifier is not referential to some signified, but rather *deferential* to yet another signifier, which happens to be nonverbal and no final repository of meaning, either.[46] Yet semiotic language has "meaning" and can be "read" the way an infant can read facial expressions and touch long before it has entered the symbolic order or has constructed any self, as women have had occasion to witness more than men (although men have perhaps observed it in the intelligences of animals more). Furthermore, biological knowledge is as constructed as symbolic knowledge, and as ideological (with the dominant discourse that of survival), if the genetic "code" is any indication of a language so ancient that it goes back into the *pre*racial unconscious of our evolutionary forebears.

The discourse of the primeval sign system of feelings, senses, intuitions, is what women can contribute to the dialogue with men to restore to them that knowledge they may have forgotten in their "phallogocentrism." Instead of trying to resolve a chicken-or-egg conundrum between language and consciousness, or culture and biology—which remains a mystery—all we can presently do is recognize their relationship. This is what the essentialist feminists have contributed. However, the validation of women's intuition and their association with the biological or earth-mother discourses can go beyond merely confirming that place patriarchy reserves for them—which might even be regarded as superior, but monologically separate. The cultivation of a dialogic concept of self would destabilize the patriarchal notion that limits intuition and earthiness to women by restoring those subject-positions to men as well. Indeed, the macho image of the "strong, silent type," e.g., the cowboy, valorizes the very traits nonessentialist feminists decry for women, which are their silence and their immanence in nature.

While dialogue may entail more apparent conflict and disorder than a bland, repressive monologue, getting differences out into the open holds greater possibilities for innovative resolutions. Where the moral potential exists in dialogism is not in any guarantees of outcomes in the negotiating process, but in the necessity to take account of the other in one's self as a countersubjectivity, a power unto itself. For negotiating can only be conducted from a position of strength for all parties, which, in turn, restrains any one from taking over monologically and subjugating the other.[47] Women therefore must assume responsibility for exercising the power of their subject-positions rather than begging for paternalistic respect from a place of weakness, as Atwood's work emphasizes. At the same time, awareness that the subject "I" is only a mouthpiece for the socially fabricated discourses implanted in an object "me" may caution the ego against the pride of originary mastery. The subject-object split, like the mind-body split, is a linguistic illusion that has its place when there is an interplay, a dialogic relationship between the parts.

Although the split between dialogism and monologism seems to be yet another attempt to set up a binary opposition, it is unavoidable in the positionality inherent in language. The point is, however, that "dialogic" and "monologic" are only relative, depending on the situation. It is in the pragmatic world (including the world of crafting novels), where encounter after encounter, instance after instance, and reflection upon reflection prevail, that such terms become operational and where theory meets practice. The following chapters will reflect more pragmatically upon the dialogic process—where it is empowering and where it breaks down—in novels whose very forms are dialogic as an outgrowth of the authors' views of the self.

Part One
Virginia Woof's *The Waves:*
The Oscillating Self

1

The Concept of Self in
Virginia Woolf's Life and Work

Virginia Woolf's concept of self is dialogic in that it opens up the finite rules of self-narrative to an infinity game in which the selves of her fictional characters become shifting centers of interaction with everything from subtle immediate influences to those far out in time and space. The boundaries between characters, and between characters and the nonhuman world, appear and disappear in negotiated meanings that are both serious and ironically playful, disrupting conventional monologic self-narratives.

Woolf's ability to play with self-boundaries might be considered a distinctly feminine talent in the light of Nancy Chodorow's psychoanalytic theory, which claims that the female child develops a fluid or liminalized ego-boundary by her early merging with the mother in contrast to the male child, who develops a more rigidly centered and demarcated ego by more radically separating from the mother.[1] Hence, males tend to exclude otherness, such as the feminine, while females more easily include otherness, even the masculine. Chodorow attributes such male-female differentiation to the cultural practice of primary caregiving by women, which Woolf's close relation to her own mother would attest to, and which might account for her bias toward the feminine in spite of her ideal of uniting the masculine and the feminine in an androgynous self. Chodorow, too, strives toward an androgynous ideal of self-formation by proposing that men share equally in primary caregiving so that children of both sexes will be able to merge and separate equally well in relation to caregivers of both sexes.

But Woolf had to give birth to her androgynous self from her greater attachment to the feminine, which made it more difficult. She probably would not have espoused such a prescriptive formula as Chodorow's for advancing androgyny as a "solution"; for Woolf's way is only to suggest androgyny implicitly in her fiction and explicitly in her long essay *A Room of*

41

One's Own. In that essay she asserts the differences between masculine and feminine orientations, but seeks to reconcile them into a harmonious whole in the ideal of the androgynous mind. The nub of her thesis occurs when Woolf describes having seen a man and woman meet to share a taxi, which becomes her image of androgyny:

> One has a profound, if irrational, instinct in favour of the theory that the union of man and woman makes for the greatest satisfaction, the most complete happiness. But the sight of the two people getting into the taxi and the satisfaction it gave me made me also ask whether there are two sexes in the mind corresponding to the two sexes in the body, and whether they also require to be united in order to get complete satisfaction and happiness? . . . The normal and comfortable state of being is that when the two live in harmony together, spiritually cooperating. If one is a man, still the woman part of his brain must have effect; and a woman must also have intercourse with the man in her. Coleridge perhaps meant this when he said a great mind is androgynous. It is when this fusion takes place that the mind is fully fertilized and uses all its faculties. . . . But it would be well to test what is meant by man-womanly and conversely by woman-manly, by pausing and looking at a book or two. (*R*, 101–2)

The book we shall look at here, *The Waves*, contains no character with as fully androgynous a mind as she and Coleridge attributed to Shakespeare. She recognized that most of us are skewed, and her novel is faithful to observable, not ideal, behavior.[2]

Woolf's concept of androgyny, however, has come under attack from both essentialist and deconstructive feminists. One essentialist, Frances Restuccia, speculates in her article that Woolf contradicts herself when she asserts feminine difference, and that her attempt to reconcile, or apparently fuse, that difference in androgynous union with masculine qualities is only a devious concession to cover her true essentialism, although Restuccia concedes the double-bind that essentialism poses.[3] That Woolf's characters are quite traditional is not an indication of what she thought to be inevitable essentialism, but rather an honest representation of the way people in her world already had been polarized, as Chodorow observes. Thus, women characters tend to be more intuitive, global, and fluid in their thinking and empathic in their behavior, while men tend to be rational, domineering, and egotistical. She clearly had a prejudice in favor of the feminine configuration of traits over the masculine, insofar as she objected to the domineering egotism and violence of men; yet she valued rational and disciplined qualities associated with masculinity, too. She strove to demonstrate the best of both sets of qualities in her art and life, as suggested by the title of her essay collection *Granite and Rainbow*, a title oscillating between masculine solidity and ephemeral feminine diffuseness.

For their part, deconstructive feminists object to the retention of the essentialist binary opposition implied in the term *androgyny* itself, which, as a term constructed by male discourse, does not reflect the multiplicity of female experience. Some, like Monique Wittig and Luce Irigaray in their different ways, would prefer to alter the language itself to reconstruct female experience outside the terms of gender, whereas Judith Butler rejects their vain attempt to forge an identity that transcends the terms of sex and gender. Instead of discarding gendered terms altogether, she favors a strategy of creatively playing different gender "styles" in various contexts, which would disrupt the sense of any fixed sex/gender identity and expose those categories to be constructed rather than essential.[4]

That is exactly the effect Woolf achieves in her fiction, in contrast to her own theory of androgyny enunciated above in which such terms as complementarity, reconciliation, harmony, and completion figure so prominently. Indeed, the fusion and completion she speaks of seems to suggest the stasis of an idealized identity—the androgyne—which Butler, for one, finds objectionable as yet another fixed category or substantial state of being, imposing a new patriarchal and monolithic unity of "wholeness" on the self.[5]

But Woolf never spells out in her theory exactly what that fused state might consist of. It is only by examining her practice that a dialogic picture emerges. It is not that "wholeness" signifies something like filling up a half-empty storehouse with fixed quantities of previously missing traits (a static spatial metaphor), but something more like a dynamic process in which thoughts, feelings, and behavior endlessly form, giving each aspect its due moment as it alternates or oscillates with different, even contrary, aspects of self in the stream of time. While she allows characters moments of equilibrium or harmony in timeless states, even those moments stand in a dialectic relation to the destabilizing factor of time. The readiness to assume a particular boundary or subject-position and then relinquish it according to the flow of events (redefining inner and outer) depends on a fine ability not only to grasp the boundary of the moment with precision but to sense the larger rhythms in which it appears and disappears. That is, the assumption of this position or that in the dialogue is continually surpassed by an integrating (or what she might call androgynizing) impulse that relates diverse positions to one another without destroying them, regardless of how contradictory they may be.

Although Woolf's dialogic impulse might be derived from the feminine, it is able not only to contain the masculine but to deconstruct the very terms of gender by the convolution of discourses in her characters' minds.[6] Like Butler, Woolf observes constant disruptions of fixed identities or states because life is too variable to maintain such fictions for very long. She makes it clear that both men and women can cross gender boundaries according to their readiness rather than their sex. Indeed, in the richness of her characterizations she goes even further, for superimposed on the categories of sex and gender are discourses that do not correlate with those distinctions at all, but render characters in other terms altogether, as we shall see in *The Waves*. Hers is a way of destabilizing all categories, not just those of sex and gender.

Her method is to weave various personal points of view into a fabric that is cut along an impersonal bias (in the sense of diagonal), which is itself a "bias" or angle of vision, but a relatively cross-sectional one compared to each of the "personal" points. Each of those personal points, in turn, can attain a further cross-sectional bias, creating new dimensions that intersect in a complex multilayered web. The cross-sectional or cross-fertilizing impulse that cuts across boundaries and categories to create new subject-positions or relational possibilities is what drives Woolf's concept of self and art. In such a concept the unifying impulse coexists with a differentiating impulse in a dynamic tension between finite and infinite games.

The very designations of "impersonal," for transcending or integrating subjectivities, and "personal," for limited subjectivities, are deeply implicated in gendered discourses. Indeed, Woolf sought to achieve liberation from the personal—constructed as narrowly feminine—both in her writing and in her life. She would not have wanted to write autobiographical fiction, as women writers tended to do, but to write impersonally, as Shakespeare did.[7] However, writing in the early twentieth century, she still labored under constraints that limited a woman to private rather than public life. Thus, like many other women authors, writing what she knew best turned out to be writing mostly about her personal and "inner" world in her fiction.

Another reason impelling her to explore her inner states through writing was its therapeutic value, for her particular psychological and physiological problems were serious enough to cause major and minor breakdowns in her mental and physical health. Not only was her life closely represented in her work, but her work was a means of managing her life, as three writers about her life—Quentin Bell, Thomas Caramagno, and Roger Poole—would agree (despite their sharp differences in other respects).[8] She herself tells in her diary how writing empowered her to find some equilibrium between mood swings: "It is this writing that gives me my proportions" (*WD*, 164); and in " A Sketch of the Past" she speculates how writing enables her to meet existential shocks of awareness breaking through ordinary "cotton wool" (un)consciousness and threatening to overwhelm her in what she calls "moments of being":[9]

> [M]any of these exceptional moments brought . . . a peculiar horror and a physical collapse; they seemed dominant; myself passive. . . . as one gets older one has a greater power through reason to provide an explanation; and . . . this explanation blunts the sledge-hammer force of the blow. . . . though I still . . . receive these sudden shocks, they are now always welcome. . . . And so I . . . suppose that the shock-receiving capacity is what makes me a writer. . . . [when] I have had a blow . . . [it is] not as I thought as a child, simply . . . from an enemy hidden behind the cotton wool of daily life; it is or will become a revelation of some order; it is a token of some real thing behind appearances; and I make it real by putting it into words . . . [which] make[s] it whole; this wholeness means that it has lost its power to hurt me. . . . From this I reach . . . a philosophy . . . that behind the cotton wool is hidden a pattern; that we . . . are connected with this; that the whole world is a work of art; that we are parts of the work of art. . . . we are the words, we are the music; we are the thing itself. (*MB*, 72)

In keeping with this insight, Woolf's fiction connects an art of the self to a sublime art of the universe.[10]

Just as she would have eschewed a narrow personal basis in her writing, so did she try to eschew the "damned egotistical self" in her life (*WD*, 23). If there were an original sin for Woolf, it would have been the fall from Edenic unself-consciousness to the agonized knowledge of her own naked self, when, in recollecting a scene from early childhood reminiscent of Lacan's mirror stage, she perceived herself as through the judgmental or intrusive gaze of others: "At any rate, the looking-glass shame has lasted all my life. . . . Everything to do with dress—to be fitted, to come into a room wearing a new dress—still frightens me; at least it makes me shy, self-conscious, uncomfortable" (*MB*, 68). Being a woman was not being without ego boundaries, but rather feeling ego as an imposition, which Woolf felt perhaps more acutely than most.

The condition of being a woman in her time meant inheriting a different kind of ego problem from that of a man. The ego, conceiving of itself as a thought-object by originally being the third-person object of others (Mead, Lacan, Jacques), was empowered for a man and disempowered for a woman by society. That is, feeling his separateness, he was encouraged to assert his interests; feeling her separateness, she was encouraged to sacrifice her interests to his. Thus, whatever path his subjectivities may have taken—like claiming to know the "objective" truth through classical rationalism, scriptural revelation, or modern science, or claiming to know the subjective truth through Cartesian subjectivity, German idealism, or romanticism—a man assumed the active orientation of gazing outward from a center and appropriating objects; whereas, whatever path a woman's subjectivities may have taken, she assumed the passive orientation of a center being gazed at and directed by men and determined by nature. Her "objectivity" was directed toward recognizing herself as biologically immersed in her sexual function in contrast to the man's intellectual function, while her "subjectivity" was directed toward recognizing herself as idiosyncratic and whimsical in contrast to a man's "universal" or "transcendental" insights. Grasping the political nature of this bifurcated social channeling of the human ego, women could either capitulate to and/or subvert it. The more the capitulation, the smoother one's apparent adjustment to the social order. In carrying this baggage of a woman's lot, Woolf did both, but tended more to subvert and suffer.[11]

She suffered with particular sensitivity at an early age, protesting inwardly any appropriation of her beauty by the male gaze, or of her body by invasive male fondling. (Bell, Caramagno, and Poole dwell at length on her sexual abuse by her half-brothers, from her account in *Moments of Being*.) In addition to sexual sensitivity, she was crucified by ridicule and could be tormented into "purple rages" by the occasional cruelties of her full siblings when they were young children. Later, extending that sense of being the center of intrusive attention to being judged publicly by her fiction, which was an exposure of herself, Woolf dreaded impending publication dates so intensely that they seemed to precipitate breakdowns almost as traumatic as deaths of beloved family or friends did.[12] Such an extreme ego sensitivity may have also been part of a bipolar physiological imbalance in addition to an imbalance from social and psychological factors (Caramagno), and only suggests how much more complex the construction of the self is than any one of these theories—social, psychological, physiological—can explain. However complex the sources of her ego sensitivity may have been, it is clear that Woolf sought to claim the male right of an impersonal gaze upon the objective world in order to escape her sense of an invaded female ego that was self-defeating in its extreme vulnerability, and that writing was her path to it.

The novels themselves attest to this struggle between the tyranny of self-consciousness and the relief of an impersonal subjectivity. It is *subjectivity* rather than *objectivity* because Woolf 's detachment is not just *from* the self as ego, but *through* multiple subjectivities of self. As an observer of the universe, Woolf realizes it to be the very stuff of herself, its flux her flux. Thus she vaults out of being "immanent" and personal as a woman to being "transcendental" and impersonal like a male writer (Simone de Beauvoir's terms) through the back door of the self, deconstructing the binary opposition between such gendered notions in her fiction, since this kind of transcendence reaches the outer through the inner—and vice versa—and is related to the receptive faculty called "feminine intuition" in women or openness to "the muse" in men.

The central problem Woolf's fiction addresses is how to preserve the integrity of the self as multiple subjectivities of the universe without either feminine ego effacement or masculine ego aggrandizement in the social world. Because of suffering from a bipolar disorder, she aimed for the equilibrium of a classic golden mean among dynamically related oppositions rather than the extremes of fixed polarizations. By exploring her own extreme states of bipolarity in her writing, she achieved greater equilibrium (Caramagno), suggesting that it is not one's condition that determines the value of one's life, but the struggle to deal with it honestly. Woolf sought in all her written discourses—diary writing, literary criticism, and essays, as well as fiction—to represent herself to herself and to her public with artistic and intellectual integrity. That integrity asserts no absolute truth as a form of ego claim, but is free to assert any honest point of view in the universe that its subjectivities may be conscious of.

The subjectivities of the impersonal universe that Woolf's fiction represents generally assume two broad phases of consciousness: (1) a dark, chaotic phase of fallowness, which state of dissolution, or formlessness, seems necessary for the return to (2) a creative phase of the outwardly manifest play of forms. This outer world of form ranges through multiple levels, from an impersonal way of relating or creating to a personal, ego-bound way. That is, the creative phase is always in a dialectic relationship with chaos. For example, Woolf regarded her periods of illness as fallow phases necessary for her productivity: "If I could stay in bed another fortnight . . . I believe I should see the whole of *The Waves*. . . . I believe these illnesses are in my case . . . partly mystical. . . . It [my mind] becomes a chrysalis. I lie quite torpid...then suddenly something springs" (*WD*, 153).[13]

For convenience, these phases of formlessness and form will be referred to as the *night self* and the *day self*, respectively, based on Woolf's second novel *Night and Day*. There the female protagonist representing Woolf, Katharine Hilberry, and her male counterpart, Ralph Denham, are matched in the realization that they have secret inner lives (their night selves) that they cannot share directly, but because they mutually respect that inner connection to the universe, that sanctuary from the demands of their own as well as the other's ego, they can then also relate less egotistically and more lovingly on the interpersonal, sharing level (their day selves).

The more sharply defined and firm one's identity in the world is, the more it might be thought of as day-dominated; the vaguer and more incoherent the forms, or the less attachment to any form there is, the more the night dominates, including intermediate "twilight" states of dream or fantasy in which the ego still hovers. These phases run the gamut from the black nothingness of midnight to the crystalline clarity of high noon, and should not be thought of as mutually exclusive or static states. Woolf's universe is as paradoxical and dynamic as the Taoist symbol yin-yang suggests, for although one phase may dominate the consciousness at any given time, the other is always implied in it somehow, moving along the underside, as the whole earth is both shadowed and illuminated at the same time from the perspective of outer space.

Often, the freedom to pursue an impersonal, more egoless state unscrutinized or judged by others—either in the fallow phase or the creative phase—brings peace to Woolf's characters, as in the example of Mrs. Ramsay in *To the Lighthouse* :

> And that was what now she often felt the need of—to think; well, not even to think. To be silent; to be alone. All the being and the doing . . . evaporated; and one shrunk, with a sense of solemnity, to being oneself, a wedge-shaped core of darkness, something invisible to others. . . . There was freedom . . . peace . . . most welcome of all, a summoning together, a resting on a platform of stability. Not as oneself did one find rest ever . . . but as a wedge of darkness. Losing personality, one lost the fret, the hurry, the stir; . . . and pausing there she looked out to meet that stroke of the Lighthouse, the long steady stroke, the last of the three, which was her stroke. . . . Often she found herself sitting and looking . . . until she became the thing she looked at—that light, for example. (*TTL*, 95–97)

However, in contrast to Mrs. Ramsay's feeling of liberation in the egoless state, one may feel anxiety, terror, or despair from a feeling of powerlessness to prevent self-annihilation in the impersonal universe of chaos. It depends on whether at any given time one is fearing or welcoming the loss of ego. Thus, within the night self as well as the day self emotions oscillate.

Yet there is a still greater threat than the loss of ego: the loss of subjective integrity, that is, the invalidation of any honestly felt or perceived subjective position, including that of egolessness. Paradoxically, the ego may serve to defend what Woolf called a "virgin territory," that is, the integrity of its subjectivities to enter or maintain an "inner" sanctuary, some area of formlessness, just as the ego defends "outer territories" of manifest form, such as one's body or accomplishments. When the ego is threatened, it will try to preserve its form, but when the integrity is threatened, the renunciation of one's form may seem to be the only way to preserve it, as in the case of Septimus Smith in *Mrs. Dalloway*, who commits suicide in defense of his integrity when society (especially the medical establishment) ignores his reality of having been shell-shocked in World War I and only attempts to control him. Septimus is alienated by a doubly monologic situation: he is mad insofar as he ignores others, being fixated on his own states, while those who ignore his truth are equally as mad, as Mrs. Dalloway (taking Woolf's point of view) understands.[14]

Woolf's intense need to work out of herself (in every sense), to come to grips with the issues of self, led her to the novel as her natural genre because she considered the main business of a novelist to be character portrayal, as she makes clear in her essays "Modern Fiction" and "Mr. Bennett and Mrs. Brown."[15] In them she criticizes novelists like Arnold Bennett, John Galsworthy, and H. G. Wells for depicting character by external means, which she calls "materialist," rather than by examining the process of internal self-formation. Again, however, the external-internal dichotomy does not hold up in her own works; neither does a label like "materialist," since she avails herself of the material environment extensively in the delineation of character. Her method of character portrayal differs from theirs in the subtle process by which "otherness" becomes internalized, a process reminiscent of the way Dostoevsky's characters generate heteroglossia in the novel.

Furthermore, her "external" is a divergent set of particulars and perspectives that conventional novelists tend to overlook. The "materialists" are more interested in the macrosituation—the gross and rationally coherent events of plot and character, rather than the random-seeming microevents that Woolf includes as part of subliminal consciousness. She shows how crucial the brush of a butterfly wing may be to a larger event in the life of the perceiving subject, anticipating our current theories of chaos that hypothesize the amplified effects of microevents.[16] Since she foregrounds the microevents that enter into thought and feeling and marginalizes the macroevents, her work defamiliarizes conventional narrative and tends to induce altered or subversive states of attention in the reader. For example, in *The Years* there is a scene at a party in which a character observes everything at knee level, just as a child might spy on adult legs under the table, which Woolf did in childhood—a view conducive to undermining adult authority.[17]

Woolf's way of revealing subtle lines of thought and influence in character could be compared to iron filings arranging themselves in ever-flowing patterns to reveal the otherwise invisible forces that surround a magnetic pole. One symbol of Woolf's vision appears in the scene where Katharine Hilberry recognizes that her lover Ralph Denham's representation of her in a little doodle is exactly her own vision of every entity in the universe: a small dot with rays like flames emanating from it. That is, everyone and everything is surrounded by an unseen aura, a radiance of forces that intersect in it, connecting it to all others. That aura, that pattern of radiance surrounding every entity with innumerable filaments of connectedness and disconnectedness (attraction and repulsion for other entities), is part of what one might call the "spirit" or "quality" of a character. Another part of "spirit" would be the original force, the underlying principle of magnetism (to return to the metaphor), which is the same regardless of the diversity of patterns of interaction.

As a professed writer of the spirit, Woolf's goal is to evoke a sense of the infinite play among entities—human and nonhuman—by representing both the visible and the invisible in the minds of all her observers: narrators, characters, readers, and herself as author. Though an agnostic, Woolf was spiritual and even mystical in her insights. She saw spirit in the meanest flower that blows, and included the material in her idea of the spiritual. This is in contrast to "materialist" writers who convey the outline of appearances well enough, but not the rich aura of spirit connecting them.

Unlike the strongly *out*lined characters in a "materialist" novel, Woolf's characters emerge in the view of the whole like figures in a pointillist painting when one stands back from the intermingling dots of color that obscure character boundaries close up.[18] Woolf's general choice of an omniscient narrator, who whirls from one subjectivity to another, intermingling the personal and the impersonal, is the most suitable narrative strategy to convey character as being diffused and inextricably relational. Her narrator's voice generally does not comment as much as it observes characters' states of mind and behavior directly. Another way to put it is to see the narrator's persona as egoless; here is where an Olenka-like plasticity has its uses as an artistic device because it can shape itself to any object, but unlike Olenka, it does not get stuck in personal attachment to anyone, alighting upon everything in its path with equal interest. And yet each work as a whole does have a path around and through the main characters.

Not only is her narrative "dialogic" in the social sense, a polyphony of human voices within and between her characters (in terms of Bakhtin's theory), but she incorporates the "voices" or felt influences of the environment upon the mind, which precede human discourses, and is conscious of the "semiotic" power of her language.[19] That sense of an Edenic state of consciousness prior to human discourse is captured in her earliest recollection, which she says in "A Sketch of the Past" is the "base" of "purest ecstasy" upon which the rest of her life stood. It is

> the feeling, as I describe it sometimes to myself, of lying in a grape and seeing through a film of semi-transparent yellow . . .
> . . . . Everything [is] large and dim; and what [is] seen [is] at the same time heard; sounds . . . come through this petal or leaf—sounds indistinguishable from sights. (*MB*, 64–66)

This "wholeness" of impressions seems to defy the categorizing separateness of experience (sights distinguishable from sounds) that discourse constructs, and yet Woolf is impelled to capture such unbounded, fluid moments in word forms.

The fluidity of her style and content is often remarked by commentators, and indeed water imagery predominates.[20] That she ultimately drowned herself is taken by some (e.g., Poole) to confirm her affinity to water, and water (or fluidity in general) is seen as a symbol of her process of dissolving the world into her consciousness and holding heterogeneous and contradictory fragments together in tension with one another. Moreover, diverse fragments are not merely blurred into some neutral or resolved homogeneity; they are *dis*solved, dispersed, rather than *re*solved (until they precipitate out of the mind into some form of resolution, perhaps for action). This state of holding all subjectivities in readiness to enter new dialogic combinations corresponds to the "negative capability" Keats attributed to Shakespeare. Woolf sought to be like Shakespeare and to reach that "incandescent" state of androgynous thinking by holding all personal subjectivities within her impersonal states.[21]

The female reader who comes to Woolf's work seeking some model whereby to affirm a female self will not be given a simple answer to an identity crisis. Instead, she will be treated to a way of seeing multiple possibilities within the given conditions of her culturally constructed experience. If, as Roberta Rubenstein suggests,[22] she envisions her self standing on the seashore looking out to the open sea, partaking of both land and sea in her liminality and feeling the rhythmic intermingling of all the elements in endless variations of the same patterns, she will capture the spirit of self that Woolf does in *The Waves*, which the next chapter will plumb in depth.

2
The Waves

THE DIALOGIC DESIGN

Of all Woolf's novels, *The Waves* is the one that most brings the stark consciousness of the self to the fore. The voices of direct subjectivities speak inner soliloquies as six protagonists, without benefit of an omniscient narrator describing what is outside their minds—except for the trace of a voice that identifies each speaker and puts each of their soliloquies into quotes. The virtual disappearance of the narrator approximates the "objectivity" of a play, and yet the work retains the scope of a novel. Unlike either traditional plays or novels, however, the usual logical and causal connections among events, the "facts" usually acted or narrated, recede into the background and are fragmented as part of the flotsam and jetsam of thought. Yet it is not a stream-of-consciousness technique like James Joyce's, with words that might literally run through the characters' heads. Neither is there any actual dialogue heard, despite the characters' frequent intense intercommunication. Woolf did not consider conversation her forte, as her other novels confirm, since it is usually represented only in snatches, with sentences often broken off.[1] Rather, the characters' voices are poetical prose representations of states of perception, feeling, and thought that include inarticulate subconscious as well as conscious levels.

The style and design, characterized as mythopoetic by Jean O. Love,[2] has features of an allegorical morality play like *Everyman*. Its nine sections (chapters or acts) represent the life span of the protagonists in the course of a mythic "day" ending with the final encounter with Death. Woolf called it a "playpoem." Each section is introduced by an interlude, written in italics like the setting for a play and describing the part of the "day" corresponding to that section's stage in the life of the characters. This biographical form is in keeping with Woolf's emphasis on character and biography in her novels. Hence *The Waves* has features of myth or allegory, poetry, drama, biography, and the novel. It constitutes a new kind of textual "self" made up of aspects of traditional genres.

The vision is held together by the interludes describing the impersonal world that is the subtext of the characters' personal soliloquies.[3] The voice of the interludes is the only sign of an omniscient narrator (other than the "he said, she said" voice introducing each soliloquy). The scheme of these interludes is to establish a traditional beginning, middle, and end: from the dawn of childhood and the morning of youth, to the high noon of the prime of life and the afternoon of middle age, and finally to the evening of old age and the night of death. Within the descriptions of the time of day are corresponding hints of the time of year, another age-old analogy: the spring of youth, the summer of maturity, the autumn of middle age and the winter of old age and death. The final interlude of all-consuming darkness also hints of spring within it, while the following night soliloquy anticipating death hints of a return to dawn. Thus, the linear trajectory of time appears to be cyclical, so that the whole generation being portrayed might be a wave, and each character a ripple in the vast ocean of time, going nowhere but repeating itself in endless variation. Woolf's vision is of a perpetual oscillation between the formation of selves by day and the dissolution of selves by night, with no evolutionary or teleological "progress" implied.

Besides the cyclical progression of time, the interludes establish a cyclical progression of space from impersonal to human and back, starting with descriptions of the sea, sky, and landscape; moving to the birds—wild creatures whose activity parallels that of humans in their ability to come together or to part company; coming into the garden—full of life that is nonhuman, yet cultivated and influenced by the human; and ending at the house where all the inanimate objects are shaped by human design but partake of the mystery of the impersonal world. At that point the scene is set for the entrance of the characters, each of whom vibrates between the impersonal and the personal.

The representation of the sixfold protagonist suggests a kaleidoscope in the way each of their facets reflects bits and pieces of both the impersonal and the social worlds, and in reflecting the same bits and pieces among themselves, they create an intricate pattern that shifts with every turn of thought, similar to what Bakhtin observes of Dostoevsky's method. At times the six characters seem very distinct, like separate individuals, and at other times they seem to merge into one, so that there is an oscillation between unity and diversity. One factor uniting them is the uniformity of style in the soliloquies, which counterbalances their polyphonic content and suggests a single subjectivity behind them all.[4] Another method is the positing of a seventh character, Percival, around whom their thoughts and feelings center, attracted to his charismatic "presence," but whose own thoughts are absent. A third unifying device is the use of the character of Bernard as the chief spokesperson of their relationship. He includes them in his own consciousness: "[W]hat I call 'my life,' it is not one life that I look back upon; I am not one person; I am many people; I do not altogether know who I am—Jinny, Susan, Neville, Rhoda, or Louis: or how to distinguish my life from theirs" (*W*, 368). It is he who begins most of the sections directly after the interlude, and who is the only consciousness in the last section summarizing the entire sweep of their lives as friends, suggesting that the uniform style is his, that he narrates them all. Bernard, in his need to find the right phrase and to imagine stories of others, may represent that part of Woolf's self that must articulate her experience, while the other characters might represent other facets of her self.

If these characters, who are peers, are taken together to represent a "whole" person, then the equal balance between three males and three females might represent her idea of the androgynous self. However, these characters balance each other in a general array of qualities that are hard to classify as masculine and feminine, so subtly distributed and permuted as these are. In their soliloquies, the characters often contrast and compare their qualities, as if trying to measure themselves relative to the others along some dimension. The total effect is to strike a rough equilibrium among them as a group, even though each is "unbalanced" as an individual in some respect or other. At the internal level within each character there is another balancing act between complementary qualities in order to retain enough equilibrium to make life tenable as a distinct individual. Some of the qualities that oscillate among and within them are degrees of orderliness and randomness, sociability and alienation, sensitivity and callousness, idealism and pragmatism, self-centeredness and self-diffusion, and stability and changeability, to name several ways of categorizing uncategorizable and cross-referential traits.

Related to these oscillating qualities are dominant images and metaphors peculiar to each character. Each of these individual motifs is sensed intuitively by the other characters and picked up by them in their soliloquies like a reflected bit of colored glass in a kaleidoscopic pattern. For example, Bernard speaks of his phrases as if they were bubbles streaming up in boiling water, forming and then disappearing. This motif conveys his effervescence and his transience of thought, qualities related to a volatility-stability dimension. Other characters then pick up on this motif of Bernard and, in a telepathic way, incorporate it into their thoughts about him. (This telepathic attunement might simply signal a unified narrator, except that they also misjudge or misconstrue one another, which suggests the opacity of separateness.) Bernard himself is most aware of the others' motifs, as well as his own, since it is he who is most empathic in his fascination with the stories he imagines about people (including his own personas), and most apt to sense and articulate their unspoken motifs.

While *The Waves* is culturally specific to Woolf's milieu—upper-middle-class British in the late nineteenth and early twentieth centuries—the basic qualities of the characters are more universally recognizable. Indeed, the poetic language surrounding the characters' dominant traits seems to be derived from the ancient discourse, prevalent in cultures both east and west, of the four basic elements—air, fire, water and earth. Although that essentialist theory of personality is not recognized today as scientific, it is still richly suggestive. Perhaps Woolf intuitively adopted it as appropriate to her mythic and allegorical method in this work. In any case, each of the six characters presents an inner discourse strongly reminiscent of the ancient scheme of four basic elements. This scheme helps both to clarify the qualitative differences among them and to obscure the gendering of such qualities.

The character primarily related to air is Bernard, the chief spokesperson, since the spoken word is related to the breath, and the breath, traditionally, to the "spirit" of the thing, which he tries to capture in phrase-bubbles. Like air, he himself has a very fluid quality of imagination; he easily adapts to wherever he is and to whomever he happens to be with, shifting like a breeze. Since his thought "molecules" tend to be diffused, he belabors himself for being "vague" and, as an aspiring writer, he is unable to see a story through to a conclusion, always fizzling out. Since he is never firmly one thing or the other, he is likely to exhibit very contradictory qualities (like the weather), such as romantic and prosaic or eccentric and conventional, depending on his current frame of mind. Thus Bernard comes closest to the Olenka-like protean quality of the omniscient narrator; but because he never totally loses his self in others, as women like Olenka do, he can extract himself and bounce along to the next involvement, appearing "indifferent" to his friends in his impersonal leave-taking. Indeed, he achieves a kind of impersonal universality by being ubiquitously personal. He retains his own self's continuity by collecting all his experiences in notebooks of phrases, and in memory, unlike the disconnected Olenka, for he is always preparing to write. But he cannot even write his own biography, because conventional narrative would never contain his notes.

Although Bernard is stable enough to marry and earn a living at a regular occupation, and although he enjoys modest contentment with the comforts and securities of everyday life (even identifying with ordinary people like shopkeepers, immersed in their cotton-wool affairs, who appeal to his need for security), he is nevertheless restless, questioning, and able to distance himself from it, that is, to float free into his preferred twilight zone that is neither day, weighted down with too solid an ego, nor lonely, "mystical" night, too empty of human solidarity. He can only tolerate fallow states of complete dissolution briefly. In the following speeches, Bernard clearly places himself at the level of egolessness that is still recognizably human: "I am not one of those who find their satisfaction in one person, or in infinity. The private room bores me, also the sky. My being only glitters when all its facets are exposed to many people" (304), and "it is the panorama of life, seen not from the roof [the cosmic view], but from the third story window [society] that delights me" (344).

The element of fire is exemplified in Jinny, who radiates energy and is always "dancing" like a flame, fascinating the gaze of others, which she welcomes. She is sexually promiscuous, setting men afire wherever she goes, consuming herself and them in passion, leaving only ash for the gray years of her life—without regrets. A motif of hers is the image of herself in a red dress, sitting on a gilt chair, intensely attracting some male in the room with her "signals," like a moth to a flame.

Here Woolf attributes to the character with her nickname the very kind of ego and body-centeredness that is opposite to her own dominant mode. While Woolf was slender, beautiful, and energetic like Jinny, we have seen how she could not have doted on clothes and makeup to accentuate her body as Jinny does. Sexually, Woolf seemed uninterested in men and is assumed to have been frigid in marriage. However, there may have been something in her of a Jinny, who is portrayed sympathetically as having flare and even a kind of glory. Jinny's adoration of the social whirl is per-haps reflected in Woolf's admission that she is something of a snob ("Am I a Snob?" in *Moments of Being*). Woolf, in her Bernardian ability to empa-thize, may well have imagined what it was like to be such a woman as she undoubtedly encountered.[5] (Jinny is like another of Woolf's characters, Mrs. Manresa, the "wild child" sensualist in *Between the Acts*.) Furthermore, even if Woolf's sensuality with respect to men had been frozen at an early age, it seems to have thawed in other directions—probably towards other women. This might explain her glorification of Jinny—as a kind of sex object of her own whom she herself might have been fascinated by (as opposites attract) and imaginatively drawn into, like a lover assuming the identity of the be-loved.[6]

Besides representing sexual passion in the fiery character of Jinny, Woolf has other ways of conveying passion, ways closer to her longing for the impersonal universe rather than romantic affairs solely on the human level. Perhaps she seeks something like a Whitmanesque "madness"—to be in direct contact with the stuff of nature, a pan- or multisexuality rather than either bi- or homosexuality. In keeping with such a universal sensuality is Woolf's affinity for the element of water, which brings life everywhere impersonally; the character dominated by that element is Rhoda, the "nymph of the fountain, always wet" in Bernard's phrase (256). Rhoda is also associated with another symbol of sensuality: flowers. If there is any object of the universe toward which Woolf's sensuality in her writing is more directed than women, it is flowers. After water imagery, floral imagery seems to prevail. Indeed, flowers are significantly paired with water in a motif of Rhoda's—a brown basin of water with white petals floating in it, her conscious representation of the earth containing the sea and a fleet of ships. The white petals may also unconsciously represent the fragmented sensuality of a pure flower torn apart or violated, as Rhoda feels herself to be much of the time, like that most raw and vulnerable side of Woolf.

As fire and water oppose each other, so do Rhoda and Jinny: Jinny commands attention and attracts desire, whereas Rhoda hides from any kind of gaze—even the shock of recognition by an old friend when they meet is unbearable torture to her. Jinny scintillates and dances, poses, gestures, and dresses, centered in the here and now of her body and its "come hither" signals to those around her, whereas Rhoda slinks and cringes, clumsily trying to imitate the self-assured postures and actions of the other women. She feels herself to have "no face" and no taken-for-granted sense of her body's place in the world (which may be related to some neurological imbalance, as Caramagno suggests), and longs to flee from the here and now into an ideal twilight world of fantasy (as with her basin of water and petals). Jinny's energy is inexhaustible, never tiring of activities and social adventures, wishing never to sleep, being like the sun, a perpetual day self, whereas Rhoda longs for night, sleep, oblivion, and dissolution, particularly associated with water, which she finally achieves in her suicide (much as Woolf herself was to). But while alive, and within a twilight zone, she still retains images from the day world that she has gleaned from her friends as material for dreams. At the same time that Rhoda is terrified of the assertive egos of others, she also longs to have more solidity of her own to make her life in society more tenable, which is a countercurrent to her night longings.

The construction of dreams in an ideal imaginary world rather than in society is where Rhoda's power and creativity lie. Her repeated fantasy of the white marble pillar by a pool (another motif) hints of classical Greek ideals, like the Platonic ultimate reality of pure form compared to which this world is shadows.[7] For her day and night seem to be inverted, with the splendor of spiritual light illuminating visions of eternal perfection, in contrast to the darkness of this fallen world, where, to extend this to a Christian vision, she is crucified daily. Rhoda is like Olenka in being an empty non-entity unable to retain an integrated self in the world; but Rhoda can construct another world of her own, whereas Olenka is helpless in solitude. On the other hand, Olenka achieves social viability by completely assuming the mask of a beloved, whereas Rhoda remains helpless in society.

All of the fluid characters have creative power, but their fluidity destabilizes any appearance of a tangible "product." Jinny's creative power is directed to preparing for and becoming involved in peak moments of ecstasy in this world, without creating anything to leave behind, not even a sentimental lock of hair (*W,* 330). She rides her wave of immediate encounters, then moves on to the next adventure. Jinny is much like Bernard in her roving voracity for incident. He, too, leaves no finished work behind, nothing but a memory of bubble-phrases that is too complex to generate anything like a coherent piece of writing. However, as a role-player, he does marry and leave progeny, so that his sexuality and role as bearer of cultural tradition at least bears fruit, while with all Jinny's sensuality and pride in her culture, there is no lasting trace, except memories in all those with whom she was involved. Yet Jinny achieves completion in each encounter, and is satisfied, whereas Bernard leaves dangling ends and is never satisfied. So Jinny and Bernard create, but their flashing moments and bubbles are evanescent, while Rhoda adheres to a vision of eternity so otherworldly—like a tableau at the bottom of the sea—that she, too, leaves nothing here but a memory for those in her wake.

Now we turn to the three characters of solid accomplishment in the world, those with a stake in the element of earth. The most obviously earthy of these is Susan, whose deep ancestral attachment to the fields of her farm and hearth makes her into a kind of pagan earth-mother figure. Susan's self-discourse is that of nature domesticated, which is the human version of animal territoriality. Like a tigress guarding her cubs, she is fiercely maternal and paces within her domain with watchful and possessive care. Susan may be the part of Woolf that loved the countryside and that longed for maternity.[8] Among her motifs are recollections of her parents, who pad through the house as reminders of what place she will inherit in an ancient legacy. Physically, she is short and "squat," close to the earth and very stable; she does not doubt who she is, like Rhoda, or fly off in all directions, like Bernard. What she wants is here and now, like Jinny, but it is rooted in fecundity, unlike Jinny's flitting and unproductive urban hedonism that blazes, leaving a path of ashes behind it. Susan achieves all her worldly ambitions in her single-minded pursuit of them; she is firm about what (or who) she loves and what (or who) she hates. Her day self is so fully developed that there is hardly any room in her mind for a night self, but it is there, underpinning the solid accomplishment of day; that is, her daytime side is already in harmony, or in equilibrium, with the primeval, impersonal cycles of nature, and she deals with death and decay with hardy acceptance.

Louis is another character with a strong stake in the earth—literally, in the motif of his childhood fantasy:

> I hold a stalk in my hand. I am the stalk. My roots go down to the depths
> of the world, through earth dry with brick, and damp earth, through veins
> of lead and silver. . . . Down there my eyes are the lidless eyes of a stone
> figure in a desert by the Nile. . . . I am green as the yew tree in the shade
> of the hedge. My hair is made of leaves. (182–83)

But his kinship with the vegetative world and with the legacy of the human race, while resembling Susan's, is conflicted by the demands of a competitive male society that requires more from a man than a simple bucolic existence. If in nature animals compete simply in order to survive or to have their genes selected, that competitive instinct becomes enlarged (and even corrupted) in human animals by the cultivation of the ego in a civilized world that allows unlimited imaginative possibilities for constructing ambitions beyond the simple necessities. Louis's problem lies in his being torn between a natural man's respect for the earth in providing for his animal needs, like Susan (and her farmer husband), and a civilized man's desire to fulfill the claims upon his ego for "success." (Another Woolf character like Louis is the embittered Giles in *Between the Acts*, who wanted to be a farmer, but was pressured into an urban profession he hates.)

Under the influence of classical Greek and Roman ideals of beauty and reason, Louis's vegetative night self, attuned to the collective unconscious of the race, becomes rarefied into a vision of eternal perfection, much as Rhoda's is; however, since he is more earthbound, with the active ego of a man of the world, his dream of a past golden age becomes a utopian impulse to reform decadent modern civilization through poetry. Although he longs for the idyllic arcades of Greece, or its nearest approximation in the halls of "Oxbridge," he feels pressured by his situation into channeling his brilliance along the commercial lines valued by modern British culture. The most brilliant scholar of his school class, Louis nevertheless feels hampered by his origins as the son of a failed Brisbane banker and by his Australian accent, which makes him feel like an outsider in English society. His brooding sense of social inferiority, coupled with his conviction of intellectual and moral superiority, produce a character dominated by the need for the worldly day self to succeed at all costs, including at the cost of suppressing the precious visions of union with the earth of his night self. Another of Louis's motifs from childhood is the image of a great chained beast stamping (from the sound of the waves breaking), which might be his feeling of the great night self being chained by civilization.

Unlike Rhoda, whose violated female ego flees from the invasions of the world, Louis's sensitive male ego is goaded to fight back and not merely retreat into the night or twilight self. His goal-oriented day personality becomes domineering and arrogant, not only in his drive for success but in his attitude of judge and would-be reformer. Unlike Susan, whose life is already integrated with the larger-than-the-individual cycles of the earth because society allows a woman's ego that "immanence," Louis feels compelled to "transcend" his immanence in the earth and beat "the boastful boys" at their own game. Therefore, Louis swings between extremes—one, his idealism based on identifying with ancient racial aspirations, and the other, his accommodation to a corrupt modern world where he must exert his ego: "I have signed my name . . . already twenty times. I, and again I, and again I. Clear, firm, unequivocal, there it stands, my name. Clear-cut and unequivocal am I too" (291).

Unable to achieve a moderate kind of equilibrium in his life, Louis is unhappy as he condemns the very world that gives him material success; with his intelligence and emotional drive, he becomes a big corporate executive, but takes no hedonistic pleasure in riches. Like many moral purists, he has a streak of ascetic self-denial that impels him to retreat to a slum attic where sordid sights give him a perverse solace in confirming his moral superiority; he needs to maintain a view of extreme polarization to support his superiority. He admits he has a cockney mistress over whom he can feel socially superior as well. Thus his domesticity is not centered like Susan's, but divided between the extremes of his private attic and his public mansion.

The last character with a close affinity to the earth is Neville, who is like Susan and Louis in his tenacity for achieving worldly success and in his need for being established in a domicile, in contrast to Bernard, Jinny, and Rhoda, who are nomadic. Neville's motif is the hearth, the cozy, private, fire-lit room where he can retreat from the world into intimate relations with a single beloved individual, the boy or man with whom he may be homosexually involved at any given period of his life. Like the territorial animal Susan is, he is fiercely attached to whomever he loves and rejecting of whomever he hates, and is racked with pain by any slight by the beloved. Like Louis, he is intellectually gifted, a lover of classic ideals and poetry, critical of mediocrity, and conscious of his superiority. Both Neville and Louis reflect that side of Woolf that was inspired by classic ideals and felt contempt for the gross materialism of modern society.

Unlike Louis, however, Neville is in a position to fulfill his intellectual and poetic aspirations of achievement in the arcades of academe, unclouded by any social inferiority in his situation and feelings—except for his homosexuality. But his aberration can be kept in the closet, unlike a foreign accent. (It should be noted that these childhood friends of his do know his sexual orientation and accept it, suggesting that they constitute a small, more sexually liberated subculture apart from the rest of their class, similar to Woolf's Bloomsbury circle.)[9] Neville can afford to indulge his night self without the kind of conflict Louis has, because his worldly achievement as a literary man allows him more freedom to consort with the night-related Muse than the world of commerce allows Louis. Neville's greater integration of his night and day selves enables him to enjoy the here and now, seeing poetry even in simple things, in contrast to Louis's need to feel contempt for little ordinary things and to impose a "blue steel ring" of exalted poetry to bind the world back to idealism.[10]

Yet Neville feels awe and dread when the impersonal universe assumes a threatening aspect, as when he is haunted by images of death at a moment of solitude imposed by his delicate health:

> I will use this hour of solitude . . . to . . . recover . . . what I felt when I heard about the dead man. . . . He was found with his throat cut. The apple-tree leaves became fixed in the sky; the moon glared; I was unable to lift my foot up the stair. He was found in the gutter. . . . His jowl was white as a dead codfish. I shall call this stricture, this rigidity "death among the apple trees" for ever. . . . the implacable tree with its greaved silver bark. The ripple of my life was unavailing. I was unable to pass by. . . . And the others passed on. But we are doomed, all of us by the apple trees, by the immitigable tree which we cannot pass. (191)

Neville, like Louis, is morbidly fascinated by decay and death, in contrast to Susan's more down-to-earth acceptance, which is untrammeled by high intellectual idealisms. His fascination and dread are embodied in the tree, just as Rhoda is unable to cross a puddle that transfixes her: "I came to the puddle. I could not cross it. Identity failed me. We are nothing, I said, and fell" (219).[11] Like Neville's, hers is an insight into the abyss of the human condition, and in her dread she must clutch at something solid (a brick wall here) to get past that terror of dissolution, which she dreads as much as she seeks. Neville just waits till the spell passes, till he can pull himself together as Rhoda never quite seems to, but he, too, seeks something solid to cling to. Because he is sickly and afraid, he needs a cloistered life, a space intensely personal, to counteract the terrors of the night, and an ivory-tower profession that partly protects him from the terrors of the day—Louis's world of cutthroat competition. (Although even academe and the literary world have the pressure of "publish or perish," Neville seems more at ease in his arena than Louis in his.)

To sum up, the three characters with fluid self-concepts of air, fire, and water have the advantage of liberation from being earthbound, but the corresponding disadvantage of being unaccomplished by society's standards, which they may or may not internalize as their own. For example, while Jinny's lack of marriage is unacceptable socially, she willfully defies that convention because she is fulfilled without it, whereas Bernard alternates between accepting and disapproving of his lack of ambition. As for Rhoda, her lack of a facade is even more intolerable to herself than it is to others, and because she cannot negotiate between inner freedom and social demands as Jinny and Bernard do, she is forced into solitary fantasy. The other three have the advantages and disadvantages in reverse. Established achievers, they nevertheless tend to be constricted in their clinging to their domains possessively and self-righteously. While on one hand all six have a certain amount of inertia, on the other hand they all have enough fluidity to lose whatever appearance of static individual essentialism they otherwise might exhibit.

If we regard them all as one composite "whole" character, then the advantages and disadvantages would be balanced out in a multiple and contradictory larger "self." However, if we regard them as fixed essences, or merely types, as the foregoing analysis based on the four elements might suggest, then we lose the sense of how their interrelationship creates a dynamic flow among them, which is not merely a static collective of a whole and its parts but an active participation in the balancing process Woolf sought. Part of the advantage of combining the discourse of day and night selves with that of the four basic elements to describe the characters is that any suggestion of static gender essentialism is dismantled by the night self oscillating with all the forms of day (and twilight).

In addition to their interrelational dynamics, time is the crucial dimension through which their wave forms rise and fall. The following section will give an idea of the major effects that the characters have on each other as well as the effects of time and the impersonal universe on them, all of which deflect the stream of their self-narratives into a marbleized dialogue.

The Dynamics of the Characters' Lifetime Relationships

That such a group of disparate spirits came together in the first place and remain friends for life can hardly be accounted for by any "materialist" facts. All the text does is place them in early childhood in a house and garden by the sea where they play outside and have lessons inside in a nursery schoolroom, much as Woolf and her siblings did at their summer house in St. Ives. What keeps this group together is partly that they have been their own earliest peer contacts, having shared experiences that imprint upon one another for life. As Bernard says, "All these things happen in one second and last for ever" (342), and these first faces are "cut out," not "confused" or "featureless" like those that come later (352–53). Despite their differences, they can depart to some degree from their dominant tendencies; being sensitive to all the influences of the world, they are all capable of experiencing "moments of being" like Woolf, and of achieving solidarity at peak moments by entering fluid states of consciousness that overcome fears and antipathies.

The very first influence on them is that of the natural world, as each one responds with feeling and imagination to different sensory objects. Their characters are almost indistinguishable, impersonal, in the early dawn of their awakening and playing in the garden, as simple observers without any purpose. Like the birds described in that interlude, their "melody" is "blank" (180). Their observations move from nature toward anticipating human purposes in the house, paralleling the direction of the interludes, and signaling the beginning of personality differentiation. Louis is the first to have a purpose: to resist assuming his ego fully through social "hailing" (Althusser) by staying hidden from the others in a bush, where he is his vegetative self "down there" in his roots, although he is still partly aware of his ego as "the boy in grey flannels [up here]" (182).

Louis's fall from the grace of the impersonal comes when Jinny makes eye and then lip contact with him. The gaze and the kiss destroy his solitude and, as the sin of Adam and Eve set in motion consequences for all of humanity, so does this violation set in motion the major themes for the rest of their lives. When Louis's trance is shattered, he is forced to defend his ego, beginning his conflict between remaining unknown, buried in the earth, and having to build a reputation above-ground. Jinny is excited with the discovery of her ability to recall him from an otherworldly stillness to her center in the here and now, which sets her in motion to arousing men. Meanwhile, Susan, having spied Jinny kissing Louis, is consumed with jealousy, which sets up her pattern of general possessiveness and particular rivalry with Jinny. Her motif is a handkerchief screwed into a ball, representing her intensity of feeling and attachment. Into this little mythological drama Bernard enters as the "omniscient" observer of Susan's woe; not content to merely observe her dispassionately, he compassionately runs to comfort her, thereby leaving his present companion Neville in the lurch.

This precipitates Neville's jealousy and possessiveness toward his future lovers, and the feeling of being abandoned by them.

Only Rhoda remains outside all this intrigue, rocking her basin of white petals on water in a mystical world of her own. She identifies with the solitary bird and with the single petal in her bowl that stays afloat beyond the foundering others, indicating her wish to survive—not in the fallen world of society, but in an eternal Eden where she is mistress of her own destiny. She could be compared to the Buddhist seeking Nirvana, or to the martyred saint seeking salvation. On the other hand, she struggles to find a viable form in the world. In her flailing attempt to comprehend a lesson on the chalkboard, she resorts to fantasy, personifying the hands of the school-room clock as travelers in a desert seeking an oasis, with herself as the slow hour hand stumbling painfully behind the bold minute hand; she imagines the loops of chalked writing as filling up with the time-bound world as she cries, "Oh, save me, from being blown for ever outside the loop of time!" (189). When Louis sees Rhoda unable to formulate meaning from that school exercise, he is moved with sympathy, intuiting her very thoughts:

> There Rhoda sits staring at the blackboard. . . . Her shoulderblades meet across her back like the wings of a small butterfly. And as she stares at the chalk figures, her mind lodges in those white circles; it steps through those white loops into emptiness, alone. They have no meaning for her. She has no answer for them. She has no body as the others have. And I . . . do not fear her as I fear the others. (189)

The butterfly, his symbol for Rhoda, is a particular motif of Woolf's for fragile beauty; indeed, her original title for this work was *The Moths*, emphasizing the nocturnal side of the sensitive creatures of her imagination who flit towards the light. Louis is free to feel compassion for Rhoda's plight because she poses no threat to him. His understanding of her, in turn, assuages her fear. Their relationship is thus a rare opportunity for each to achieve some kind of solidarity with another human being, enabling them to breach their protective shells. Not only do they have a similar purpose in wanting to retain the integrity of their dreams, they also have a common cause as a subgroup of outsiders or "conspirators" apart from the others, seeking refuge in each other in their social alienation. This is why they become lovers for awhile in later life. But Louis and Rhoda cannot remain together, because, while they respect each other's night dreams and ideals as fellow outcasts, his controlling day self intimidates her.

Despite Louis's and Rhoda's greater separation from the others than from each other, there are still forces binding them to the others, forces that

overcome their fears at times. For example, Louis is capable of solidarity
with them when he realizes how vulnerable they all are as children: "Now,
... we all rise. ... When we are sad and trembling with apprehension it is
sweet to sing together, leaning slightly, I towards Susan [whom he admires],
Susan towards Bernard, clasping hands, afraid of much ... yet resolute to
conquer" (192). The orderliness of being led by the firm hand of the teacher
and the beauty of music and poetry bridge their separation, influencing
Louis, like a latter-day Shelley, to put his faith in an order of poetry as
redemptive of humanity. Rhoda's moments of solidarity with the others,
however, do not come from her recognition of their common frailty, but
from those moments when they seem non-threatening and allow her to be.

The chief unifying force for all of them is their sympathy and caring for
one another, which is always being strained by their divergent paths. As
remarked earlier, Bernard operates as an integrative force among them
through the power of his caring. Without him it is hard to imagine that they
would remain in touch all their lives, since their paths are so separate. From
the first section the focus is more on his relationships with each of them
than with any other set of relationships among them, since he is more inclined to seek them out. For example, although he may leave Neville "dangling," he returns sooner or later and manages to overcome Neville's an-
noyance by entertaining him with stories. Because of love, Neville learns to
tolerate Bernard's vagaries and becomes a little more free-floating himself
over time, although at first he prefers to make nice distinctions between
himself and Bernard, because he is coated with the "thin, hard shell" of
youth (377). But even as a young man, Neville confides his first poem to
Bernard trustingly (236).

In the first section we follow Bernard at greater length than anyone else
in his effort to comfort Susan by distracting her from her tight little balled-
up ego. He takes her to a spot in the garden where they spy a lady writing,
a place he calls Elvedon because he has transformed it into a mysterious
fairyland where he pretends the gardeners sweeping the lawn with brooms
are guards of the lady and enemies to intruders (him and Susan). Susan is
drawn into the pretense as they flee for their lives when the evil guardians
approach. She has loosened her hold on her wish to die of jealousy. But
upon reaching safety, Bernard's plot fades as he rambles along on other
trains of thought, eluding Susan who says, "Now you trail away ... making
phrases. Now you mount like an air-ball's string higher and higher ... out
of reach. ... You have escaped me" (186). But in her autumnal years Susan
recalls that flight with him, that loosening of her hold on who she is, and
reflects that not only Bernard had escaped her, but what he had to offer has
escaped her—the free play of imagination of entering into a larger world

than her limited prosaic one. She has been too engrossed in the hard facts of day and feels she has missed something of the night. He has additionally given her a key to release her from the suffering ego's isolation when he replies: "But when we sit together, close . . . we melt into each other with phrases. We are edged with mist. We make an unsubstantial territory" (185). In short, she eventually realizes she must expand her definition of her territory.

Elvedon is more than a representation of what Bernard has to offer earthbound Susan. It also has the postmodern effect of textual self-referentiality, which, in a work about the self, suggests that the lady writing is the appearance in the text of the author herself, who is an alter ego of Bernard's just as he is one of hers. As she creates him, he creates her, the emblem of his fleeting ambition (except that Woolf succeeded in disciplining her writing by balancing out the mistiness of his rainbow with some granite from her other subjectivities). This incident of self-reflexivity is part of the text's deconstruction of any notion of self that can be grasped in strictly referential, "materialist" language. For example, while Susan says "I see the beetle. . . . It is black, I see; it is green, I see; I am tied down with single words," Bernard is nudging her to let go of hard meanings; just as time and new adventures release her possessiveness toward a single person like Louis, so do "words, moving darkly, in the depths of your mind . . . break up this knot of hardness, screwed in your pocket-handkerchief," as he says to her (185). Phrases that are suggestive, with multileveled and deferred meanings (not approved of by the precise Louis and Neville, either) are Bernard's way in contrast to Susan's hard-edged referentiality. But she is still too young and encased in her shell to follow his meandering meanings.

Woolf deftly shows how fluidity of language corresponds to the fluidity of selves in achieving, not solidity, but solidarity in Bernard's phrase "we melt into each other with phrases" (185). Her frequent repetition of the signifier *I* in "I see it. . . . I see it" or Louis's "I, I, I" deconstructs the signified "subject" more convincingly than Derrida's academic theorizing, according to Ruth Porritt.[12] Yet Bernard's subjectivity is not null and void, or "dead" as some postmodernists may claim—just infinitely deferred into others. Another example of how Bernard's use of language tears down ego barriers is his approach to a complete stranger on the train: "I at once wish to approach him; I instinctively dislike the sense of his presence, cold, unassimilated, among us. I do not believe in separation. We are not single"; and then with airy "smoke ring phrases wreathing" off his lips, notes: "His solitude shows signs of cracking. He has passed a remark. . . . A smoke ring issues from my lips . . . bringing him into contact. The human voice has a disarming quality" (221).

However, even phrases may be too binding in the face of the unspeakable. Bernard sometimes turns to "the little language of lovers"—sighs, cries, moans—the primitive signifiers that precede abstract symbolic language. And beyond even that lie the infinite discourses of silence, which all three women appreciate, but which are for Bernard an unbearable "pressure of solitude. When I cannot see words curling like rings of smoke around me I am in darkness—I am nothing" (267). Yet even in that state of night he is conscious; although the subject experiencing night is not dead, the ego is even more dismantled than when it merges into persons. Only later in life does Bernard value his night self more and tolerate the chaos:

> These moments of escape are not to be despised. . . . I see far out a waste of water. A fin turns. This bare visual impression is unattached to any line of reason, it springs up as one might see the fin of a porpoise on the horizon. . . . Visual impressions often communicate thus briefly statements that we shall in time to come uncover and coax into words. . . . A meaningless observation, but to me, solemn, slate-coloured, with a fatal sound of ruining worlds and waters falling to destruction. (307)

The pendulum then swings from the dismantling of the old order to the coming of a new form, sensed by his feeling a "drop" forming on the roof of his mind. From the faceless subject of wordless chaos, Bernard turns to recreate himself as his own partner (307), thereby reinventing referentiality in the wake of the unreferential fin, which is Woolf's image for a blank signifier in a waste of infinitely deferred meanings, an image that came to her as the harbinger of this work within herself. The problem with the deconstructed "subject" is that it remains far out at sea, carried off like Rhoda. The self must continually form new drops, ripples, and waves and come in to shore to be viable in the world. As Woolf gives us words of the self, so does she take them away.

Returning, then, to the shore of Bernard's and the others' oscillations through school and young adulthood, we encounter that other unifying force—the figure of Percival. He has a power that brings them to solidarity by setting aside their fears and rivalries, thereby bringing them individually as well as collectively to a greater equilibrium between the order and chaos that otherwise polarizes them. Like Jacob in *Jacob's Room*, Percival is known through his absence more than through his presence because his presence is so powerful that it becomes part of them. He enters their lives as a schoolfellow of the young men who is somehow brought into contact with the young women, just as Woolf's brothers brought their friends home.[13]

Before discussing his specific effects on them, it is necessary to inquire, based on clues in their thoughts, about Percival's role in the novel and why he is so central a figure. On one hand, they idolize Percival, but on the other hand, they allow unflattering observations about him as a fallible human being to slip out. He is quite ordinary in his clumsiness (like Jacob), is apparently unquestioning of his conventional education, and is quite willing to take up his role as colonizing sahib in India—where Bernard imagines him "applying the standards of the West, . . . using the violent language that is natural to him. . . . [solving] the Oriental problem [as the] multitude cluster around him, regarding him as if he were—what indeed he is—a God" (269). In his adoration of Percival, Bernard is overlooking the violence and colonizing mentality, or justifying it as the prerogative of a superior being. Here Woolf gives us a glimpse into the underside of the mythmaking process by simultaneously showing Bernard's enthrallment on one level and a basis for his disenchantment on another. In effect, she demystifies the myth, at least for the reader, as the significance of Percival's name, "to pierce the veil," suggests. Thus, Percival can be regarded from a dual perspective—as a situated self and as an ideal, mythological self— which dual strands Woolf weaves together into an inseparable fabric.

As Kathy Phillips has abundantly documented in *Virginia Woolf Against Empire*, Woolf disapproved of violence and colonialism, and feminist readers like Makiko Minow-Pinkney and Maria diBattista therefore assume that Woolf's main purpose in setting Percival up on great heights is to knock down all the harder the patriarchy he represents.[14] This is a valid assumption, but it does not account for the consensus among Woolf scholars that Percival represents her favorite brother, Thoby. Since Woolf adored Thoby, the question arises as to whether Percival affirms any of her positive values, and what those might be.

As a situated self, this ordinary young man inspires general adoration. At school he is so charismatic that flocks of boys follow him and imitate his every gesture ("unsuccessfully"). This charisma should not be easily overlooked as a given or dismissed out of hand by feminists as something of mere patriarchal value, i.e., a "leadership" quality. For although a natural leader, Percival is not like Mr. Kurtz in Conrad's *Heart of Darkness*, because he seems to have an "indifference," as Bernard remarks, an unself-conscious, unassuming detachment from his ego. He does not glory in his power over others, which suggests an alternative use of power that is benign. Bernard notes that although Percival was "not the least precocious," he nevertheless "thought with that magnificent equanimity . . . that was to preserve him from so many meannesses and humiliations" (344).

One explanation for Percival's equanimity despite his lack of precociousness lies in his social position. As a member of the British upper class, he is so thoroughly confirmed in a tradition of fixed roles in the order of society that he has no self-doubts, not a shred of a modern identity crisis, particularly in his role of privileged authority. That his every gesture becomes a command is not simply because underlings are fawning, but because he does everything with an air of unquestioning and supreme self-assurance that is impossible to imitate by those not equally in the thrall of the rightness of their existence, for imitation is only a "materialist" approximation of an inner spirit. Woolf is acknowledging through Percival how a spirit of self-assurance can be magnetic, just as she was more captivated by her older brother Thoby, who had audacity and verve, than by her younger brother Adrian.[15]

However, this charisma could not be simply determined by external circumstances, e.g., birthright, but by his inner disposition, either an attitude of conviction or enthrallment. That everyone is entranced by Percival is probably due to his own naive enthrallment by the stage set he was born into. He is very conventional and plays his part to the hilt—and yet the part he plays has so much authority built into it that he can take liberties with convention with the "indifference" that comes of complete self-confidence. In addition, because he is detached from seeking power (since he already has it), Percival never feels compelled to jockey for position or prove himself and can afford to be relaxed enough to accept others as he does himself. (The underside of this relaxation might be the complacency implied in his "lack of precociousness.") His naive magnanimity endears him to his friends and enables them to relax their own intrapsychic self-doubts and interpersonal conflicts. He is like a catalyst that promotes a certain kind of interaction without itself changing, and he has a paradoxical stimulating and calming effect on their inner and outer dialogue.

Yet Percival himself seems to balance on the razor's edge between full-hearted Dionysian involvement—his favorite music is "wild hunting songs" (350)—and the ability to walk away, much to the distress of Neville, who is in love with him and wants to possess him. "He had the kind of beauty which defends itself from any caress" says Bernard (344), which puts his "indifference" in an ambiguous light. Negatively, as a situated self, he seems not very caring about others, but positively, as an ideal cast in terms of a classic pagan hero or noble knight, he is too "indifferent" (detached) to be either possessed or a possessor. While Woolf approves of his power of Dionysian *jouissance*, which is innocently amoral like that of a prelapsarian child of nature, she condemns him as soon as he is conscripted in India to suppress it in others. Thus Percival, like Jacob going off to World War I, must die.

And Percival's death is unheroic—just a random riding accident due to his (literally) cavalier carelessness. He who confers so much meaning upon life for the main characters disappears in a meaningless death, like Thoby, who died of an illness contracted abroad. That Percival's absurd death is an anticlimax to the buildup of his heroic image, suggests the folly of carrying on an aristocratic tradition that has long since exhausted its original vitality, the folly of the colonial adventure he associated himself with, and the folly of worshipping an ordinary human being, follies that Woolf felt subject to in her mythologizing of the deceased Thoby (and of her deceased mother as well). All these strands of patriarchal hubris are undone by the power of feminine chaos to puncture the inflated ego and pierce the veil of an illusory solid self (to use a metaphor that confounds gendered notions).

While Percival's death undermines his idealization, that idealization serves functions more central to the novel than his demotion to fallibility. Woolf is distinguishing between two kinds of order that are conflated in Percival and liable to be confused. One is the monologic patriarchal order, which is the ideology that happens to be situated in him (or him in it). The other is his participation in something like a principle of order in the universe, a principle corresponding to Woolf's intuition of an underlying pattern of connectedness when she pierces the veil of ordinary cotton-wool perceptions. It is this impersonal cosmic order that allows Percival to cohere as a presence.[16] (While this "manic" belief of hers could be taken for a foundational one, she herself oscillates between it and belief in chaos in her depressed states.)[17] That cosmic order is an ordering *process* rather than an immutable regime. Thus, Percival symbolizes a divine process that reaches the zenith of form by day, the apogee of order in the universe, while his absent thoughts and his death represent the oscillation of chaos and order, absence and presence. That is, his destruction at the point of fullest embodiment of self at midday, when form is at its sharpest and clearest, is the most dramatic statement of the underlying nothingness of the self. It is as if one must be able to embrace one's form fully, and then to let it go fully, like Nietzsche's indifferent (super)man who dies at his height. As a symbol of pure assertive form and pure indifferent formlessness, the larger symbolic function of Percival in the novel amounts to the balance of forces Woolf is striving for—he becomes a symbol of androgyny, that is, dialogism, not just masculinity. By personifying an ideal of perfect balance between being nobody and being somebody, the figure of Percival also acts as a foil by which to measure the imbalances of the six main characters.

We see them best—in the light of Percival—when the great wave of their lifetime reaches a peak at the center of the novel just before the high noon of their life's day when they are all gathered to wish him bon voyage. The scene begins with their feeling awkward and distanced, keyed up with anticipation and the "shocks" of recognition. As each arrives, he or she comments on the next. They observe one another with mixed emotions of admiration, pity and/or rivalry. Neville's comment on Bernard serves to heighten our expectations of Percival by contrast:

> He does not look in the glass. His hair is untidy, but he does not know it. . . . He hesitates on his way here. . . . He half knows everybody; he knows nobody (I compare him with Percival). . . . But now, perceiving us, he waves a benevolent salute; he bears down with such benignity, with such love of mankind (crossed with the humour at the futility of "loving mankind"), that, if it were not for Percival, who turns all this to vapour, one would feel, as the others already feel: Now is our festival; now we are together. But without Percival there is no solidity. (259)

Percival is beyond compare because Neville idolizes him. Poor Rhoda, also in love with Percival, feels Neville's anxiety most when she says, "The sharp breath of his misery scatters my being" (259–60), so it is to her relief and Neville's when Percival finally appears. Now they are transformed; as Neville says, "Now. . . . My heart rises. . . . All impediment is removed. The reign of chaos is over. He has imposed order. Knives cut again" (260).

Bernard, picking up on the looking-glass cue, notices that Percival smoothes his hair (without looking in the glass) not from vanity, "but to propitiate the god of decency. He is conventional; he is a hero" (260). Bernard has interpreted Percival's gesture as typifying the heroic figure who knows when to bow to convention and when not to, e.g., he is late and, as Jinny notes, has not dressed for the occasion. This is an example of how Percival is the kind of person who might get away with certain violations of the rules, as a leader with prerogatives rather than as a slavish follower. While Bernard can bend the rules to some extent, he imagines that only Percival would have the audacity to commit himself fully to a major breach of convention. As he speculates in later life, Percival "would have done justice. He would have protected. About the age of forty he would have shocked the authorities" (345).

Percival's entrance affects them all profoundly. After rambling through the memories of their previous encounters as children and in school, reviewing their strengths and weaknesses compared to each other, they suspend their usual modes of being. Louis, for example, says, "Now let us issue from the darkness of solitude" (260) and is released from his alienation. Jinny surpasses her usual body-centeredness, saying, "Yes . . . our senses have widened. . . . Membranes, webs of nerve . . . have filled and spread themselves and float round us like filaments, making the air tangible and catching in them far-away sound unheard before" (269). But it is Rhoda's soliloquies that reveal the most marked alteration in Percival's presence. "Look," she says, "listen. Look how the light becomes richer ... and bloom and ripeness lie everywhere; and our eyes . . . seem to push through curtains of colour . . . , which yield like veils and close behind them, and one thing melts into another" (268). This speech is remarkable for its utter peace and acceptance of the world at midday, in contrast to the terror or lament of her previous thoughts just a moment before. She pierces veils as the sharp forms of noon melt benignly.

Rhoda's peace takes the lead in this section and enables her to enter upon a great mystic vision of a pure white shape, a living form that seems to undergo transformations, but is not in the form of any one of them:

> It makes no sign, it does not beckon, it does not see us. Behind it roars the sea. It is beyond our reach. Yet there I venture. . . . And for a second even, now, even here, I reach my object and say, "Wander no more. All else is trial and make-believe. Here is the end." But these pilgrimages, these moments of departure, start always in your presence, from this table, . . . from Percival and Susan, here and now. (271–72)

It is as if she has a vision of the protean quality of the "soul" that takes on all form provisionally, without being essentially any form. She can only reach this nocturnal abstract vision through the concrete forms of day—through all of them, especially through Percival and Susan. Thus, Woolf shows that there is neither pure spirituality nor pure matter and that they are realizable only through each other.

Rhoda's mystic trance is not solitary, however, not in that moment when all of them are transformed by Percival. Louis engages her in a dialogue apart from, yet in the same context as, the others: "('Look, Rhoda . . . they have become nocturnal, rapt. Their eyes are like moths' wings moving so quickly that they do not seem to move at all')" (272), in which they seem to be observers of a savage ritual around a fire, decking their beloved (Percival) with laurel and flowers—violets, symbolizing death even at the height of honor. Percival has returned them all to a primitive past, and they have become like nocturnal moths entranced by fire, their wings oscillating so quickly between the darkness and light that an equilibrium resembling stillness is achieved.

Bernard cannot even call it "love" that has united them as his symbolizing impulse reaches for a better way to express their state:

> No, that is too small, too particular a name. . . . We have come together to make one thing . . . not enduring—for what endures? —but seen by many eyes simultaneously. There is a red carnation in that vase. A single flower

... but now a seven-sided flower, many-petalled ... —a whole flower to
which every eye brings its own contribution. (263)

Although Bernard later refers to Percival as their missing center (282), this
particular symbol is a *seven*-sided egalitarian structure, with Percival just
another decentered petal. That small detail of Bernard's symbol radically
alters our perception of their relative positionality and takes Percival off his
pedestal momentarily. This image in effect makes each one of them equal
in their alternating ability to be both centered and decentered, just as light
can be theorized as either waves or particles. Their equality is based on
sharing that generative inchoate space which may be conceived of as either
an *inner* center or an *outer* decentered space surrounding the subjectivities
already marked. This equal creative blankness is the basis for respecting
persons regardless of the particular voices and discourses that proliferate
and circulate through them.

The trance, of course, cannot endure. They all depart wondering what
shapes their futures will assume, especially Neville, who would hold onto
that union with Percival forever. His absence in death has as profound an
effect on them as his presence in life.

Neville's wish to hold onto personal love is sorely tried by his love for
the impersonal stark truth, which, in the glare of high noon, takes the form
of Percival's death. He is again transfixed by his old vision of the immiti-
gable apple tree and refuses to rejoin the stream of life in his grief. The only
other characters who appear in this section are Bernard and Rhoda. Rhoda
belittles each of the others, even Neville, for being capable of going on with
their lives much as before, whereas her life's course has been radically altered by his death. Not only does she feel the loss, but she is impelled to a
kind of resolution. It is as if his death enables hers: if he who is the giver of
meaning and order can charge into death, she, too, can fling herself upon
the cruel, indifferent world with courage. Instead of crumbling passively at
the news, as she appears to at first, she turns her gaze boldly upon the
world, judging it instead of being judged, as she says,

Look now what Percival has given me. Look at the street now that Percival
is dead. The houses are lightly founded to be puffed over by a breath of
air. Reckless and random the cars ... hunt us to death like bloodhounds.
I am alone in a hostile world. This is to my liking. I want publicity and
violence and to be dashed like a stone on the rocks. (286)

This time she pierces the veil and finds this illusory world to be as chaotic as
herself, and to have a threatening aspect. But in further meditation on
Percival's gift, she sees that there is some order, some tangible meaning

after all, and in this revelation, and through her newfound courage, realizes in the following mystical vision that the world is not the threat she thought:

> —but what is the thing that lies beneath the semblance of the thing? Now that lightning has gashed the tree and the flowering branch has fallen and Percival, by his death, has made me this gift, let me see the thing. There is a square; there is an oblong. The players take the square and place it upon the oblong. They place it very accurately; they make a perfect dwelling-place. Very little is left outside. The structure is now visible; what is inchoate is here stated; we are not so various or so mean; we have made oblongs and stood them upon squares. This is our triumph; this is our consolation. (288)

James Naremore interprets this soliloquy of Rhoda's to be a "bitter irony," as if she is mocking the worldly order that recognizes "very little left outside," i.e., where her world lies.[18] However, irony here would be too consistent with a fixed notion of Rhoda's identity as a creature of disorder; it would disregard her general need to hold onto something solid, and her immediate need to honor Percival and attest to his gift of order and stability, which no one else can give her. While Louis only supports her night self, Percival, who is like some unself-conscious child or animal with whom she can relate, frees her to engage in a dialogue with the day. Only he has enough power to validate order for her and enough indifference to allow her to partake voluntarily of some "semblance" of that order without feeling it imposed upon her. The passage is ambiguous as to whether order is "the thing" or "the semblance" of the thing: chaos may be "the thing" underlying apparent order or order may be the thing underlying chaos. In any case, she has encompassed some order and has now enough substance to make a pilgrimage to the sea to make an offering of violets to Percival upon the waves. They represent her promise to meet him in the perfect balance of an austere afterlife where "We will gallop together over desert hills where the swallow dips her wings in dark pools and the pillars stand entire" (289), which validates both her dipping into dark chaos and Percival's standing as a pillar of cosmic as well as social order.

Bernard, too, has been jarred to the roots of his being. For him Percival's death means the loss of a standard by which to measure, define, or balance out what is missing in himself:

> Now, through my own infirmity I recover what he was to me: my opposite. Being naturally truthful, he did not see the point of these exaggerations, and was borne on by a natural sense of the fitting, was indeed a great master of the art of living so that he seems to have lived long, and to

have spread calm round him, indifference one might almost say, certainly
to his own advancement, save that he had also great compassion. (284)

But is Percival opposite to Bernard in compassion, truthfulness, or indifference to his own advancement? We can find evidence that Bernard demonstrates all of these, and yet not quite the way he idealizes Percival as doing.
In measuring Bernard by the standard of Percival, not only does the source
of Bernard's sense of opposition become more clear, but that standard also
serves as an ideal model of the dialogic self. Although Bernard may seem as
dialogic as they come, Percival contributes something to the dialogue that
Bernard lacks.

Since the text gives us little or no factual evidence for these attributes of
Percival as a situated self—for example, in showing his compassion, which
Bernard merely asserts—the explanation lies in his idealization. While
Bernard's compassion is clear from the way he melts barriers between people
with words, working as a sympathetic do-gooder, Percival does nothing overt.
Every action they remark about him seems almost too trivial to account for
his impact on them. Yet it is precisely the subtle influence of his self-assured
spirit that is more palpable and effective in Woolf's universe than any "material" deed. That his very presence produces benign effects in people may
account for Bernard's impression of Percival's compassion.[19] Thus, Percival
becomes for him a type of Emersonian charity, which, instead of active do-
goodism, only inspires others to enhance themselves. But what is it that his
very presence does for them? Another attribute—his "natural truthfulness"—needs to be analyzed in contrast to Bernard's "exaggerations" as a
factor in such an Emersonian compassion.

In his own truthfulness, we cannot judge Bernard insincere in his caring for real people. However, in his "exaggerations" we might justify some
of his harshness to himself. Whenever his imagination slips into poses or
gets carried away, like his assumption of a Byronic self-discourse, he might
be guilty. And yet, Gergen would claim that Bernard may be the ideal
postmodern man in a world where there is no absolute truth, where such
notions as "sincerity" and "authenticity" are as archaic as Woolf's discourse
on Percival. Bernard's personas may be just part of the richness of the fragmented, multiple self, in which contradictory positions and poses may be
improvised to suit the occasion, as in eastern cultures like Japan.

One problem with this light and airy model of carnival role-playing,
however, is that it may not be taken seriously, especially by the authorities
who permit it only to reinforce their hegemony. In recognizing this lack of
strategic ability to seriously challenge the authoritative order, feminists such
as Diane Price Herndl argue for a dialogue between feminine and masculine

modes of discourse, telling women "to examine our own authority within the academic carnival" with a view to both assuming and questioning that authority.[20] Indeed, the very diversity of postmodern or eastern self-discourses—to be consistent with their inconsistency principle—must allow such traditional western notions of truth, sincerity, and authenticity to exist on a relative and provisional basis. If no position is ever occupied honestly and all positions appear to be equally false from a metapositional perspective, then logically that perspective is false, too, and therefore *something* must be true. Another way to look at it is that if there is no truth, then there is no diversity either: if everything is reduced to the same nullity, the result is a uniform void. On the other hand, if everything were regarded as equally true, a positive chaos of diversity would result. And from a positive chaos it might be possible for any truth to emerge and assert its ascendency for a time, yielding when necessary to other truths in the play of forms, whereas from a metaposition of uniform lack of truth, nothing can ever take form or be asserted except that metaposition itself.[21]

In the case of Bernard and Percival we can make some useful distinctions. As a situated self, Percival's "truth" begins with his simple belief in appearances. Because he is so sure of himself, his belief becomes a force that must be reckoned with as "authentic," "sincere," or having "integrity," without which no position can be maintained long enough to have an effect, whereas Bernard's questioning of appearances, especially those that are overconstructed by his imagination, weakens their authenticity and therefore their effectiveness. Thus, Percival's faith in *any position he takes* has the advantage of focusing energy, whereas Bernard's rapid shifting between romantic self-constructs and ironic doubts scatters his force, or, to use Emerson's metaphor in "Self-Reliance," Percival is like a sailboat that keeps to its course by tacking with the wind in a "fitting" way, i.e., he makes every turn into an act of self-confirmation, whereas Bernard, without a taken-for-granted self to confirm, tacks in many directions helter-skelter.

The dissipation or paralysis of energy that results from lack of belief is perhaps the greatest source of alienation and disempowerment of the self in the modern age, which is why so many cling to some kind of foundationalism. Percival, in his aspect of symbolic *presence*, represents that felt need, and is validated in a positive way by Woolf as a counterweight to the meandering Bernard, not as the vindication of any given foundational belief (because she also endows Percival with symbolic *absence*), but as a way of empowering any serious subject-position to assume its rightful place in the dialogue, with perseverance if necessary. Thus, the charismatic confidence of the situated Percival becomes magnified into a source of strength and courage for Bernard, carrying him through the rest of his life and rallying him to meet death, just as a belief in God might.

Bernard willfully chooses not to dismantle Percival's feet of clay (which he easily could), because he senses that Percival makes palpable that divine principle of order larger than his situated self. Percival's naive absolute faith in his existence turns him into a walking (though unwitting) "moment of being," piercing that veil for Bernard and the others if not for himself— hence his name. It is ironic that Percival can construct so powerful a faith from something as fleeting and illusory as appearances, but his faith is nevertheless sound because by affirming any form he affirms all forms.

In this way, Percival's "presence" dismantles the originary agent of the Cartesian subject by affirming merely that *something* must exist—not necessarily the "I" of the cogito. Indeed, he does not even need to think to prove his existence. His every gesture affirms a principle of existence, which could be conceived as a positive chaos from which all forms, including word forms (thoughts), ascend as constructs. (Of course, such a metapositional concept is itself a construct.) "I" is itself only such a thought construct, not a universal subject that causes thoughts. It is a grammatical artifact mapped onto a continuum of subjectivities with shifting boundaries.[22] Percival does not appear in the text as thoughts, because it is enough that the other characters register his existence. He *is* the words; he *is* the music.

As an ideal, Percival not only gives Bernard some impersonal and inchoate truth beyond bubble words, but also a measure of what is "fitting" in the world of form by which to judge his own fitfulness. That is, as an exemplar of classical standards in his supposed equanimity, Percival looks like a person of *moderation* (despite his actual excesses), which is not the same as *mediocrity*. Moderation aims for *right* action, neither more nor less than what is required by the situation, whereas mediocrity settles for less than right action. By examining what makes action fitting, the workings of the dialogic self can be clarified. For example, the test of what makes a self-concept of Bernard's insincere, imitative, or *un*fitting, like his Byronic pose, is not whether it is a "real" aspect of himself (or even of Byron, for that matter) but whether it takes into account not only his own impulse but also the here-and-now context in which it appears—including other persons and the impersonal environment. Caramagno's analysis of the dialogues between subjectivities of the self and the objective world is apropos here:

> In a "moment of being," life and Virginia Woolf co-create a space in which self and world can exist. They are mutually enhanced, made whole and good . . . involving, paradoxically, . . . mutual fusion and a gain in

distinctiveness. . . . manic depressive modes are reconciled when subject and object connect but are not completely subsumed in each other. It is only then, and not by looking directly into the mirror (which aggrandizes egotism or destroys ego, depending on mood), that the truth is captured. . . . World and self must meet.[23]

A discourse can easily become inappropriate or exaggerated when it does not correspond to the constantly shifting variables of the situation, which no single discourse can account for. When such a slippage is perceived, a feeling of falseness ensues. Throughout the text, the characters, especially Rhoda, have to keep checking their perceptions for something to believe in—like reaching for something solid. She is neither ratified by the world nor the mirror. On his part, Bernard is so responsive to shifts in his perceptions of reality that his awareness of those slippages is partly why he does not usually maintain a given discourse for very long.

Therefore, whether to shift or not may also depend upon his grasp of the scope of the situation. If every passing encounter is defined as one's "situation," one might feel justified in living a life from one moment to the next, with little continuity. The extreme case of that would be Rhoda's, whose fragmented scope is untenable to her. Bernard and Jinny already have a larger scope than Rhoda's for what they define as "the moment," but even they are more focused on the smaller ripples of life compared to the earthbound characters, whose "here and now" may stretch to include one's life span, or even to the continuity of the race. Thus, the "situation" can expand and contract, oscillating with subject positions as short as a nanosecond of thought or as long as the cosmic wavelength of the expanding and contracting universe. Or the situation may be perceived as the timelessness of eternity within the nanosecond of clock time. Bernard is constantly slipping out of measurable time into a position as timeless observer of the passing scene. But as observer, he tends to lose his place as participant, to lose touch with the pulse of a particular timed situation by aborting it prematurely through ironic distance or by getting involved in another situation before the first has run its course. The implication of Percival's "mastery" is not any willful control of situations, but a putatively fine attunement to the course of whatever particular wavelength(s) he might be on; by sensing the scope of large as well as small situational waves, he behaves like a surfer keeping his balance minutely while staying the course, that is, believing in it as long as it must run. But as an unideal self, he gets wiped out.

In retaining one's balance among conflicting subject positions in a situation, the postmodern self still has to suppress or "falsify" certain alternative positions in favor of others. The danger is to impose an abstract "best account" principle as the guide (Taylor), rather than to trust one's spontaneous responses (which includes general principles only as available discourses, not as absolute dictators). For example, when Bernard allows himself to chase rainbows, he, as his own ironic narrator, recognizes that he is sacrificing some sustained effort, some larger commitment, for the joy of effervescing. Instead of assuming responsibility for his own way of being— which might be justifiable some of the time, but not all of the time—he condemns himself generally as being flawed compared to Percival and sets up a judgmental subjectivity whereby the polarization in values is likely to lead neither to change nor to satisfaction. By devaluing or overvaluing the road not taken he gets deadlocked by "shoulds." Thus, to pursue a given identity or self-image or to strive for a certain quality in the abstract is to deny oneself alternative ways, perhaps more "fitting," of interacting in concrete cases.[24]

For example, neither Bernard nor Percival strive to be kind; neither are they deliberately unkind. When Bernard comforts Susan he is kind to her but unkind to Neville, and Percival is also unkind to Neville. Their "unkindness" to him is perhaps unavoidable, considering what he contributes to the situation. And their spontaneous sympathy cannot be imitated, even by themselves on different occasions. Kindness and unkindness do not nullify one another, but may even be exercised simultaneously, depending upon one's point of view in the situation. Cultivating an "identity" or set of qualities in general is tantamount to turning the gaze in on one's own subjectivities in a closed-circuit, solipsistic interplay that loses touch with ratification in the world. But paying close attention to the world (even to oneself as just another object in it) through multiple subjectivities is an art, and timing is crucial to the interactions that are "fitting."

That "ripeness is all" is borne out as the characters change through time over the wavelength of their lives. In the lengthening shadows of their falling waters, the characters assess their span in retrospect and begin to prepare for their merger back into the timeless ocean from the shores they have reached. Jinny, on seeing herself in the glass once, recoils saying, "How solitary, how shrunk, how aged!" (310), and momentarily feels the shadow of night make her cower in fear. But she rallies by surpassing her self-centeredness and adopting a triumphant solidarity with the march of civilization against the impersonal jungle. "I am a native of this world [urban, not primitive]. I follow its banners" (311). She will still powder her face, not so much for her private conquests anymore, but as a badge of pride in being part of that great collective (un)consciousness beyond her individual body.

Susan also feels the chill of the shadows falling:

> Where can the shadow enter? What shock can loosen my laboriously gathered, relentlessly pressed-down life? Yet sometimes I am sick of natural happiness, and fruit growing, and children scattering the house with . . . trophies. I am sick of the body, I am sick of my own craft, cunning, of the unscrupulous ways of the mother who protects, who collects under her jealous eyes. . . her own children, always her own. (308)

There is more to being human than attachment to animal territoriality. Susan has now become detached from her own situation, closer to the disillusioned existential ironist.

Neville joins her in disillusionment and alteration of hard-edged stances. He knows he will always be disappointed by lovers, but he will, since "there is no end to the folly of the human heart—seek another" (301), oscillating between romance and existential irony. His fierce exclusiveness has mellowed to the point that "One must put aside antipathies and jealousies and not interrupt. . . . Nothing is to be rejected in fear or horror"—not even imprecision, as he tolerates a modern poem that has "no commas or semicolons"; although it is irregular and he judges much of it to be "sheer nonsense," he goes on to say, "One must be skeptical, but throw caution to the winds and when the door opens accept absolutely" (314).

Unlike the others, but more like Rhoda, Louis has only intensified the extremity of his situation over time, and seeks death as a release, as he ponders the anonymous medieval poem "O western wind, when wilt thou blow . . . / Christ! that my love were in my arms, / And I in my bed again!" (315–17)—which suggests his longing to be back in the bed of earth that he loves.[25] It is with such a poem that he still hopes to bind to the ages the recalcitrant world of the low-class eatery he frequents. But his idealistic wish to unify that disorderly world is irreconcilable with it:

> My task, my burden, has always been greater than other people's. . . . I have driven a violent, an unruly, a vicious team. . . . yet never forgotten my solemn and severe convictions and the discrepancies and incoherences that must be resolved. . . . It would have been happier to have been born without a destiny, like Susan, like Percival, whom I most admire. (315)

He supposes Susan and Percival were not born with a "destiny" because, unlike him, they make no vain attempt to reconcile an overly rational ideology with nature, accepting their destiny without too much conflict. In his

severe need to unify, he becomes the most divided character of all. And lest
we file Louis away as "essentially" deserving of the bind he is in, as the chief
victim of his own frowns, Bernard occasionally reminds us of the sudden
laughter that can leap into his eyes (345), which is the signifier of some
mysterious potential that might release him from his burden.

For Bernard, time has exposed the limits of his scope; he releases his
hold on unrealized ambitions to travel and to experience many more things,
saying, "I am not so gifted as at one time seemed likely" (305). It is with a
kind of relief that he relinquishes the "rings of identity" (like a tree) that
bound him complacently to his marriage, his proprietorship over his children, his possessions. He returns to something like that detachment he had
when he was first engaged:

> But . . . I do not wish to assume the burden of individual life. I, who have
> been since Monday, when she accepted me, charged in every nerve with a
> sense of identity, . . . now wish to unclasp my hands and let fall my posses-
> sions, and merely stand here in the street, taking no part, watching the
> omnibuses, without desire; without envy; with what would be boundless
> curiosity about human destiny if there were any longer an edge to my
> mind. But it has none. I have arrived; am accepted. I ask nothing. (253)

Only now, after many years, his detachment is derived more from disap-
pointment than satiety. In middle age Bernard has become, strangely
enough, like Byron as the romantic-ironic narrator of *Don Juan* (the one
work of Byron's Neville notes on Bernard's shelf). Bernard has been the
"disillusioned but not embittered" narrator jumping into adventure with
gusto, then swinging into endless digression of commentary detached from
material plots.

However, for all his multiplicity and capability of detachment throughout his life, which has made him resilient, a survivor, Bernard still has to
confront the final detachment in the last section where he alone speaks to a
mysterious Other. His subjectivities oscillate rapidly in a struggle with his
lifelong enemies—the struggle to overcome the unspeakable with an apt
phrase, the struggle to push back brute nature with orderly civilization,
joining his voice in the chorus and marching with Jinny. In one crisis after
another, he loses his phrasemaking capacity to feel human solidarity, then
he loses his ability to clench his fist and "bang his spoon" of self-assertion
against utter chaos, each time feeling vanquished, and then, miraculously,
recovering, but becoming increasingly liberated as he swings between exal-
tation and despair. He experiences different kinds of detachment, rising to

cosmic detachment one moment and descending to mocking satiric detachment at his presumption the next. Each state is destabilized by the undertow from a previous one meeting the surge of the coming one, as he realizes:

> [H]ow incompletely we are merged in our own experiences. On the outskirts of every agony sits some observant fellow who points. . . . Thus he directed me to that which is beyond and outside our own predicament; to that which is symbolic, and thus perhaps permanent, if there is any permanence in our sleeping, eating, breathing, so animal, so spiritual and tumultuous lives. (348–49)

That "observant fellow" who keeps appearing like a new untitled window on a computer screen is designated as if "he" were singular, but he might only be one of a succession of endless subjectivities that momentarily assume the office of "speaking subject," entitled by the signifier "I," which arise simply by the process of ring formation, or the drawing of "Circles," as Emerson describes them in his essay by that title. That is, every subject position might be conceived as a "mark" upon a "wall" of blankness around and beyond it (as in Woolf's story "The Mark on the Wall"), which invites speculation. Soon the blank wall becomes filled with commentaries—new marks surrounding the original one—like the Talmud, which is printed concentrically, with a small passage of the Torah in the center of the page surrounded by consecutive rings of commentaries added by generations of rabbis. This "observant fellow," then, could be regarded as a generic and generating subject, one that represents a species: the detached observers of ourselves, endlessly re-forming between rings of identity and involvement, as one subject begets the next. These spaces between the rings are the inchoate states in which detachment from the previous formulation can occur in preparation for the next one. Thus a new "panoptic," or integrating subjectivity, may continually re-form, no matter how wide-ranging prior subjectivities may have been.

But for every human being's life, including Bernard's, there is an end to the waves of commentary. Even near the end he manages to keep hold of the world as a disembodied observer, a ghost, clinging to what he always needed most—an audience, for he has been telling all this to a stranger, as we all tell our inner narrative to that "stranger," that perpetual listener we imagine ourselves talking to. When the time comes to bid that person good-bye, Bernard can at last say:

> Heaven be praised for solitude! . . . Let me be alone. Let me . . . throw away this veil of being, this cloud that changes with the least breath, night

and day, and all night and all day. While I have sat here I have been changing. . . . Now no one sees me and I change no more. (381)

His book of phrases slips to the floor. All he needs is "a howl, a cry," and silence (382).

But even when he clearly recognizes that his life is spent, that the waters of darkness are falling around him, he still feels "a sense of the break of day," and as he recognizes his old enemy as Death, he renews his struggle and becomes young again, charging heroically as he imagines Percival doing in India, "Against you I will fling myself, unvanquished and unyielding, O Death!" (383). Then Bernard speaks no more, and the last words, "*The waves broke on the shore*" (383), are in italics, like the interludes. It is "the lady writing," the subject containing his, as he contained hers and the others, who concludes. The next wave that arises is the question on the reader's mind as to what these nesting male and female subjects imply about female "identity."

IMPLICATIONS FOR THE FEMALE SELF

Woolf avoids the representation of any singular "female subject" in this work at the same time that she opens up the minds of both men and women characters to various feminine and masculine subjectivities. Of all her novels, this one least emphasizes the material social conditions that situate her characters in masculine and feminine discourses. By their tasks, roles, attitudes, and power struggles, the polarizations between male and female subjects in the other novels are much more in evidence. In *To the Lighthouse*, for example, Mrs. Ramsay knits and bows to her husband's "superior intellect," while he demands her sympathy and attention. In *The Waves*, traditional demarcations of gender are there, but they are muted in favor of qualities of thought, feeling, and action that are interchangeable between men and women.

To begin with, all the characters have ego rivalries with one another that might place them within a "masculine" discourse. On the other hand, they all suspend those ego boundaries to feel sympathy and solidarity on the human level, or loss of self in the impersonal universe, which might place them within a "feminine" discourse. Therefore, these aspects of self become gender-neutral by being distributed universally between both sexes. It would also be difficult to maintain a strict gendering of the day and night discourse, i.e., by regarding day as masculine and night as feminine, for Jinny and Susan would be the best exemplars of the day, while all the men would have too strong a night self to make this simplistic division work. The discourse of the four basic elements also completely obscures any simple gender classification of qualities.

However, the characters are undeniably gendered in material ways of education, occupation, and social roles. The men are distinguished by having a classical education and taking up positions in business and the professions, whereas the women's schooling shows little trace of the classics and prepares them for no perceptible occupation. Indeed, Susan, the only one of the women who seems to work—as a farmer's wife, not for her own remuneration—rejects her schooling as hateful and irrelevant. One cannot imagine Rhoda as being employed, nor Jinny, although the latter might have been a professional dancer and/or courtesan in more straitened circumstances. Since there is no allusion to their material support, and neither are married, one can only assume they have independent means, as certain upper-middle-class women were privileged to have (like Woolf herself, in part). That neither Jinny nor Rhoda, nor indeed Louis and Neville, ever marry is deviant by the standards of their class, although more acceptable for the men, and acceptable even for the women in their subculture. But there is no social problem on that issue registered in any of the character's minds, unlike in Woolf's early novels, *The Voyage Out* and *Night and Day*, to which the faint mothball odor of Jane Austen's marriage-mart novels clings.

That the female characters appear to conform to certain social expectations of women is a matter of contingency—they can only take paths that are open to them. But *how* the women pursue these paths, i.e., by their inner dispositions, is more important to Woolf than the material paths themselves. The disadvantage of this text in not developing the material struggles of women in the world is offset by the advantage of focusing on the quality of the women's characters that deconstructs the appearance of genderedness in their pursuits, as the following discussion will show. The same could be said of the men. This work does not engage the political battle of the sexes, such as the clash of Lily Briscoe and Charles Tansley in *To The Lighthouse*, but it does make available self-discourses for both sexes that undermine that battle.

All three women are feminized in different traditional discourses: Susan in the maternal, Jinny in the erotic, and Rhoda in the incoherent mystical. While the maternal and the erotic are more directly related to biology, other feminine discourses in which they are cast are more clearly cultural. For example, one of the few conspicuously gendered discourses is Bernard's appropriation of Susan as a quasi-muse figure:

> It was Susan who first became wholly woman, purely feminine. It was
> Susan who dropped on my face those scalding tears which are terrible,

beautiful. . . . She was born to be the adored of poets, since poets require safety; some one who sits sewing. . . . who is neither comfortable nor prosperous, but has some quality in accordance with the high but unemphatic beauty of pure style which those who create poetry so particularly admire. (348)

Tears and sewing gender her culturally. Bernard may think of her as "feminine" in order to account for his attraction to her, for without a woman to remind him of his masculinity—as his wife is the "muse" to inspire him with masculine ambition—he tends to float away from it. Because he needs to exaggerate and totalize Susan from the cultural imperative to construct himself as masculine, he does not perceive *her* in terms of any masculinity.

Within the women's primary feminine roles, however, certain masculine discourses can be discerned. Susan, "wholly feminine" to Bernard, is quite masculine if one converts her "protective mother" discourse into a warrior one. In other mammals like bears and lions, it is the female who is the more formidable fighter as defender of her interests. She is also the chief hunter, not only for herself but for her family. In addition, she is the bearer of her culture as chief educator of the young. These subject-positions for females have been all but forgotten in human history (except in legends like that of the Amazons). Susan, however, has appropriated her space, her mate, and her children, and dominated her enterprise. These attitudes and behaviors of hers, traditionally the human male's prerogatives, suggest that, basing themselves on some models in nature, women can reinvent "feminine" discourses that challenge patriarchal claims of what femininity is (just as men appropriate analogies, such as comparing the harem to practices of animals in herds or packs). Thus, "maternal" or "motherly" would suggest not only nurturing tenderness and images of madonna-like suffering and compassion, but also fierce combativeness and territorial possessiveness.

Jinny is another example of a woman whose masculine qualities can be modeled on a discourse from nature, but in her case, the models are males—birds, to be exact. Flamboyant plumage is her forte in the dance rituals of courtship. Like a strutting peacock who "passively" signals to the peahen, she tries to get one of the opposite sex to join her. Who is the initiator and who is the follower? Who the active and who the passive? The naked eye cannot tell, so rapid are the oscillations of attraction and desire. It is she who kisses Louis, she who is bold enough to seize the fruit from the Tree of Knowledge, while he would have preferred to remain passively egoless and obedient to his deity Mother Earth. She is not merely the *object* of the male gaze, but the *subject* that commands it. Jinny is also in the human tradition

of the bachelor playboy in her sexual, materialistic, and ego-centered subjectivities, except that she might be called a "femme fatale" or "coquette,"
which connote (in the double standard) something more culpable—"fatal"
seductress or tease, respectively—than the "boys-will-be-boys" connotation
of "playboy." Related to Jinny's playgirl lifestyle of lavishing the products of
British capitalism and colonialism on herself in carefree consumerism, she
is more completely socialized in the modern patriarchal idea of "progress"
than Louis, who is divided within himself as a collaborator.

If these traits seem morally reprehensible, the dark side of her masculinity, they can be balanced by her masculine virtue of courage—by accepting her fate fully, in the heroic tradition of a Percival. Bernard says that
"Without illusions, hard and clear as crystal, she rode at the day with her
breast bared. She let its spikes pierce her. When the lock whitened on her
forehead she twisted it fearlessly among the rest. So when they come to
bury her, nothing will be out of order" (368). Because Jinny is integrated at
the level of society, i.e., is attuned to the games people play, she has the self-
confidence, the chutzpah, to satisfy the demand for coherence by creating a
different coherent illusion for each member of her audience, one by one.
Her authenticity consists of being true to her desires as well as to her partner's,
recognizing that desire itself is a construct she can stylize (the way Butler
envisions) as well as a biological drive.

While Jinny easily shifts her faces without losing her integrity, Rhoda is
completely devastated by the demand for coherence. Yet even Rhoda, who
seems to be the ultimate female victim in her hysterical day self, harbors a
masculinized twilight subjectivity in which she regally asserts her ego, for
example, in her childhood dream as the empress of her brown bowl of
water where she cruelly sinks those who would dominate her (213). It is as
if only in a static world of eternity can she assume a face, the face of the
ultimate controller whose pretensions go unchecked by dialogue with the
temporal world. She seems to illustrate Nietzsche's argument in *The Genealogy of Morals* that mystics who renounce the world (that they cannot control)
are engaged in the ultimate will to power.[26]

Paradoxically, her insistence on her own vision by withdrawing from
society appears to Bernard as a form of self-assertion, for he admires Rhoda
for her courage to be "authentic." Bernard has a fine intuition of the integrity of Rhoda's position. Since she is precariously located on the verge of
society, facing toward a plane of otherworldliness while turning her back
facelessly upon the world, she appears, from his point of view in the world,
in the paradoxical position of being fixated on nonfixation (facelessness).
Therefore, she would falsify her position by assuming any worldly mask
whatsoever, which is why she berates herself for complicity with society

when "imitating," unlike Jinny who is free to masquerade with her integrity intact.

If society in its masculine consolidation of conventional forms desires to control those who are incoherent like Rhoda and Septimus, it is only because most people are afraid to confront their own incoherencies. In the rush to deny the incoherent in themselves by setting up a binary opposition between masculine order and feminine disorder, both camps become fixated and frightened of the other instead of dialogic. Therein lies the insanity. Instead of judging "insanity" by that incoherent otherworldliness, that *ability* to see meaninglessness in loops of time (which is not a disability by the "standards" of the night self), it would make more sense to judge by the degree of *fixation* on that (or any other) mode of being, or by fixation on its opposite pole, both of which can be pathological, considering the pain and loss of function they entail. If Rhoda were to be balanced (biochemically and otherwise) and could expand her scope (or contract it), she might be capable of both the putting on and the taking off of masks, depending upon the contingencies of social and personal situations. It is to the credit of her friends in this group, who all have acknowledged night selves, that Rhoda is valued, though she suffers, supposing them to be more cruel than they are when she is immersed in her fear and not free to be sympathetic to them. Under the benign influence of Percival, however, she does achieve greater equilibrium, suggesting that the balance of a person is a function of more than individual biochemical makeup—that human relations, and even dialogue with the nonhuman world (as Rhoda has with cats), play a part.

The character who best illustrates the insanity of inner polarization as opposed to the sanity of balance through dialogue is Louis. Ironically, as a power-driven masculine ego by day, he is the opposite pole of the violated feminine self by night, like Rhoda. His problem and the problem of women is that of dismantling the discourses on hierarchy, especially that of superiority and inferiority that underlie power struggles. It is not that there is no place for such rational discourses when particular goals have to be met and standards of performance assessed, but Louis's case shows the effects of totalizing and essentializing those discourses when it comes to persons. Because society tends to reduce an individual to his or her salient qualities, Louis's superior intellect becomes equated to a "core self" that is superior. He is forced to maintain that facade, to "prove" himself, for he cannot afford to be eliminated from the competition by allowing his intellect to become fallow in deference to his visionary night side. Similarly, his accent assumes such large proportions in his mind that he becomes paranoid and afraid of being rejected as totally alien and inferior. His assumption of these reductive social discourses is what makes him exaggerated rather than "fitting." Thus, his exertion of power is perceived as an imposition on others rather than as an inspiration for them to follow by their own spontaneous recognition of some superiority of his, as is the case with Percival, whose only superiority is his attitude of not having to prove it.

One way to achieve balance is that of the only female character in the novel who grapples seriously with the male-dominated symbolic order in the attempt to inscribe her feminine vision—the lady writing. The phrase "lady writing" does not fix her identity beyond placing her in a context as a privileged female; otherwise, she is identified as someone "writing," emphasizing unself-conscious attentiveness to an ongoing task instead of to any self-conscious image as a "writer," which would be Woolf's way of suggesting her impersonal orientation.

This cameo of the author not only makes her point about balancing gendered traits in the act of writing, but if *The Waves* might be *what* the lady is writing, it also contains the nested examples of how her characters measure up to her standard of relating dialogically to language. She appears more balanced than her less verbally empowered women characters, such as Rhoda, who flees loops of writing that would reduce her fluid soul to mere constructs; she prefers the silent semiotic power of Percival. Or Susan, whose hard-edged masculine referentiality is baffled by Bernard's bubbling over (to put it into prosodic as well as thetic terms). The closest to the lady in a dialogic relation to language is chief articulator Bernard, who, despite his love of words, can reject his own move to symbolize, as when he, after waxing eloquent to compare the late Percival to a lily, says, "[T]he sincerity of the moment passed; . . . it became symbolical; and that I could not stand" (360). Neither could Jinny, whom he loves because she "respected the moment with complete integrity" (360). Her eloquent tribute to Percival is to powder her face to meet the here and now. Here Bernard moves toward the feminine with Jinny, who turns from the order of words to a body-coded discourse. Woolf regretted that she could not have written frankly of her "own experience as a body" because of prudish impositions on ladies' writing,[27] but she managed to translate Jinny's silent knowledge into the symbolic by entering into a dialogue with the precise wordcraft of a Neville or a Louis.

Although the women may seem to reject the symbolic order more than the men (as if adhering to a feminist discourse that devalues patriarchal abstraction in favor of concreteness or of silence), the men never sneer at the women for feminine inarticulateness or incoherence; only Bernard is criticized by the other two men and by Susan for his vagueness of language. It is as if those three expect greater linguistic competence of him as a man, while allowing the women to be different. Although they may have a linguistic gender bias, Susan's actual practice straddles that issue by being polarized into the extremes of silence and reductive referentiality. Since Louis and Neville accept both her difference and her similarity to them, they undermine their own gender bias. For her part, Susan is only biased by not expecting linguistic clarity of the other women, but in excepting herself she degenders her practice. Woolf sets up gendered discourses and unravels them in a complex way that allows tensions and contradictions to occur in the fluid medium of tolerance and friendship.

Perhaps that is why there are surprisingly few "battles of the sexes" between the men and women in the group on other issues besides language. For example, while there is a suggestion of Jinny's sexual power over Louis, they never confront each other in an affair. He seeks her sympathy and wants to impress her (because they're both snobs), but also resents her power to command that from him (263–64). Since both want to retain their independence and exert power over others, they tacitly recognize their incompatibility in the sex game. Similarly, although he admires Susan, Louis is also afraid to be "nailed" by her. Bernard might have been "nailed" by a woman, but not by Susan, because Susan does not seek to inspire a man's ambitions, as his wife does, but must devote herself to her own ambitions. If Bernard does not fit her specifications, if he baffles and escapes her purposes, then even if he may have the power to excite her imagination and love, she must go her own way, exerting her power of refusal, as she does with Percival (363). As for the relationship between Rhoda and Louis, one might sense an element of paternalism in his sympathy for her, but there is enough commonality in their ideals and in their camaraderie against the others to mute that. He sets aside his daytime severity to allow the frightened moth Rhoda to be attracted; yet in recognizing the danger of his harsh light, Rhoda finally exercises her power of flight. Another gendered power struggle to note might be that between Susan and Neville, a competitive rather than sexual one. Because men's successes are more recognized publicly than women's domestic successes, he flaunts his acclaim, his "credentials" over her obscure accomplishments. But this little "clashing of antlers" is quickly set aside by their deeper goodwill and respect (325).

In sum, although the characters have assumed some of the gendered attitudes of society, they do not oppose one another along sex divisions. The power distribution in this group is remarkably balanced compared to society at large, and indeed, even weighted in favor of the women, who seem capable of pursuing their own agendas rather than simply tailoring themselves to please men and society.

The strength of this work is that the dialogic self is represented in a great range of subjective experience, from the consciousness of cosmic impersonality to the minutest oscillations of the ego, and it is shown to be interdependent with other forces and entities on many planes. The characters represent varying degrees of fixation and nonfixation that affect their balance and their power, but no conclusions can be drawn about remedies to their situations, except to develop a larger, more sensitive awareness of the contingencies and of the discourses available to meet them. Woolf is not preaching pragmatic answers and therapies for women in general just because her own therapy included writing. However, by realigning old discourses into new forms and increasing the play of possibilities among subjectivities that make up the self, the text releases women from having to construct "a female subject." That is the function of a visionary work: to make new insights available.

However, because Woolf does not judge her characters from any overarching feminist position, but only has them judge themselves and each other from various (sometimes contradictory) positions, her work might appear to be too impartial and apolitical. She herself recognized that art and politics were not easily reconciled, and her inclination was to shrink from the platform in her fiction, although she takes strong positions in her nonfiction. Alternatively, her apolitical approach might not be so much a shrinking from taking a political position as it is the assertion of yet another position, one transcending the polarizations that political debate tends to fall into. For example, it may disturb some feminists that a Nietzschean character like Percival is given such a positive image, or that the capitalist Louis is made to appear the poor victim, which might seem too supinely "sympathetic," in the view of women who need to express anger at the dark side of machismo. That Percival is so central and charismatic may disturb women readers who seek female models of power at the center, like Mrs. Ramsay, the great absent presence of *To the Lighthouse*, or Clarissa Dalloway, about whom it is enough to say in the final sentence, "For there she was" (*MD*, 296), even if these two are compromised in their power. Similarly, Rhoda's discourse of violence and will to power as the underside of her pathetic helplessness would seem to justify male scorn for the feminine as weak and hysterical, or to justify male fears of the feminine as demonic or weird. This work might therefore seem deficient by the standards of politicized feminism, because it does not dramatize the gendered power struggle and take a clear stand on the point of view of women in that struggle.

Indeed, if this work is biased, it is toward the deconstruction of the ego, which might seem to serve women ill just when they think they need to assert an ego. Anne Herrmann, for one, claims that Woolf's historical need to counteract the patriarchal male ego accounts for her deconstruction of subjectivity at the expense of female self-affirmation. Herrmann would affirm female subjectivity, not as univocal like the patriarchal ego, but as a dialogic inner community of all female voices.[28] Such a view, however, would only invert a patriarchal dialogism that still excludes an/other gender. Herrmann does not recognize that Woolf's valorizing all voices, however gendered, valorizes female subjectivities (though not a univocal female subject) after all. For Woolf also deconstructs the men's egos, which levels the playing field, and then restores full worldly assertiveness and integrity to Jinny and Susan in their own right through the play of multiple discourses. This is a liberating move for both sexes.

Furthermore, by giving some legitimacy to the masculine discourse of a Percival, Woolf is acknowledging differences between men's subjectivities and women's and avoiding the move to totalize and legitimize only feminine discourses, which would lead to an imbalance in the opposite direction. While women need to validate their own feminine discourses, both personal and impersonal, they also need to validate their own suppressed masculine ones. Paradoxically, women are capable of championing, not only their basic human rights, but the "feminine" qualities society needs to valorize for men as well. Such a social recognition of multiply gendered selves would enable the Louises of the world to recover their liberty of fusion back to the mother without losing their autonomous and masculine subjectivities. What stands in the way is the fear each camp has of the darker side of the other, without acknowledging their own dark side or the positive values the other can contribute. Woolf fearlessly sets forth the dark and the light of both the feminine and the masculine toward a more comprehensive and versatile self for women as well as men.

In order to balance out Woolf's mythopoetic method and bias toward the oceanic feminine, we will turn to another woman novelist whose method is more "material" in the patriarchal tradition of the *Bildungsroman* and whose context for the self is located more on the terra firma of international politics than in mythical space-time. Not only does Doris Lessing's *Four-Gated City* dramatize social situations and deal directly with problems of political ideologies in the discourses of the self, but it also swings wide to encompass the collective (un)conscious and the cosmos, suggesting another broad dialogic model as a way to restore the integrity of women's subjectivities.

Part Two

Doris Lessing's *Four-Gated City:*
The Comprehensive Self

3

The Concept of Self in
Doris Lessing's Life and Work

A study of Doris Lessing's writings and interviews shows her to be both committed to her integrity and yet capable of radical change. The key to her ability to change is a commitment to bearing witness to her experience without becoming locked into any single position or discourse. She has remarked, "I really do feel . . . about every two years—what a fool I was two years ago."[1] Indeed, she has not only changed opinions, but even her authorial identity at one point in her career, when she wrote two related novels under the pseudonym of Jane Somers to try to depart from her usual authorial persona.[2] The ability to be both committed and independent requires the paradoxical duality of being both a naysayer, "I am not this, not that," and a yea-sayer, "I am this and this and . . . and . . . and . . . ," instead of "I must be either . . . or . . ."[3]

Her commitment is not just to the general principle of staying uncommitted, however, for she takes strong positions on specific issues and events, and has long-term beliefs and convictions. Although she is bold in taking positions, she is just as bold in modifying or even repudiating them, wherever the naysayer encounters some slippage or contradictory evidence. The kind of consciousness Lessing conveys in her writing is that of constantly testing ideas, assumptions, and discourses against what she senses is happening, being alert and listening to divergent and alternative points of view or even to unarticulated intuitions that run counter to prevailing assumptions.

Because of being both a naysayer and a yea-sayer, Lessing is a paradox: she favors a collective view of humanity, yet defends individual liberties; advocates equality across classes, genders, races, and ethnic groups, yet affirms their differences; seeks harmony and unity, yet testifies to discord and disorder; is optimistic about the potential for human evolution, yet pessimistic about the forces of repetition and the potential for regression; is a

moralist, yet admits her own immoral impulses. Although she has her pref-
erences among all these oppositions, she testifies to the inclusion of all of
them in her comprehensive view of herself as a microcosm of society and
the universe: "To my mind the whole push and thrust and development of
the world is towards the more complex, the flexible, the open-minded, the
ability to entertain many ideas, sometimes contradictory ones, in one's mind
at the same time" (*P,* 89). It is this rigorous inclusiveness, the seeking out
and refusal to deny whatever she may find in her consciousness, even if it is
ugly or contradicts something else that may be dear to her, that gives her
writing its integrity. And it is that inclusiveness which incorporates the impersonal stuff of the universe and the transpersonal relations of society into
her personal life and work.

Doris Lessing, like Virginia Woolf, cycles and recycles the impersonal
through her personal experience as a woman. Her work takes up where
Woolf's leaves off around mid-twentieth century, and continues to demonstrate that the subjectivities of women are not confined to narrow domesticity and immediate personal relations, but may encompass larger social
collectives in the material historical world and in the imaginative ahistorical
world of the collective unconscious, which extends to visions of the cosmos.
As with Woolf, this comprehensive self is not a static achieved state, but a
perpetual interplay of subjectivities relating to create new possibilities. Although she, too, is extensively autobiographical,[4] the selves she inscribes
are like Woolf's in that they are force fields that draw the macrocosm into
their microcosmic space (or inversely, expand from the small to the large)
by the power of the observer's acuity and honesty.

While they both undertake a comprehensive scope, Lessing departs
from Woolf in both the content and form of her representations of the self.
One notable difference is that while Woolf's dominant images are of water
(*The Waves*), Lessing's tend to favor hard-edged human constructions with
walls (*The Four-Gated City*). Woolf acquiesces, flows along with the cycles of
nature; Lessing builds structures that aspire to enhance nature. This difference may be a function of their discernible gender biases, assuming a traditional dichotomy of the feminine as nature versus the masculine as culture.
Although both seek to degender the qualities of the self in their work without losing their female-specific subjectivities, cultural biases still influence
them in that Woolf tends to favor virtues associated with femininity, whereas
Lessing tends to favor those associated with masculinity. For example, in
Going Home, her autobiographical account of her first return to Africa from
England, Lessing compares the African sun to the English sun in a gender-
coded motif that reappears in various works:

Here [in Africa] the sun is a creature *of the same stuff as oneself; powerful and angry,* but at least responsive, and no *mere dispenser of pale* candlepower.

When I was first in England I was disturbed all the time in my deepest sense because the sun went down at four in the middle of an *active* afternoon, filling a cold, damp remote sky with *false pathos.* Or, at eleven in the morning, instead of blazing down *direct,* a hand's-span from *centre,* it would appear on a *slant* and in the *wrong* place, . . . a *swollen, misshapen, watery ghost* of a thing *peering* behind chimney pots. The sun in England should be feminine, as it is in Germany. (*GH,* 7–8; my italics)

In short, she conceives of herself here as powerful, angry and responsive, no mere subservient dispenser of false pathos, and no watery Rhoda-like creature. Lynne Sukenick observes how contemptuous Lessing is of "feminine sensibility," much as Jane Austen takes the side of "sense" versus "sensibility" (sentimentality) with her dry irony.

A conspicuous explanation is that while Woolf nearly idolized her deceased mother, valuing the strength of her feminine sympathy and feeling beholden to that benign power, Lessing resented her mother's pathetic need to overprotect and nurse her into a delicate feminine creature fit only for polite society. Both mothers were strong personalities with a bent for nursing, which they practised particularly on their husbands, but Julia Stephen found wide social outlets for her caring, whereas Emily Tayler, in her frustrated isolation on an African farm, focused her attentions and social ambitions on her daughter. Lessing staunchly resisted her mother's attempts to dominate her by toughening herself and defying her mother's conventionality, a position she poignantly recalls in "The Story of Two Dogs," in which a young female protagonist, an autobiographical figure, defends her choice of an untamable outcast dog for a pet.

Thus, Woolf reacted primarily against the intrusiveness of male domination, and only secondarily against the thrall of her mother (as Lily Briscoe's ambivalence to Mrs. Ramsay represents in *To The Lighthouse*), while Lessing reacted primarily against an intrusive mother who represented a sentimental, hypocritical society in contrast to the honest impersonality of the African sun and landscape.[5] As a girl often solitary in nature, Lessing took her subjective gaze for granted, like Wordsworth, Emerson, or Thoreau, in contrast to Woolf's painfully socialized self-consciousness as an object of the male gaze. Instead of being frozen by male intrusiveness, Lessing boldly affirmed her feminine sexuality in defiance of her mother's prudish delicacy, even disgust. Being treated as a sex object may have seemed ridiculous or annoying rather than traumatic to Lessing, hence her impatience with what might seem to her like pathetic feminist plaintiveness. If anything,

Lessing sympathizes with beleaguered males, in sympathy with her father who was dominated by his wife.[6] Young Doris felt closer to him because he did not try to impose on her and because she valued his visionary idealism in spite of being critical of his ineffectuality. Her parental biases are incorporated into the following self-portrait, generalized into that of an androgynous artist:

> To the creation of a woman novelist seems [*sic*] to go certain psychological ingredients. . . . One . . . a balance between father and mother where the practicality, the ordinary sense, cleverness, and worldly ambition is on the side of the mother; and the father's life is so weighted with dreams and ideas and imaginings that their joint life gets lost in what looks like a hopeless muddle and failure, but which holds a potentiality for something . . . better, on a different level, than what ordinary sense or cleverness can begin to conceive of.[7]

Although Lessing values her mother's qualities, she favors her father's, which exactly inverts Woolf. While both Woolf and Lessing had ambivalent feelings of respect for and criticism of their fathers, their relation to their mothers is more crucial to the distinction not only between their self-concepts as women, but also between their attitudes toward women (and men), feminism, and their art.

Indeed, Lessing has remarked that she wanted to write what Woolf left out.[8] What Woolf "left out" in the way of content, Lessing assiduously and overabundantly supplies: the material facts—the accurate historical record of fully dramatized situations, including, on the personal level, frankness about female bodily awareness, which Woolf was still too Victorian to be explicit about; and on the political level, documentation of local and global events. Lessing's forte (and perhaps weakness, too) is meticulous reportage. As for style, Lessing's conventional prose with its cerebral explicitness seems detached and often cumbersome compared to the fluid and aesthetic modernist style of Woolf. Although Woolf's narration lacks explicit bodily content, her poetic style is driven by the semiotics of the body, whereas Lessing often speaks *about* the body in the *dis*embodied voice of an omniscient narrator.[9] This form-content reversal has raised the important question of whether Lessing's vision is that of a transcendental subjectivity that seeks to gain control of her contingent worldly self (and art) with the lucidity of the intellect, or whether she, like Woolf, equally values the dark knowledge of the body-self, balancing the Dionysian and Apollonian aspects, so to speak. Whether this difference in style is related to their gender biases must be considered.

Lessing defended her choice of realism in spite of the advent of modernism in her essay "The Small Personal Voice":

> For me the highest point of literature was the novel of the nineteenth century, the work of Tolstoy, Stendhal, Dostoevsky, Balzac, Turgenev, Chekhov; the work of the great realists. I define realism as art which springs so vigorously and naturally from a strongly-held, *though not necessarily intellectually-defined*, view of life that it absorbs symbolism. . . . or any other ism [my italics]. ("SPV," 4)

> I reread . . . the old giants continuously. So do most of the people I know, people who are left and right, committed and uncommitted, religious and unreligious, but who have at least this in common, that they read novels as I think they should be read, for illumination, in order to enlarge one's perception of life. ("SPV," 5)

> I was not looking for a firm reaffirmation of old ethical values, many of which I don't accept; I was not in search of the pleasures of familiarity. I was looking for the warmth, the compassion, the humanity, the love of people which illuminates the literature of the nineteenth century and which makes all these old novels a statement of faith in man himself. ("SPV, 6")

Built into her defense are major assumptions from the liberal-humanist tradition of individual authenticity—an authenticity that goes so deep that it lies beyond intellectually defined discourses—and the rights of individuals that society must protect so that its collective self can be reformed by the voices of its most moral individuals. (Thoreau's influence on her early ideas was great.) Her fiction is so driven by a moral imperative from a sense of twentieth-century apocalypse that it often becomes didactic, or perhaps Socratic,[10] but either way, hers seem to be "novels of ideas, not characters."[11] In "The Small Personal Voice" her assumption of realism's transparency-to-truth reinforces her didactic inclination. Although her particular moral bent was first attracted to Communism, by the time she wrote "The Small Personal Voice" early in her career, she had repudiated the crude didacticism of socialist realist works as boring and sappy propaganda. Yet Frederick Stern is right to say, "Doris Lessing is certainly an intensely political writer,"[12] not just because she made some of the same assumptions as socialist realism in her early work, but because a radical humanist worldview drives her critique of not only the racist, colonialist-bourgeois society of Southern Rhodesia where she was raised, but also of Communist societies.

Her worldviews and politics, however, are always grounded in the personal. Even her first novel, *The Grass is Singing*, a tragedy of the wasteland of colonialism, is more psychologically complex than socialist realism. And the political views in the *Children of Violence* series spring from the deeply felt personal experience of her semiautobiographical heroine Martha Quest, whose *Bildungsroman* is "a study of the individual conscience in its relations with the collective" ("SPV," 14).[13]

Lessing later changed her assumptions about form, if not her ethics of literature, as she called into question the realist novel with her writing of *The Golden Notebook*, which is carefully structured in a self-referentially postmodernist way that deconstructs the assumptions of order and plenitude in its nested conventional novel (the "Free Women" sections). Protagonist Anna Wulf, Lessing's alter ego, is the author of and protagonist in "Free Women" and other nested novels in one of her notebooks. These color-coded notebooks contain the raw materials of Anna's writings about different aspects of her life, which seem separate, and thus color-bound. A culminating section, "The Golden Notebook," conflates all the other notebooks into one big jumble instead of compartmentalizing them, and is the symbol of Anna Wulf's integrative self-realization after a mental breakdown. But this new integrative notebook /state is not so much more comprehen*sible* as it is more comprehen*sive*. Anna's act of assuming responsibility across her whole spectrum effects a breakthrough in the paralysis of being both locked into, and out of, her separately colored notebook personas. Through the disorderly fecundity of "The Golden Notebook" Anna is released from her "writer's block" to circulate freely among her colors and paint creatively with them. She then writes a conventional account of herself in the smoothed-over, coherent self-narrative of "Free Women," which is an affirmation of her need for some kind of order to communicate limited aspects of her experience, and, at the same time, an ironical comment on the fictionality of all such attempts in view of an underlying disorder that problematizes authorial truth and character consistency.

Lessing wrote *Golden Notebook* during a crucial period of change in her life, in which she finally quit the Communist Party and turned from political collectives to the collective unconscious within the individual mind and across minds (transpersonally), as Anna Wulf does in her affair with Saul Green, in which they experience an androgynous interchange of personas in their joint madness. As Lorna Sage puts it, Lessing turns her urge for communality "inside out"[14]—or outside in. This novel interrupted her plan for the *Children of Violence* series, so that years later, when she came to write *Landlocked*, the fourth novel in the quintology, she increased the number of poetic passages of mystical content while otherwise remaining "landlocked" in the conventional form she had initiated. The fifth and final volume, *The Four-Gated City*, gradually departs from the fiction of Martha Quest as the focal *Bildungsroman* character, and in an appendix launches into a futuristic fantasy where the omniscient narrator disappears into documents of an apocalyptic era containing the last evidence of Martha as a person. Despite the departures in genre and depictions of mental breakdown, Lessing maintains coherent sentence structure throughout, but admits the form of *The Four-Gated City* is "shot to hell."[15]

Although she abandoned the rationalist ideology of Communism, her turn to the "mysticism" of Sufism, with its emphasis on the teaching story,[16] indicates that she preserves her need to write from a kind of Wordsworthian literary ethic—in the language of ordinary people. Her attraction to Sufism is partly because of its claim to be nonhierarchical: its teachers assume the roles of ordinary people on every level of society and they claim its teachings need not be reserved for esoteric practices, but can be integrated with ordinary life. While she has abandoned her own belief in the transparency of realistic, conventional forms, she still believes in the teaching value of her writing, in the romantic tradition of being the representative voice of a common humanity. In a 1982 interview, she maintains that a writer's task is to write truthfully no matter what point one is at, which will express what others are thinking and feeling but are too afraid or inarticulate to say.[17] Sage is under the impression that Lessing abandoned her position as a representative small personal voice, based on this 1969 quote of hers (of which Martha enunciates a variation in *The Four-Gated City*):

> Since writing *The Golden Notebook* I've become less personal. I've floated away from the personal. I've stopped saying, "This is *mine*, this is *my* experience." . . . I don't believe anymore that I have a thought. There is a thought around.[18]

Although Lessing is no longer possessive of her ideas, it does not mean she cannot claim to represent others. On the contrary, her implication is that the small personal voice is simply one microphone picking up a chorus of voices.

Lessing assumes the stance of seer or prophet who tells stories and fables that represent the *unfamiliar* ("a new way of seeing") in *ordinary* language, in contrast to Woolf, who represents even the *ordinary* in her *unfamiliar* style. But Woolf's style is the very embodiment of "a new way of seeing," whereas, to appeal to readers at many levels of understanding, Lessing's new way of seeing is disguised in the very conventions it would undermine. The unfamiliar that Lessing insists on familiarizing, despite her (post)modern insights, consists of states of transpersonal and impersonal subjectivities that are not locked into personal ego compartments (like states of extrasensory perception and Woolfian "moments of being"). She no longer defends the old unitary autonomous subject, but a collective self of the imagination that is a hologram of the whole universe, which is what makes every individual precious and "authentic" in this new sense. Thus, her use of the omniscient narrator, like Woolf's, corresponds to a concept of an imaginative subjectivity that links ordinarily fragmented consciousness within and across characters. Her panoptic narrator is *in* the text, but not *of* it, to paraphrase the Sufi ideal of selfhood—and what she is trying to teach—as being "*in* the world, but not *of* it [original italics]." That is, one should be yea-saying to one's contingency *in* the world like Woolf's day self, but be nay-saying (not *of* it) to imprisonment, or fixation, in any of its forms, like Woolf's night self.[19]

Let us return to the question of whether Lessing's general choice of a conventional style biases her toward being a unifier and controller of her text-selves as an authorial presence, or whether her texts escape her. I would claim she *is* biased toward the unifying, clarifying impulse in her style, but that she still inscribes a process that gives the irrational and contingent their due in content and structure—for example, in the play on multiple layerings of symbols, numbers, and names.[20] The next chapter will examine the relationship between the detached, transcendental subjectivities ("not *of* the world") and the attached, immanent subjectivities of material experience ("*in* it") in Lessing's work.

When this relationship is put into gendered terms, it becomes a question of whether her bias in favor of masculine qualities is related to transcendence and whether she is patriarchally suppressing her feminine subjectivities. French feminist critic Nicole Jouve rails against the dry "above-it" stance of Lessing's narrators, who suffocate the text by their plenitudinous presence, leaving no gaps of dark bodily-sensed intuition to the reader.[21] Not only does the narrator *tell* all, but Jouve complains that she *shows* little. Jouve's method is to compare passages of *écriture féminine* by Hélène Cixous and others with passages from *Children of Violence* to demonstrate the bloodless neatness of Lessing's controlling voice. Jouve does not deny that a transcendental subjectivity is possible in the psyche, but she prefers it to bubble up through the "mud" of material existence, the representation of which is the mimesis of a process that goes directly through, and does not bypass, a suitably muddy feminine style. She objects to that distant masculine subjectivity that appropriates its immanent self as an object, to be scrutinized and neatly filed away in the preterite.[22]

In analyzing passages from *Landlocked* to show how the wise narrator's point of view blots out or confuses the point of view of the heroine, Martha, by being inappropriately intrusive, Jouve is convincing, but this point is not relevant to a critique of style per se, for it merely reveals that Lessing is not always in control of that style because of her too-faithful documentation of every thought in a mishmash of omniscient narrator and character perspectives. Too much plenitude creates its own kind of mud, and is perhaps an indication of the very exuberance and disorder of an implied author whose passion for honest thoroughness overflows the text, causing disjuncture and gaps, after all. Jouve manages to have it both ways—criticizing Lessing for overcontrol by showing where she loses control.

Indeed, Kaplan and Rose dispute the gendering of Lessing's style as masculine, claiming that her very carelessness marks an urgent immediacy, a "passionate engagement [that] repudiates . . . the distancing implicit in a chilly cerebral detachment of highly wrought style." (Lessing herself rationalizes away revision by not wanting to tamper with the freshness of the first outpouring.) Furthermore, Kaplan and Rose regard her style as "'feminine'—material, solid and concrete," for example, in the way Martha "expresses her political and social consciousness at any given time by how she dresses and does her hair and by how much she weighs."[23] Adding to the arbitrariness of such gendered distinctions, it could be claimed that men's typically more ego-bound behavior is "personal" in contrast to women's more typically ego-effacing behavior, which could be called at least "transpersonal," if not impersonal.[24] Oppositions like passionate/cerebral, concrete/abstract, and personal/ trans(im)personal are not clear binaries correlating with gender.

More importantly, the very idea that any text of whatever style—coherent masculine or muddy feminine—is privileged to offer a more direct route to either a bodily perceived or intellectually perceived reality belies the abstracting, reductive function of *all* language, which leads to Felski's thesis that form does not correlate with ideology or gender. Once we know that the most plenitudinous text is full of holes, and the most transparent text is occluding,[25] all that matters is that the form is effective in creating illusion (and/or disillusion, if its form is purposely self-referential). Thus, gender is not the crucial distinction, because people do not agree on what those labels mean in terms of style. The distinction may be better put in terms of the appeal to reader intuition or to explicit articulation, since every text is an interplay between both.

Although the gendered terms of this formal issue should be discarded, many of Jouve's other observations remain valid. Her own visceral style and juxtapositions of Lessing with the French "feminine" stylists does capture what bothers many readers, and even Lessing herself, about her "dryness" (which is why she tried writing as Jane Somers). Jouve demonstrates why a reader such as myself could not shed a tear or laugh along with either

Martha Quest or Anna Wulf despite the emotional turmoil they endure. Arguments that realism is passé don't explain why even sophisticated modern readers still weep or laugh with the nineteenth-century classics Lessing admires. However, those of us who are moved by Lessing's work may be responding to an emotion too deep for tears. It is that passion of the implied transpersonal author/narrator which finally does move us more than the personal emotions of the characters. The narrator is the protagonist. We are more engaged with that passionate intelligence behind the story, and with her tenacious integrity, than with any of her incarnations represented in it. In that sense, Lessing's novels are most effective, for they produce the very level of emotional involvement she seeks: the absorption of individual identity into an increasingly comprehensive state of mind that leaves individual personas behind as mere fictions. Or rather, as *lesser* fictions than a grand, more sublime one.

What Lessing's admirers value is not so much her notions of truth, which critic Joan Didion, for one, scorns as unoriginal,[26] but her commitment to self-discovery as process, not to any self-construct as product. While some of her commitments may seem to Didion to offer "unambiguous answers" (such as her teleological and utopian leanings), they are no more than a belief in the potential of the human imagination, which can regress as well as progress, or be repetitive as well as creative. Lessing's "answer" is not in any foundational truth, but in what the individual/collective human mind makes of its condition, as she urges us to "force ourselves into the effort of imagination necessary to become what we are capable of being" ("SPV," 9).

If Lessing's realism makes something available to readers that would otherwise remain too inchoate for them to formulate as relevant to them— just as Lessing and Martha keep asking of their reading, "What has this to do with me?"—then it is valuable. Felski argues for the present need of realist feminist texts as consciousness raisers, for which *Golden Notebook* and *Children of Violence* have been acclaimed. But Lessing dismisses feminist readings as "missing the point," which baffles feminists (e.g., Claire Sprague and Virginia Tiger) who find these novels relevant to them.[27] If Lessing misses *their* point, it is because she gives priority to "the bomb" rather than to personal feminist concerns, forgetting in her urgency that feminism's personal issues are political and that they do indeed address the kind of thinking that makes the bomb a threat.[28] Lessing's other concerns resonate in a network of readers of many stripes who also find relevance in her work, as Kaplan and Rose's overview of the great range of Lessing criticism indicates.[29] Here we have touched on some of the main discourses of analysis— Marxist, feminist, and psychological, particularly Jungian and Laingian, which are closely related to discourses of the mystical or paranormal. These discourses will be invoked at appropriate places in the discussion of the text. While each makes a contribution, none is the single key to Lessing's work, for she rejects being categorized in any school of thought. She regards readers and critics who are bogged down in only one aspect as missing the whole, as she complains in her introduction to *The Golden Notebook* (written ten years after the first edition):

> Why are they so parochial, so personal, so small-minded? Why do they always atomise, and belittle, why are they so fascinated by detail, and uninterested in the whole? Why is their interpretation of the word *critic* [original italics] always to find fault? Why are they always seeing writers as in conflict with each other, rather than complementing each other . . . [original ellipsis] simple, this is how they are trained to think. (*GN*, viii)

If Lessing's nay-saying to the academy and other critics seems to contradict her yea-saying to the collective mind—which presumably must include academic minds as well—it is because she assumes they are uniformly attached to established patterns of institutionalized thinking, in contrast to outsiders who are aware of alternatives, limitations, or fissures in "received opinion." But Fishburn points out that even the academy can be a site of subversion, and advocates teaching students Lessing's introduction to *The Golden Notebook* for its direct appeal to the experience of the student before the rigor mortis of thought sets in. In it Lessing writes:

> Dear Student. . . . You don't see that you are the victim of a pernicious system. . . . if you have yourself chosen my work as your subject, and if you do have to write a thesis—and believe me I am very grateful that what I've written is being found useful by you—then why don't you read what I have written and make up your own mind about what you think, testing it against your own life, your own experience. Never mind about Professors. (vii)

Here, then, is her appeal to intuition, as if her textual message is available unproblematically to an ideal reader or critic who can independently see the author's whole point without fragmented academic interpretation. But Lessing is not that naive. It is not that she expects individuals to be ideology-free, but that she expects there to be a naysayer, at least potentially, in every person. Her collective mind is not a monolithic uniformity. That is just what she objects to about the lockstep indoctrinated mind. The wholeness she advocates derives its vitality from an open dialogue among diverse minds that are both naysayers and yea-sayers. Consequently, her conclusion to this introduction swings 180 degrees from demanding holistic comprehension to recognizing the value of fragmentation as a form of such open dialogue:

> And from this kind of thought has emerged a new conclusion: which is that it is not only childish of a writer to want readers to see what he sees, to understand the shape and aim of a novel as he sees it—his wanting this means that he has not understood a most fundamental point. Which is that the book is alive and potent and fructifying and able to promote thought and discussion *only* [original italics] when its plan and shape and intention are not understood, because that moment of seeing the . . . intention is also the moment when there isn't anything more to be got out of it. . . . it is time to throw the book aside, as having had its day, and start again on something new. (xxii)

Here she admits that a fully comprehensible wholeness would be death, and that dialogue in the face of mystery is what art and life are all about.

With this pronouncement Lessing disclaims authorial control over reader response, but still evokes authorial intentionality, the other side of the coin of the author-reader relationship. However, Lessing's claim to authorial intention is met with the suspicion by Eve Bertelsen, for one, that she is claiming some isolated originary presence (in spite of her other pronouncements to be merely representative, not originary?) and that she uses her extratextual commentary, in interviews for example, as a backdoor to control the "meaning" of her texts for readers, in privileged competition with other interpreters.[30] Bertelsen sets herself the task of calling into question Lessing's specific authoritative claim, as well as the general illusion of the authority figure that the institution of an interview reifies, by practising conversation analysis on her own interview with Lessing. In analyzing the unedited tape according to her categories of analysis, Bertelsen reveals that the "famous author" persona is a master manipulator of the interview (but not of her texts?). Instead of dismantling the author under her Foucauldian assumption that discourse control is not locatable in an individual, Bertelsen exposes Lessing to be "controlling" (at least as an interviewee).

Yet the control Lessing exercises is a function of her *relationship* with the interviewer, and thus not locatable in either party, but in the nature of their dialogue. That dialogic relationship includes not only conversational strategies (e.g., denials, changes of topic), but also *content*. However, Bertelsen purposely omits the *content* of the interview, which Wendy Hollway's method would include as crucial to the analysis of any dialogic process, because it reveals *what* the assumptions of the contenders are, not simply *that* they are contending. Thus, Bertelsen can only admit her own assumptions, that she is pursuing Lessing "to fill in the lacunae" (which?) of previous interviews (is that completely possible?), so that her own attitude of trying to pin Lessing down (to what?) might very well account for her elusive prey's controlling defensiveness. She also admits that when she, the interviewer, attempts to "repair" the conversation (which is merely incidental to her purpose), Lessing is not at all nay-saying and evasively controlling, but forthcoming and egalitarian by taking an equal interest in Bertelsen's experience. This repair fills a lacuna in Bertelsen's project: her experiment demonstrates that when relationships are conceived as egos competing with egos for control (as in the hierarchical structure of an interview, an authority-challenger contest), walls are erected, but when they are conceived as gateways to welcome the contributions of each, they become enhancing and cooperative. Which is a point of Lessing's.

The point is that the process of becoming a personal-transpersonal-impersonal-and-comprehensive self is a dialogic, relational one, not locatable in any single point. This process might be epitomized in "the game" that Anna Wulf recalls from her childhood (reminiscent of the geography game Stephen Dedalus plays in Joyce's *Portrait of the Artist as a Young Man*):

First I created the room I sat in, object by object, "naming" everything . . . till it was whole in my mind, then move out of the room, creating the house, then out of the house, slowly creating the street, then rise into the air, looking down on London, at the enormous sprawling wastes of London, but holding at the same time the room and the house and the street in my mind, and then England, the shape of England in Britain, then the little group of islands lying against the continent, then slowly, slowly, I would create the world, continent by continent, ocean by ocean (but the point of "the game" was to create this vastness while holding the bedroom, the house, the street in their littleness in my mind at the same time), until the point was reached where I moved out into space, and watched the world, a sunlit ball in the sky, turning and rolling beneath me. Then . . . with the stars around me, and the little earth underneath me, I'd try to imagine at the same time, a drop of water, swarming with life, or a green leaf. Sometimes I could reach what I wanted, a simultaneous knowledge of vastness and of smallness. (*GN*, 548)

Molly Hite takes issue with Anna's game by ascribing to it a single controlling transcendental point of view that is literally at a point in outer space.[31] But, as Lessing might say, that isn't the point. That is, remaining fixed in outer space isn't *the* point. This little game of concentration is only a paradigm of the process of expanding consciousness, one that can be repeated with *new contents* that achieve new points of transcendence at any time, while alternating between the microcosm, the importance of the individual, and the macrocosm, through the integrating function of the mind. It is a paradoxical view in that it is a method of circulating among views, relating them rather than isolating them. Every point of integration can, in turn, be subsumed or undermined by any other position. This game cannot hope to establish final control by a single point of view that contains and manages all other positions, for although the integrative impulse arises from a need to manage for survival, that survival requires constant reckoning with new data and new perspectives on old data. If there is such a thing as *the* point, it is the dialectic between transcendental integration (unity) and local particularity (diversity), and between yea-saying and nay-saying to unity and/or diversity.

Lessing represents the process of the dialogic self in her *Children of Violence* protagonist Martha in two broad stages: the early years in the first three volumes—*Martha Quest, A Proper Marriage,* and *The Ripple Before the Storm*—which are dominated by her development as a naysayer (dissenter), with the yea-sayer in embryonic form; and the later years, beginning in *Landlocked* and culminating in *The Four-Gated City,* which are dominated by her development into a yea-sayer (a joiner). It is not that the early Martha does not try to be a joiner, but that the emphasis is on her disillusionment with the kind of collectivity that excludes the naysayer. A passage that reveals this double longing can be found in "The Story of Two Dogs" when the young girl (another incarnation of Martha) feels excluded from the camaraderie of hunting:

> We set forth each morning, first my brother, earnest with responsibility, his rifle swinging in his hand, at his heels the two dogs. Behind this time-honoured unit, myself, the girl, with no useful part to play in the serious masculine business, but necessary to provide admiration. This was a very old role for me indeed: To walk away on one side of the scene, a small fierce girl, hungry to be part of it, but knowing she never would be, above all because the heart that had been put to pump away all her life . . . was not only critical and intransigent, but one which longed so bitterly to melt into loving acceptance. An uncomfortable combination, as she knew even then—yet I could not remove the sulky smile from my face. . . . myself unwillingly following. ("STD," 168)

As a girl, she is excluded from the community of males, but she is not a naysayer to the community of hunters. Nevertheless, she is excluded here because maleness and hunting are equated, forcing her to deny either her femaleness or her wish to join the hunt. Not only does this passage reveal her hunger for solidarity, but her reactive, defensive nay-saying independence (in the uncomfortable combination of a controlling third-person point of view stepping out of the suffering first-person narrator). In *The Four-Gated City*, however, Martha finds a path to human solidarity through psychological, including paranormal, dialogues that are comprehensive enough to include the naysayer. Since the analysis of this culminating process in *The Four-Gated City* depends on recycling her previous life, the discussion in the following chapter will be divided accordingly.

4

Children of Violence

The central image of the archetypal four-gated city appears very early in *Martha Quest* as a metaphor articulating adolescent Martha's longing for her missing self, i.e., what is largely missing in her inner-outer relations: that which is at home in the world, not excluded from it. For by the age of fifteen she is already embittered and alienated, struggling to find the key to where and how to belong. She longs for loving human solidarity and harmony, not only as the social parallel of self-love but as the crucial juncture, the very constituency, of that self-love. Yet Martha's most frequent feelings throughout the series are anger, resentment, scorn, frustration, and inner conflict as she repeatedly "grind[s] her teeth with resentment"—at herself as well as others. She is harsh to herself from a principle of toughness that eschews sentimental self-pity. Her dream city is the antidote to her poisoned self, especially when her sympathies are aroused: "But the pity she refused herself flooded out and surrounded the black child like a protective blanket" (*MQ,* 10), as she slips into her "familiar day dream," gazing across the veld:

> There arose, glimmering whitely over the harsh scrub and stunted trees, a noble city, set foursquare and colonnaded. . . . There were splashing fountains and the sound of flutes; and its citizens moved grave and beautiful, black and white and brown together; and these groups of elders paused, and smiled with pleasure at the sight of the children—the blue-eyed, fair-skinned children of the North playing hand in hand with the bronze-skinned, dark-eyed children of the South. . . . Outside one of the gates stood her parents, . . . [and] most of the people of the district, forever excluded from the golden city because of their pettiness of vision and small understanding; they stood grieving, longing to enter, but barred by a stern and remorseless Martha. (11)

Young Martha's visualization of her ideal city is tainted by nay-saying at the outset. As her wiser narrator remarks, "[U]nfortunately, one gets nothing, not even a dream, without paying heavily for it" (11). Long after writing *Martha Quest*, Lessing, as a student of the Sufi way, came to realize how "rejecting" she had been all her life ("Learning How to Learn").

Martha's primary alienation is from her family, themselves colonizing aliens and transients in a hostile land. Their "temporary" mud farmhouse (lived in for about twenty years) becomes a metaphor for the displaced person Martha remains for the rest of her life. Although Martha's family never thinks of this house as "home," and she is only too eager to escape from it, Lessing herself looks back to that original house on the veld as the only place she ever thought of as home (*GH*, 30). Her homing nostalgia is part of the ambivalent feelings toward her place in nature, as they are inscribed in Martha, for this house, unlike the eternal ideal city, represents the insignificant individual—made of clay only to dissolve back into the impersonal earth, reabsorbed by the great forces of nature. When experienced directly by the living mind as self-transformation, this dissolution into nature becomes a form of dreadful knowledge, as in one of Martha's "moments" of being:

> There was certainly a definite point at which the thing began. It was not; then it was suddenly inescapable, and nothing could have frightened it away. There was a slow integration, during which she, and the little animals, and the moving grasses, and the sun-warmed trees, . . . and the great dome of blue light overhead, and the stones of earth under her feet, became one, shuddering together in a dissolution of dancing atoms. She felt the rivers under the ground forcing themselves painfully along her veins, swelling them out in an unbearable pressure; her flesh was the earth, and suffered growth like a ferment; and her eyes stared, fixed like the eye of the sun. Not for one second longer . . . could she have borne it; but then, with a sudden movement forwards and out, the whole process stopped; and *that* [original italics] was "the moment" . . . impossible to remember afterwards. For during that space of time (which was timeless) she understood quite finally her smallness, the unimportance of humanity. (*MQ*, 52)

This experience is painful, not like religious ecstasies she has read about. Her rational mind rejects such disturbing "moments" in favor of a humanist (rather than theocratic) vision of the golden city.

The four-gated city, according to Mary Ann Singleton, is a construct that resolves this terror of the wilderness in that it acts as a buffer, a place of refuge for humanity not only against the vicissitudes of nature, but beyond even the order of nature, against the void, nada, the ultimate meaningless universe. Humans endow the city with salvational meaning through a power of imagination that turns nada into cosmos, impersonal nature into Mother Earth, society into community, and self into communion with all.[1] On the other side of the coin, it is the symbol of Martha's nay-saying to all the blind, instinctive forces that bind her to her family and to a corrupt society through fateful repetition instead of loving creativity. The constant irony is that in her rejection of the family and an apartheid society she reenacts the very disconnectedness she deplores around her, for every "real city" she knows—self, family, society—is not just walled against outer destructive nature and the void, but walled against itself by inner barriers of judgmental rejection that prevent communion and destroy it from within.

A major clue to Martha's rejection of the family, and of herself, is that relation to her mother, which may have gone wrong even at the preoedipal stage, according to a detail her mother reveals when Martha herself is a young mother struggling to make sure her baby is eating enough. Mrs. Quest recalls that she was not producing enough breast milk for Martha as a baby and was tormented by her daughter's constant crying (*PM*, 97). Thus, Martha began life feeling deprived and rejected by her own mother, and developed a hard shell to protect herself, while her mother became entrenched in trying to control the child and disliked Martha for her protests and resistance. Mrs. Quest's lack of fulfillment as nursing mother and a woman in society causes her to hang on to that nursing role beyond the appropriate stage. And the missing self for which Martha longs is what should have been fulfilled at the breast, so that she could separate from her mother without becoming locked into a rejection syndrome.

In turn, Martha becomes a naysayer to her own maternity. Not only is motherhood to be rejected because it will mean further bondage in an incompatible marriage, but it will mean entrapment in the ruthless reproductive cycle of merely instinctual nature, forcing bondings by blood alone rather than love. The image of a Ferris wheel outside of the apartment she had as a young married woman becomes her obsessive symbol of the cycle of nature encoded into the female body and into the social pressures that drive her to marry someone she knows is wrong for her in the first place. When the marriage finally breaks up, Martha, already dismayed by signs of repeating the same mother-daughter power struggle with her own daughter, abandons custody of the young child in order to "free" her from the imposition of her own regime.[2] She has no available precedent to enable her to enact a balanced relationship in which mother and daughter negotiate common interests—both in their bonding and in their autonomy from each other. The first four volumes are heavily dominated by the drag of fatalism, against which the four-gated city stands in protest.

Martha searches for some available precedent, some discourse at least, if not direct example, to negotiate her path. From early girlhood she has been a voracious reader, but not to satisfy her mother's academic ambitions for her; although going to a boarding school like her privileged younger brother would have liberated her from home, it would only have delivered her into the hands of alien authorities who would control her reading. She resists that temptation and stays home to pursue independent study in the quest for self through literature, philosophy, psychology, and whatever would articulate that missing self. "What has it to do with me?" is her perennial question, as she says nay to book after book.

For example, her response to psychology books is to recognize that the "experts" disagree —except on their fatalism, which she discerns is the common factor despite their differences. In that sense, they seem to know it all: "If we *know* it [original italics], why do we have to go through the painful business of living it? . . . The act of giving names to things should be enough" (*MQ*, 8–9). For like Anna's game, which involves *naming* everything (the most controlling aspect of it), Martha seeks verbal management over the chaos of her inner state. Because of her critical mind, perspicacity, and verbal sophistication, Jouve wryly observes that Martha has the makings of a writer. But Lessing intends to inscribe other paths of action in her alter ego.

The first affirmative answer to "What has it to do with me?" is the discourse of Marxism with its four-gated ideology, given to her by the Cohen boys, two Jewish sons of a local merchant, who tutor her in the ways of radical dissent. Martha's relationship to Jewish characters, aliens among even the whites, are among her most significant. As People of the Book, they reinforce a culture of the Word, not in its primitive magical use but as intellectual knowledge. In order to master the mud of experience she seeks transcendence through the rational ideology of Communism and political, not artistic, activism. Ironically, dialectical materialism is yet another form of determinism. But this form holds the promise of inevitable evolution toward the four-gated city.

Although the appeal of rational transcendence through ideology is very strong, there is an even stronger transcendental appeal through another form of determinism as basic as economics—sexuality. Indeed, her body is the site of both a transcendence over words and a concurrence with them. Because Martha must say no to her mother's denial of sexuality, she becomes an emphatic yea-sayer to her physical desires, taking pride in her youthful body and seeking out discourses that validate feminine sexuality. The discourse on Marxism seems one key to her missing self, and so does the modern sexual revolution, which provides Martha with yea-saying discourses that speak for her deepest urges.

On another level, as yet unacknowledged by her at this stage, her erotic potential has already been revealed in those powerful "moments" on the veld, which are a form of orgasm, a dissolution of the controlling and controlled word-self, a means of transcendence not achieved through the naming game. Sexual union is only one form of nature's process of merging, dissolving the old, to reformulate the new. When such a transformation is realized in the living mind-body, it becomes an experience often felt as an ascendency—not just of the controlling subject rising *over* its object-self/world, but also of that muddy immanence rising to immerse its observer; hence it is often realized as a paradoxical loss of control as well as an empowerment. The rational mind may formulate this as a purely imaginary utopian ideal, but it can actually occur any time, and to varying degrees, among historically situated selves at certain moments. Both the rational and irrational are grounded in the mind-body engagement in which each gains by bowing to the other.

However, privileging the rational sets up Martha's inner conflict. On one hand, she affirms the body; and on the other, tries to control it—through physical contraception and through a mental rejection of the body's betrayal of emotions in tears:

> Now she wanted to cry. But she would not allow herself tears. Just as tenderness, moments of real emotion . . . left her exposed to her need for Caroline [her daughter], so did tears, even brief tears, open her to a feeling of deep, impersonal pain that seemed lying in wait for her moments of weakness like an enemy whose name she did not know. . . . (*RBS*, 25)

> Martha watched in herself the growth of an extraordinarily unpleasant and upsetting emotion, a self-mockery, a self-parody, as if she both allowed herself an emotion she did not approve of, allowed it and enjoyed it, but at the same time cancelled it out by the mockery. "How do I know what I feel and what I don't? . . . It's all dishonest. It's as if somewhere inside me there was a big sack of greasy tears and if a pin were stuck into me they'd spill out . . . [original ellipsis]." (226)

She doubts not so much her hard, dry emotions, the anger of the mocking naysayer, but her tender, moist emotions when they arise without ideological permission, as a dark enemy. Like her mother, she is hostile to the needy, crying child in herself,[3] demanding complete obedience to reason and, because of either-or thinking, she accuses herself of dishonesty.

To complicate the conflict, her rational rejection of the dreadful fatalism of nature (the dark enemy) is undermined by her equally rational acceptance of unity with nature as one antidote to a racially divided society.[4] For example, even as she is rejecting maternity, she is envious and approving of the native women who are "whole" and at peace with their childbearing existence—only to chide herself from the opposing perspective. Her hidden affirmation of nature also creeps out irrationally, in the contraceptive "negligence" that leads to her pregnancy and to her prolonged denial until it is too late for an abortion. In spite of massive denial, her integrity is constantly breaking through, as, for example, when she momentarily admits her subversive complicity in the pregnancy:

> Not the least of her bitterness was due to her knowledge that in some part of herself she was already weakening towards this baby. . . . she understood that this long process had been one of determined self-deception—almost as if she had wanted this damned baby all the time, she thought quickly, and immediately pushing the idea from her mind. (*PM,* 102)

But she returns to that rejected idea when a friend, whom Martha admires, but envies, for her smooth control over her affairs, polarizes Martha into resisting her advice for a late abortion:

> Martha, in the stubborn, calm voice of complete conviction, found herself explaining . . . how foolish an abortion would be at this stage. . . . The arguments she now found for having this baby were as strong and unanswerable as those she had been using, only ten minutes ago, against it. She found herself intensely excited at the idea of having a baby. (103)

She now assumes solidarity with her baby—passively allowing her rational will to find itself justifying an undeniable need that her rational friend denies.[5]

In very late pregnancy, a Dionysian urge impels her to glory in the mud of her condition, literally, in a Lawrentian scene in which she and an equally pregnant (different) friend romp naked in a rainy pond:

> She heard that same shout of triumph come from her own lips, and she ran on blindly. . . . into a gulf. . . . gaping like a mouth, its red crumbling sides swimming with red water. Above it the long heavy grass almost met. Martha hesitated, then jumped straight in. A moment of repugnance, then she loosened deliciously in the warm rocking of the water. She stood to her knees in heavy mud, the red thick water closed below her shoulders. . . . She was quite alone. A long swathe of grass had been beaten

> across the surface of the water, and around its stems trailed a jelly of frog
> spawn. . . . Martha allowed herself to be held upright by the mud, and
> lowered her hands through the resisting water to the hard dome of her
> stomach. There she felt the crouching infant, still moving tentatively around
> its prison, protected from the warm red water by half an inch of flesh. . . .
> Then, across the white-frothed surface of the pool, she saw an uncoiling
> in the wet mat of grass, and a lithe green snake moved its head this way
> and that, its small tongue flickering. (134–35)

This scene is directly inspired by their observing the mud-ball fight of their
husbands, who are releasing the pent-up energy of waiting eagerly to be
drafted into World War II. The young men's irrational indulgence in the
thirst for violence is countered by the escapade of their wives, who have
been penned up—and just as pent–up—in the isolating walls of houses by
their husbands' rational protectiveness. Everything has an ambivalent value:
rational walls are protective and imprisoning; irrational nature is violent
and orgiastic; men and women are equally creatures of all of these forces of
survival and dissolution. And the interplay of all these levels breaks through
the formal constraints of a superficially coherent and realistic narrative,[6] as
the omniscient narrator describes Martha's mud bath with enough symbolic dry earth to give it substance and enough semiotic water to make it run.

Martha's nay-saying ambivalence comes closest to Louis's than to that
of any other character in *The Waves*. Like him, she must eschew rootedness
in spite of her longing for a home, and, because of her alienation in the
world, she constructs an ideal city of perfection in her imagination, a vision
pursued through relentless frowning at the flawed world, with only an occasional peal of laughter to relieve the earnestness. She, too, must construct
a tough intellectual shell to protect that sensitive inner child:

> She was engaged in examining and repairing those intellectual's bas-
> tions of defence behind which she sheltered, that building whose shape
> had first been sketched so far back in her childhood she could no longer
> remember how it then looked. With every year it had become more com-
> plicated, more ramified; it was as if she, Martha, were a variety of soft,
> shell-less creature whose survival lay in the strength of those walls. . . . she
> clutched at the bricks of arguments, the stones of words, discarding any
> that might not fit. (94)

But unlike Louis, she does not beat the boastful boys by joining them in
their game, but by dropping out of one illusion of solidarity after another—
as we backtrack , then proceed, through her chronology for the highlights
of her unfolding process.

Martha Quest begins with the young girl's illusion of a romantic "coming out" for her first dance, which takes place at the house of the Afrikaaner family of her "date," where she feels more at home than in her own house (despite not understanding Afrikaans) because of their folksy warmth and solidarity. A momentary fusing transcendence occurs in the whirl of the dance, reminiscent of Percival's entrancing effect on the farewell partygoers:

> [F]or the few minutes the music lasted, every person on the verandah lost self-consciousness and became part of the larger whole, the group; their faces were relaxed, mindless, their eyes met those of the men and women they must meet and greet in the dance with an easy exchange . . . . the responsibility of being one person, alone, was taken off them. (*MQ*, 73–74)

And a ritual of initiation into their fold nearly occurs as the paterfamilias interrogates Martha, the alien English girl. But her stand against their racism—even if she prefers their honesty to the hypocrisy of English paternalism toward the natives—breaks the spell of that moment of solidarity among them.

Leaving behind any illusion of joining an innocent rural *volk* culture, Martha gets a job in town. She is taken on another whirl, this time in the partying culture of the Sports Club, where she is flattered to be instantly accepted by the "wolves," the young men about town. Although she is snapped up by one of them who tries to dominate her (and who dubs her with the girlish nickname "Matty"), she shakes off his hold, saved by the club's code against pairing off (so that the scarce women of the colony can be shared in the temporary never-never land of all-night carousing). This hedonistic elementary communism of the pack is barely tolerated by the older generation, who have been cajoled into supporting the Sports Club by the madcap son of a prominent magistrate. The generational nay-saying is part of the appeal to Martha, who contemplates the authoritative solidity of the magistrate, Mr. Maynard, in contrast to her own self-image:

> His large elderly face had the authority of a commanding nose, jowled cheeks, strong hazel eyes deep under thick black brows. It was the English face which, . . . has been looking down so long from the walls of countless picture galleries and country houses. Handsome . . . but more—every feature, every curve, had an impressive finality, an absolute rightness, as if the atoms which composed it had never had a moment's hesitation in falling where they did.
>
> Martha thought: here is another person who is complete—finished in his way. . . . Whereas she herself was formless, graceless, and unpredictable, a mere lump of clay. She rejected even the sight of him. . . . (*PM*, 4–5)

While Mr. Maynard is a kind of exemplar of the perfectly formed, the unquestioning epitome of his culture, as Percival is in *The Waves*, he is not the naive and indifferent repository of cultural values that Percival is, but rather the pillar of the status quo, who has a vested interest in his privileged status and cynically takes measures to defend it, becoming a kind of nemesis to Martha. If Percival has the potential to shock the authorities, Mr. Maynard would be one of those authorities. Mr. Maynard's heavy authority is the disapproving counterpoint to Martha's Dionysian urges for pleasure and dissipation in the Sports Club (founded by his wayward son Binky). And yet, he himself has a discrete extramarital affair—and designs upon Martha, which shocks her.

Long before she discovers the looseness beneath Mr. Maynard's solidity, she becomes abundantly aware of undercurrents beneath surface appearances in the behavior of the Sports Club when she attempts to circumvent the norms of their ritualized sexist behavior. Slipping out of her yea-saying formulaic mouthings is an occasional intelligent voice that brands her as an "intellectual," a liability as "one of the girls" but not too damaging, since attractive women are in demand. Similarly, even though her first sexual affair is with a Jewish musician, in her defiance of their anti-Semitic code, they still forgive her while forcing her to break it off. But if her nay-saying voice is silenced, her independent observing eye makes contact with a few other eyes in moments of shared knowing that the rituals are just a facade:

> Martha watched his eyes; she was becoming obsessed by the need to look at the eyes of these people, and not their bodies; for they were serious, anxious, even pleading; while all the time their bodies, their faces, contorted into the poses required of them. It was as if their surfaces, their limbs, their voices, were possessed, it was an exterior possession that did not touch them, left them free to judge and comment. . . . Towards the end of the dance, encouraged by the intelligent seriousness of the blue eyes, she rebelled, and talked in her normal voice, . . . while she felt his arms tightening, his eyes clouding. But she went on; she was resentful because he would not accept her as *herself* [original italics]—whatever that might mean; for was she not continually at sea, because of the different selves which insisted on claiming possession of her? She meant, she wanted to establish contact with him, simply and warmly; she wanted him to recognize her as a reasonable being. . . . And, slowly, she succeeded. He was beginning to talk normally, if in a gruff and unwilling voice, . . . (*MQ*, 155–56)

From time to time Lessing locates the "true" self in the eye of the beholder, that "reasonable being" taking it all in. Sally Robinson observes that Martha subscribes to the ungendered humanist "true self" beyond discourse instead of recognizing the "reasonable being" as one of her different selves that the Sports Club does not validate in Woman. While this makes feminist, dialogic sense, Martha's very claim of subjectivity itself is more than just a patriarchal "reasonable being." Her "true self" may be the felt ability to gaze or speak in her own behalf regardless of which of her varied selves, reasonable or not, she is assuming at the moment. Like a mobile open microphone, the "true self" could refer to that open space where subjectivity is always being reconstructed in response to prior experience.[7] When this observer-self recognizes its counterpart in a subject-to-subject gaze between a man and woman, rather than in the prevailing subject-object gaze dictated by group pressure, then the female subject and the male subject become capable of genuine engagement, respecting and even enjoying their differences. But here Martha's nay-saying subject can slip into a genuine yea-saying solidarity with the man for only a brief moment before having to revert to alienation.[8]

It is ironic that the nay-saying subjectivity seeking independence is helpless to control the forces of nature and society that entrap her. Dagmar Barnouw notes the passivity of Martha's drift even as she struggles to fashion her own destiny by denying those pressures.[9] When compelled to assume that controlling, nay-saying eye that despises the mock solidarity she enacts, Martha's quest for her missing personhood becomes more like a circular chase, with an alienated subject trying to sneak up on its tail from behind, as in a scene from a Pink Panther film in which Inspector Clouseau follows his own footprints. The problem is that being the naysayer alone is commitment to the principle of noncommitment, to lack, to no positive vision. At this point all Martha has are, on one hand, an ideology, an abstract commitment to the vague ideal of the four-gated city, which lacks concrete relationships (except with the Cohen boys, problematized by the sexual attraction issue), and, on the other hand, concrete, body-celebrating relationships in the Sports Club, which lack moral ideals she can commit herself to.

The concrete continues to exert more power over her than the abstract, as the Sports Club phases out of her life gradually, overlapping with the illusory solidarity of marriage. Although she tries to drop out of the club when their racism erupts in an ugly incident, she drifts back when claimed by one of the more liberal and intellectual boys, as war fever changes communal hedonism into a coupling-off pressure. She and Doug Knowell ("Know all") become one of the couples hurrying to marry before the wolves are drafted. She wishes to resist this new wave of social mania, but allows herself to be swept up in the tide. *Martha Quest* ends in a parody of those novels that end happily ever after in marriage, as Mr. Maynard, who performs the ceremony, reflects on the coming divorce. As a partner in a marriage, she is even less free to resist the nightlife that rises to a new pitch of frenzy before the war claims the men.

After the young husbands are drafted, the town is invaded by the RAF, and a new code of partying for "hostess" wives ensues, with conflicting pressures to entertain the troops and remain faithful to absent husbands. Of course, Martha has no intention of honoring the bourgeois code of fidelity, as her liberal young husband seems to understand. When he is unexpectedly discharged early, she is in the midst of an affair with a Communist RAF officer, which eventually becomes the ostensible cause of her divorce, but not until she has endeavored to salvage her marriage by putting up with the cotton-wool life of the security-minded suburbs and in propping up her romantic image of her husband. As the narrator scornfully remarks:

> [I]t was a matter of pride for Martha not only to be attractive sexually, but to be *good in bed* [original italics]. . . . Douglas could hardly be blamed for not understanding the thoroughness of Martha's dislike for him, since . . . [she was] prevented . . . from ever expressing it in bed. The moment she did so, it would have meant the complete collapse of the romantic picture she maintained of him. A young woman of this type will expend immense energy on arranging her image of her husband into something admirable and attractive. (*PM,* 280)

Throughout all these driftings with the tide of social/psychological pressure, Martha's naysayer has been dragged protesting, for she is helpless without something concrete to say yes to.

That is finally provided by her RAF lover, not because their love is so compelling (she finds fault there, too), but because he introduces her into a fledgling Communist cell composed mostly of newcomers—RAFers and refugees, like Anton Hesse,[10] a part-Jewish German whom she later expediently marries as a gesture of camaraderie against bureaucratic authorities. Fired by enthusiasm for the group, Martha dedicates herself with a self-sacrificing zeal she could never summon for matrimony and motherhood. Her missing self is already being realized as dispersed in a dialogue on an international scale rather than confined to the nuclear family and the stifling security of the suburbs. She "selfishly" abandons her own child to minister to the needs of the world's children, for home is everywhere else but the private hearth. Her political activities are the real downfall of her marriage, as she finds in the small group of Communists enough inspiration, camaraderie and clout (infiltrating local organizations) to create an illusion of accomplishment—due to the fluke of patriotic sympathy for Russia as "our gallant ally" in the war effort. Martha seems to have found herself in the words with which Anton mesmerizes them:

> She was swung because of the calm and responsible certainty of Anton Hesse's voice into a state of quiet elation and purpose. She knew that everyone in the room felt as she did. She was linked with them all, and from the deepest needs of her being. The people in the room, listening, exchanged small trusting smiles with each other; eyes, meeting, pledged faith with each other and with all humanity. (*RBS*, 55)

Disillusionment with their Communist cell, and with world Communism, comes slowly as factiousness eventually tears the group apart. The discrepancy between stated ideals and practice is the wedge of the Party's destruction. Anton's is the authoritative voice of organizing "Party discipline," which conflicts with democratic decision making and with ad hoc acts of human decency that do not fit in with Party strategies of *Realpolitik*, such as the rule (for expediency) against RAF members fraternizing with "colored" women, in spite of their antiracist ideals. Anton's cold "analysis of the situation" is opposed to simple acts of compassion. This mind-heart (body) split reflects the sexism, which, in spite of ideals, still prevails, although in reverse to that of the Sports Club; for while women's intellectuality is endorsed, their need to be sexually attractive is derided as bourgeois, and "personal relations" are derided as unproductive. Neither Communism nor capitalism perceive that the personal is political. As information slowly seeps in about Stalinist atrocities, Martha is one of the first in the group to recognize that it is not merely capitalist disinformation, but that nay-saying voices within Communism are speaking out, as her own naysayer intuits from what has been going on in their group.

The greatest value of Martha's association with the group is her contact with people who share her ideals, however they may falter in their practice. Since they form a composite self with Martha (like the group of friends in *The Waves*), each exhibiting various aspects of her—of which she approves and/or disapproves—a few sketches of them will help to portray her.

Although Anton is handsome, idealistic, and even sometimes commanding in his Marxist rhetoric, his cold efficiency and authoritarianism both reinforce Martha's own antiemotional stance and cause her to repudiate it. She is drawn into coupling off with him, but resents his takeover of her, for he betrays a very bourgeois instinct for patriarchal appropriation of women in his private affairs, which he rigidly keeps apart from his political activities. This is in contrast to Martha, for whom the marriage is an integral part of group action. During their marriage he becomes petulantly demanding of her, so that when she is having an affair, her body seems to sense his loss and to protest her infidelity without her mind's concurrence. By rigidly denying his own mind-body split, he eventually breaks (along the either-or fault line), with his complete capitulation to bourgeois colonial life in his next marriage. But Martha divorces the mind-body split in divorcing him.

A better example to Martha of tempering rational strategy with a spirit of immediate service and decency, is an RAF man, Andrew, who rivals Anton for leadership of the group. He offers to marry Maisie, Martha's old secretarial coworker and Sports Club friend, to give her unborn child legitimacy (against Anton's advice). When Maisie protests that even this noble gesture is too cold and abstract for her, Andrew admits some more personal feeling, which miraculously results in a truly loving marriage for them, because passion is wedded to ideals (his stated, hers implicit). Their case sets an example for Martha in her decision to marry Anton, although no such loving bond of mind-body is possible for them. However, Andrew becomes estranged from Maisie because of rivalry with her unborn child's absent father, Binky Maynard, when Mr. and Mrs. Maynard intervene to claim custody of their grandchild. This conflict of patriarchal territoriality over the woman's womb smashes one of the rare instances in which Martha sees that a marriage can be a beautiful union.

Perhaps the only man in the group who does actually live up to Martha's ideals—a man Lessing has stated is portrayed exactly as she recalls him in real life, even to retaining his real name—is Athen, the Greek guerrilla fighter temporarily displaced from his own country's civil war by the larger war.[11] His compassion and intensity of feeling are commensurate with his ideology, not only on the abstract level but on the immediate personal level. Whereas Andrew becomes emotionally disabled by his possessiveness turned to repugnance for Maisie, Athen becomes a gentle comrade and lover to her, treating her with utmost respect, even though she is a simple and unpolitically minded person. His relationship to everyone is caring and empathic, as a woman is supposed to be, without being appeasing or in any way compromising of his own dignity, as a man is supposed to be. His very faults—he shows embarrassment and self-disapproval for indulging himself in a few modest luxuries—only underline his saintliness. The only reason he does not marry Maisie after her divorce from Andrew is that he must return to fight in Greece—where he is martyred, as he anticipated. His appearance in Martha's story is Lessing's tribute to his memory. He comes closest to having an androgynous ability to relate the political and the personal by concretely nurturing and fighting for that abstract principle.

Martha loves and admires, but cannot emulate him, for she is still too much of a naysayer and not enough of a yea-sayer to herself to be as open to others as he. During her landlocked years of marriage to Anton, she leads a compartmentalized life, telling herself "She must keep things separate" (*LL*, 14) to survive, as she realizes from a recurring dream about houses with separate rooms that would disintegrate into rubble, meaning the ruin of her soul, without the trusted "guardian" who sends the message of her ambivalent dream:

> Keeping separate meant defeating, or at least, holding at bay, what was best in her. . . . the need to say yes, to comply, to melt into situations; . . . well, all this wouldn't do, she must put an end to it. She had simply to accept, finally, that her role in life, for this period, was to walk like a house-keeper in and out of different rooms, but the people in the rooms could not meet each other or understand each other, and Martha must not expect them to. She must not try to explain, or build bridges. (15)

She is already foreshadowing what she will have to go through in *The Four-Gated City*, when she spirals out to nay-saying separateness on another level, leading to further levels of communion.

In this waiting period of separateness, her belief in organized political collectivity shattered, Martha articulates her old longing for a missing self in terms of a "center":

> If she lived, precariously, in a house with half a dozen rooms . . . then what was she waiting for, in waiting for (as she knew she did) a man? Why, someone who would unify her elements, a man would be like a roof, or like a fire burning in the centre of the empty space. (30)

The man who has the power to fill that "empty space" and to kindle Martha's yea-sayer through direct sexual-spiritual union, rather than by ideology or vicarious example, is comrade Thomas Stern, a Polish Jew, who becomes her lover during the latter part of her marriage to Anton. It is significant that "the peasant" Thomas is a gardener, who, as a cultivator of the earth, represents the archetypal citizen of the four-gated city.[12] The attainment of that center through sex has a ripple effect throughout Martha's life, as former obstacles seem to melt away:

> She had complained that her life had consisted of a dozen rooms, each self-contained, that she was wearing into a frazzle of . . . nerves in the effort of carrying herself . . . from one "room" to the other. But adding a new room to her house had ended the division. From this centre she now lived— . . . (98)

> By herself it would have taken weeks of thinking, I should do this or that, and then a drift into a decision. But now she lived from this new centre, the room she shared with Thomas, a room that had in it, apparently, a softly running dynamo, to which, through him, she was connected. Everything became easy suddenly. (108)

For his part, Thomas is as surprised as Martha to be caught up in so intense a relationship. Unfulfilled in his marriage, he has been having numerous affairs, none of which have been as powerfully releasing as with Martha. It is as if they each held the key to the other:

> [W]hat was this absolute giving up of herself and his need for it; what was the prolonged almost unbearable look at each other, as if doors were being opened one after another inside their eyes as they looked—how was it that she was driven by him back and back into regions of herself she had not known existed . . . (100–101)

For opposing reasons, Rotraut Spiegel and Sally Robinson criticize Martha for supposing she has a center to be defined by a man.[13] Robinson faults Martha's seeming essentialism, while Spiegel objects to the intrusive other in her essential self. However, the above series of quotes suggest that Martha is not simply being taken over by Thomas, like an Olenka, because their attunement is a reciprocal opening up of doorways to each other's multiplicities. Although the discourse suggests unity, which Robinson objects to in Martha's self-narrative, Lessing steers between the opposing critiques of Spiegel and Robinson by describing a process that is both other-defined and defined apart from any other. Martha's empty center can be read as a dialogic space where her subjectivities mingle with his in relaxed re-creation, each reconstructing the other. Thus, her relationship to Thomas enables Martha to attain a point of equilibrium; she is no longer stuck in fragmented denial but recognizes yea-saying possibilities as well.

Indeed, in her communion with him Martha discovers that Thomas is even more of a naysayer than she is. He is tormented by his parental family's demise in the Warsaw Ghetto. As a Jew he assumes the historical burdens of his people, and as a person he is riven by his wife's denial of his lower-class origins, all contributing to a deep self-hatred and hatred of his enemies (but not his wife, whom he loves). Thomas leaves for Palestine to fight the British in "Operation Exodus," appalled that a liberal government would prevent Jews from escaping to their homeland. His extreme bitterness about the mindless violence of the world comes through in his letters to Martha, which set the theme for their historically situated selves:

Perhaps, when Thomas and she touched each other, in the touch cried
out the murdered flesh of the millions of Europe . . . having its revenge, .
. . through the two little creatures. (159)

> Martha did not believe in violence.
> Martha was the essence of violence, she had been conceived bred,
> fed and reared on violence.
> Martha argued with Thomas: What use is it, Thomas, what use is
> violence? (195)

> The soul of the human race, that part of the mind which has no
> name, is not called Thomas and Martha, which holds the human race as
> frogspawn is held in jelly—that part of Martha and of Thomas was twisted
> and warped, . . . —she could no more disassociate herself from the vio-
> lence done her, than a tadpole can live out of water. (196)[14]

If Martha's historically situated self is that of a child of violence, then
her ahistorical self, the one that causes her to claim to be nonviolent, is that
which envisions the four-gated city of peace and love. It is that ahistorical
self which is positioned at the "center," a mandala self in Jungian terms. Its
attainment at the level of social systems may hardly be approximated, but it
is available to transpersonal consciousness through sexual union such as
theirs, and through powerful impersonal "moments" of interconnectedness.
It is significant that flowing through their ahistorical union are the historical forces they feel so deeply. The claim that the timeless state is the only
"true" one is another form of denial, which can result in isolation from
historical "reality."[15] Martha carries about her timeless yet time-bound union
with Thomas as an inscription in her body-mind, for even in his absence he
is present to her.

But when he returns from Palestine, he is more absent to her than ever,
possessed with his work on behalf of the natives. After he goes off to remote
villages to report on conditions, to the sorrow of the natives he dies of an
illness. In transcribing his final report for the leftist society that sponsored
him, Martha realizes he must have gone mad. She types an incoherent text
on onion-skin paper, which she superimposes on the coherent sections, much
as Anna Wulf's chaotic notebooks might be juxtaposed against "Free
Women"—except that Thomas's incoherencies are even wilder and more
fragmented than Anna's notebooks. Martha intuitively knows this text has
a bearing on her own self-inscription, and carries his manuscript with her
to England.[16]

While the men of the Communist group partly define Martha, she is
also defined by a number of women, both in and outside the group, who

influence her. Her old friend Maisie appeals to Martha because of the down-to-earth honesty of her feelings, with little sentimental investment in being widowed (more than once) by the war. Maisie is a large, sensuous woman whose self-respect Martha notices especially in the repose and grace of her hands. She is not a complicated intellectual having to ratify her intuitive responses to people by any internal ideological monitor, and that makes her a breath of fresh air for Martha.

More her intellectual equal, Martha's closest Communist friend is the dedicated Jasmine Cohen (cousin of the Cohen brothers), who bears most of the burden of organizing on her petite, overworked shoulders. Martha grows to admire her and emulates her devotion to the cause. But Jasmine is not merely a cardboard zealot; she is a woman of flesh and blood whose intellectual discipline is based on passion and body-knowledge, including the sexual. Jasmine reinforces Martha's observations of the sexist hypocrisy of the men in the group who condemn them for "bourgeois" makeup and clothing. But Martha never comprehends how Jasmine can tolerate living at home with her very bourgeois parents when she is just as antifamily as Martha. This is a kind of heroic renunciation Martha is not ready for. When Jasmine leaves for South Africa, marking the final dissolution of their cell, she carries to her new cadres an unshakably pure idealism and faith in political organizing that Martha can no longer maintain.

A closer alter ego for Martha is Marjorie, another party comrade. She has a similar kind of looks and need to be attractive mixed with her idealism. In contrast to Martha and Jasmine, both of whom undertake comradely marriages for the expedient purpose of eluding bureaucratic authorities, Marjorie marries out of a need for a stable personal relationship with a fellow comrade, but not for love either. As outlets dry up for meaningful political action, Marjorie and several other young enthusiastic members find themselves marooned in the dull pattern of settled bourgeois housewives and mothers:

> [T]hey watched their own deterioration like merciless onlookers. . . . Lives that appear to them meaningless, wasted, hang around their necks like decaying carcasses. They are hypnotized into futility by self-observation. It is as if self-consciousness itself has speeded up the process, a curve of destruction. . . . And it is these people who are at twenty the liveliest, the most intelligent, the most promising. (205)

They envy Martha for leaving the colonial backwater, but feel like traitors to themselves, unable to do likewise. This kind of "self-observation" is the voice of the self-hater, not the transcendental observer. Marjorie is what Martha would have been.

Unlike the idealistic women who consider family life to be an albatross around their necks is Mrs. Van der Bylt, the one older woman outside the young Communist group whom Martha wholeheartedly admires as a political power in her own right. The striking difference between Mrs. Van and the young neurotic women is her enormous determination to be politically active and still committed to her family in the Afrikaaner tradition. In one of the few digressions from Martha's point of view, the narrator tells Mrs. Van's history: of how, when she discovers at the outset of her marriage that her husband has no sympathy with her convictions, she solemnly resolves to eschew all emotion (self-pity) and to carry on by devoting herself to her children first, to her husband second, and to her need to work for human rights in society. With sheer will and energy (and servants, of course) she accomplishes all three—raises a large family, caters to her husband, and becomes mayor of the town and power broker in the Socialist-Democrat (Labour) Party, where she agitates against the color bar. Behind these credentials is the quality of her commanding personality—her immediacy and insight into people and situations is graced by warmth and compassion. However, she must pay a price with a painful back due to overwork, and a marriage that is a duty rather than a fulfilling relationship.

From a Jungian feminist point of view, Lorelei Cederstrom argues that Mrs. Van has "compartmentalized" her life, and is not operating out of her center. Thus, her fragmented life is "falsified."[17] However, this judgment, while claiming to privilege one's state of mind over one's circumstances, is focused on the *circumstance* of her imprisonment in a certain kind of marriage—not on the strength of her state of mind about it. For Mrs. Van chooses to make what she can of a bad bargain, honor-bound to accept a contingency she cannot alter, rather than to succumb, like so many women, to powerless complaining and self-defeating passive resistance. The Jungian illusion-reality discourse inverts one that would value Mrs. Van's pragmatism as "realistic" because it does not deny contingency. And Mrs. Van is more rigorous about refusing to deny the incompatibility of her marriage than the "type of woman" Martha once was. Indeed, that integrity of Mrs. Van's to confront this and every other contingency of her life without surrendering her values is what connects the "compartments" of her life and falsifies the appearance of external fragmentation. The integrity that does not deny contradictions, but lives with them, is a kind of unity that acknowledges it cannot unify the incompatible.

Although Mrs. Van stands up for her values, she is nevertheless mistaken to impose her judgment on Martha, whose situation is very different. The alternative Martha chooses—to sever herself from her marriages—is the one thing Mrs. Van disapproves of about Martha, while Martha, for her part, does not understand the conservative code of honor about family in Mrs. Van. Martha must be true to her own needs and values, not to Mrs. Van's. While abstract justifications can be maintained for both their points of view, what is most important is the timing, the readiness of an individual to take a given position at any point in her particular process. In *The Four-Gated City* Martha moves into stages of experience that will give her retrospective insights into Mrs. Van that she could not possibly have had earlier.

Martha's relations to these women have enabled her to ratify herself as a woman, despite their differences, as she could not with her mother. Whereas with her mother Martha's sexual affirmation is reactive, a case of reverse psychology, with these other women it becomes a more positive confirmation of the prerogatives of the body and its dark knowledge, because it is combined with intellectual and/or moral integrity. Their influence has moved her body awareness into a position more balanced with that of her intellect in the dialogic makeup of her self, especially in the context of her divorce from the cerebral Anton and her union with the earthy and irrational Thomas.

Martha's being landlocked on a high and dry plateau is symbolic of that controlling position assumed by her nay-saying voice. Anticipating her release from that landlocked place in Africa, Martha becomes obsessed with the counterpart to the high and dry controlling voice, as images of the sea inundate her in poetic, almost Woolfian, prose that suggests the transformative nature of the ocean as the origin and dissolution of life's processes. Martha's seagoing passage to England, to the roots of her intellectual tradition, represents her transition to a state of being that contains within it all the old roots, including the cadres of men and women whose influence she has gathered into the collective dialogue of her ongoing self.

THE FOUR-GATED CITY: YEA-SAYING AS OPENING GATEWAYS

Martha's state at the beginning of *The Four-Gated City* is the envelope into which the rest of the novel, the rest of her life, drops. Or it is the conduit through which it passes, for its chief characteristic is its emptiness. It is not the bitter emptiness of an Olenka or an Anna Wulf, to whom being a "free woman" is a galling irony (even though Anna has a golden notebook full of material to create selves, while Olenka's self-discourse is disconnected). They both are still longing for the man-woman relationship, and, in Anna's case, for the solidarity of an idealistic society. But, after a voyage of dissipation at sea, Martha's rebirth in London is into an emptiness that is affirmative, more like that of Mrs. Ramsay's peaceful liberation in her lighthouse trance. (Martha's metaphors for this state are being a "lighthouse" or a "radio set" [*FGC*, 44]). She has been emptied of her need for refuge in a utopian dream and of her dependence upon a man to define her missing center, because she has caught up with that missing self to find that it has been there all along: "This was loneliness? Yes, she supposed so. But . . . , since she had been in London, she had been alone, and had learned that she had never been anything else in her life. Far from being an enemy, it was her friend" (37). The very thought of any attachment, any particular identity or solidarity, would spoil it:

> For a few weeks she had been anonymous, unnoticed—free. Never before in her life had she known this freedom. Living in a small town anywhere means preserving one's self behind a mask. Coming to a big city for those who have never known one, means . . . freedom: all the pressures are off, no one cares, no need for the mask. For weeks, then, without boundaries, without definition, like a balloon drifting and bobbing, nothing had been expected of her. (4)

Her new drift is not fraught with anxiety, conflict, and confusion. The "self" without a mask is like the socially unformed, preoedipal child, a purely open subjectivity, receptive to whatever comes. One by one, she watches her old personas (Matty, Martha, Mrs. Hesse) and a few new ones she has improvised for strangers in London (Phyllis, Alice) drop off. She cannot even describe this "self": "But who then was she behind the banalities of the day? A young woman? No, nothing but a soft dark receptive intelligence, that was all" (38). In short, not any banal day self, but a night self. Unlike the sudden moments on the veld that would overwhelm her and leave, this state is prolonged and brought on by her cultivation of alertness:

> She had learned that if she walked long enough, slept lightly enough to be conscious of her dreams, ate at random, was struck by new experiences throughout the day, then her whole self cleared, lightened, and she became alive, light and aware. (36)

> And she had been walking and alert all day. The conditions were right then. First, before the lit space, a terror: but slight, nothing that could overwhelm. . . . it was always her heart that first fought off the pain of not belonging here, not belonging anywhere, and then, resisted, told to be quiet, . . . and after that the current of her ordinary thought switched off. Her body was a machine, reliable . . . for walking; her heart and her daytime mind were quiet. (37)

The naysayer of the night self does not control by naming, but by shaking off labels and bringing fears "to heel" (37) by clearing the mind and simply being there, intensely alive to what is happening. But even though she had no identity

> she was connected still with—a feeling of being herself. She was able to see herself as if from a hundred yards up, a tiny coloured blob, among other blobs, on top of a bus, or in a street . Today she could see herself, a black blob, in Mrs. Van's coat, a small black blob beside a long grey parapet. A tiny entity among swarms—then down, back inside herself, to stand, arms on damp concrete: this was what she was, a taste or flavour of existence without a name. Who remembered. Who noted. And not much more. (17)

But into this quiet floating state in which she freely takes the panoramic view or zooms in for a close-up, as in Bernard's moments of detachment, there comes the rub: Necessity. Memories. Since her arrival, she has resisted any attempts at obligating friendships, even warm and sincerely offered ones, by people from a range of classes—the working-class people who rented her rooms, and the upper-middle-class contacts who were offering hospitality and jobs. No longer seeking solidarity or a home, she would like to prolong this separateness like a long exhale before breathing back in the "silly banalities" of everyday life that remind her of how tired and hungry she is, and how "scared stiff" she is down to her last bit of money (39). This naysayer who is not of the world is more mellow—even has a sense of humor—compared to the old caustic Martha. The only trace of scorn here is a view of necessity as silly. Yet even that is modulated by an amused voice that observes, "The most interesting discoveries were made through banalities" (39), as the silly, frivolous voices break into the empty space and force that aloof subjectivity to listen to their urgent messages of survival; thus, the dialogue of her responsibilities to herself and to other people is reengaged.

It is not enough to have found that missing self, as if it could be definitively found once and for all, for Martha keeps forgetting and then remembering it, as transcendental subjectivities oscillate with immanent subjectivities. Martha keeps chiding herself for continually forgetting this "lit space" when she is involved in material affairs, as if she prefers to remain continuously alert without falling into the cotton-wool trance of worldly desires. On the other hand, when necessity takes over, she chides her spaced-out self:

> That was the night when, walking, she had understood . . . but she could not remember now what it was she had understood. And she had a vio-

lent reaction against that too—posturing around she thought; making yourself important, imagining all kinds of great truths when all it was really . . . well of course if you're going to not-sleep and not-eat properly. . . . (95)

However, she balances that reaction with: "but somewhere in the back of her mind the thought held: it was here, it was here, it *was*—just because you can't get anywhere near it now, that doesn't mean . . . it doesn't exist" (96). She has realized that

> You could perhaps, during the long day of work, responsibility, people, noise, have a flash of reminder: *These places exist* [original italics], but that was because the day had lifted you towards them, like a wave, for just a brief moment. . . . That was why people did not remember. They could not. (41–42)

Thus, the banal, muddy world itself gives rise to those lit spaces, each time from a new vantage point, a rediscovery of the old in new variations:

> You suddenly understand something you've understood all your life, but in a new way. But there's a pressure on us all the time to go on to something that seems new because there are new words attached. . . . But I want to take words as ordinary as bread. Or life. Or death. Clichés. I want to have my nose rubbed in clichés. (101)

The third-person narrator serves as a mechanism to keep the dynamic moving, to remind Martha of these oscillating states. For who is it that remembers and forgets? A first-person narrator proceeds from point to point linearly, whereas a third-person narrator acts as a third-eye scouting the terrain unspoken by the speaking subject and discloses other views. In *The Four-Gated City* the narrator is somewhat like the "guardian" of her dream messages and appears to be much closer to Martha's current process than in the previous volumes, where the narrator kept a long, often ironic, distance from her protagonist.[18] Of course, the narrator still preserves some distance to create Lessing's effect of watching Martha watching her own thoughts, as if there is "a thought around" just a step ahead of her. It thus suggests an unknown knower always slightly beyond the character's immediate position.

Having established her new state of awareness, Martha must now weigh alternatives for shelter without seeking permanent resident status, since she carries "home" within herself, that is, a readiness to enter whatever edifice she needs to further work out the issues of her life. The rest of *The Four-Gated*

City is the story of Martha's sojourn in various houses, which become symbolic of the still darkened compartments in herself that she must explore and open up to inner dialogue. The first house she explores in depth is that of her friend, Jack, a South African, the only one of her initial acquaintances who understands the freedom of the empty space she's in. "The house that Jack built"—Sprague observes the inevitability of this phrase occurring to the reader—is where she confronts her sexuality and the power it has for evil as well as good.[19]

Because Jack understands her floating state, she is sexually attuned to him, although her relationship to Jack as an individual is peripheral compared to the centrality Thomas once supplied. The good part of sex with Jack is reentering that "thousand volt" energy field (60). She stumbled into it before with Thomas, since both he and Jack were plugged into that source of power, but she and Thomas were too overwhelmed, pulling back when the intensity was too great. However, Jack has developed sex into a fine art, such as one might imagine a tantric meditation to be, and he initiates Martha into it:

> [Successful] Sex, with Jack, was never an explosive, or the simple satisfying of a need. . . . Sex was the slow building up, over hour after hour, from the moment of meeting the woman he was to make love with, a power, a force, which, when held and controlled, took both up and over and away from any ordinary consciousness into—an area where no words could be of use. (61)

The problem with Jack is that he is fixated in the single room of his sexuality, while Martha has various other rooms to tend, as Thomas had (which is what they brought each other in their union). Jack's obsession with sex is based on his harrowing experience of surviving at sea when his ship was sunk during the war and he was severely wounded. He emerged with a sense of mastering his body and a bottomless longing for women (as a deprived sailor). Through sex he overcame his enemies—Time and Death. But not his enemy Hatred. He has observed that tuning into the cosmic force of sex opens up not only collective love, but collective hate: "[Y]ou discover hatred is a sort of wavelength you can tune into. After all, it's always there, hatred is simply part of the world, like one of the colours of the rainbow" (60).

Thus, besides being more comprehensive than Jack, she cannot remain with him for very long, out of "Self-preservation," because she senses he is *"paying too high a price* [original italics]" as the jingling line from the nursery rhyme "Jack fell down and broke his crown" informs her like a refrain (40).

Years later she returns to observe firsthand what that price is. Because hatred had been distilled in him by his father's abuse, the band of hatred
finally undoes him after neither Martha nor any of his other women take
him seriously enough in practical ways to stay and have children with him.
He wants them to trust him, but they sense his obsessiveness, his inability to
be a good parent because of his relation to his own father. After Martha has
left him he deteriorates into an illness that locks his mind into hatred—as
Thomas's had been, except that Thomas turned his hatred inward and did
not survive his illness, whereas Jack survives to become an archfiend exploiting women with diabolic manipulativeness, turning his house into a
brothel. Martha herself nearly succumbs when she revisits him, even though
she is tough and aware of his techniques of slowly bringing his victims down
by moral degradation, so much a master of the art is he.

Lessing describes his brainwashing method at length in a chilling account that rivals Orwell's *1984*, in order to illustrate the process of indoctri-
nation of all kinds. The key is to use people's pride in their moral principles
as the very lever of their ruin, as they struggle to trust their suave tempter
when he plays the confidence game, only to feel self-hatred and guilt for
giving in when he switches roles to castigator and tormenter. Martha learns
the devious ways of hell from Jack, which gives her an advantage when she
descends to her own depths of self-hating horror.

During the first weeks of her relationship with Jack she is still in the
dark about that (de)basement of her self. In disappointing Jack's offer to
become his chief concubine, all she knows is that she cannot be trapped in
his house. The house she does find, though it seems unlikely at first, becomes the very place where she can tend to the many levels of her being—
upstairs and in the basement. The only reason she decides to be writer
Mark Coldridge's secretary temporarily is that she needs a job and a place
to stay, and he offers her both. That "temporary" place becomes, like the
old farmhouse on the veld, her home for many years, as she becomes not
just a secretary but the housekeeper of her old dream, taking up her task,
literally, in tending to the Coldridge rooms as well as to the corresponding
rooms in herself. After an initial nay-saying period, she becomes a yea-
sayer to the aspects of herself she once rejected.

Although the room she has in the Coldridge house in Bloomsbury has
a calming, consoling effect, especially the sycamore tree outside the window, she resists sinking into the upper-middle-class, conservative atmosphere
with its neurotic family scene, and plans to move on as soon as possible.
However, she does become emotionally entangled in the skein of family
relationships with Mark's son Francis, his nephew Paul, and his "madwoman
in the basement" of a wife, Lynda, who cannot relate to Mark as a wife,

although he is devoted to her. She is a beautiful woman with classic features, but is asexual (a little reminiscent of Woolf, perhaps). Lynda's dysfunction as a wife and mother is symptomatic of her mental illness.

During the years Martha spends there, she forms a strange triad with Mark and Lynda, becoming his occasional mistress (only after several years), and descending to Lynda's basement to discover solidarity with her madness—and her sanity. That lowest region of the house symbolizes Martha's inner hell, the place from which she must learn to extricate herself with Lynda's help and Jack's example, neither of whom can extricate themselves. It is the kind of psychic trip Lessing has explored in the Anna Wulf–Saul Green shared madness, except that Martha has already passed beyond the disillusioned note "Free Women" ends with, in her disciplined attainment of the quiet space beyond good and evil, which she struggles to regain time after time.

Before Martha descends to her lower depths, she has issues on the upper storeys to work out.[20] One is her relation to politics and society at large, which she ruefully finds she cannot escape in private life. After Mark's scientist brother Colin defects to the Soviet Union (on the principle that giving the Soviets the bomb will create nuclear deterrence) and Colin's Jewish refugee wife commits suicide, leaving young Paul in Mark's care, the Coldridge house is besieged by the media and the Foreign Office, who send reporters and spies into their lives, giving the family notoriety and causing trauma to young Francis at school, as well as to his cousin Paul. Martha's years of political activism have given her the presence of mind and perspective to be steadying to the family during this crisis. Out of loyalty to his brother, and in reaction to the persecution of public agencies, liberal Mark turns radical Communist, becoming estranged from his Tory mother. In watching Mark go through stages of zeal and disillusion, Martha feels as if she is watching her old self, although his Communist phase is more superficial than hers was.

She now becomes like the narrator of herself by observing (and participating in) the stories of her alter-ego housemates, rather than primarily through herself per se; as such, she serves in the humble capacity of the biblical Martha,[21] more as a yea-saying backdrop rather the nay-saying star of the piece. As the years go by, Lynda goes back and forth between hospitals and home in cycles of struggling to get away from the medical establishment and from her dependence on pills, and of being defeated because she is still dependent on Mark from fear of the normal world—while hating his overprotectiveness. He, still hoping she will get well someday, provides a place for her in the basement, where she brings a mental patient friend back, for solidarity against the normal denizens upstairs . The boys, Francis and Paul, return home from school for holidays, each needing the stability Martha offers, yet vying for the favor of Lynda, who, having been closer to Paul than her own son during their childhood, estranges Paul in early adolescence in her effort to reopen her relationship to Francis. Paul's loss of Lynda's favor hardens an antisocial, amoral streak in him, causing his expulsion from the progressive school he liked—for theft—and his return to the house, where he is a strain on everyone. The overly polite Francis is a different kind of strain on Martha, as he plays the self-deprecating buffoon to cover up his vulnerability, like her old Matty persona. Complicating their growing up is their relationship to their girl cousins, who, in rebellion from their own broken home, seek the favor of Francis, while ostracizing Paul. Their adolescent years are a trying time for Martha, who must confront the hated enemy in herself—the matronly mother figure—as she enacts the role of adult authority against the rebellious children in a role reversal to that of Martha Quest. But now she is the observer of her roles:

> How very extraordinary . . . this being middle-aged . . . as if more than ever one was forced back into that place in oneself where one watched; whereas all around the silent watcher were a series of defences, or subsidiary creatures, on guard, always working, . . . with . . . earlier versions of oneself, for being with the young meant . . . reviving in oneself . . . that mood, that state of being, since they never said anything one hadn't said oneself or been oneself. (*FGC*, 354)

Martha's near disappearance from the center of the story and her effacement into the household as general factotum, child superintendent, counselor, and sometime sexual consoler of the male head of the house are baffling to feminists who have come to expect a naysayer like Martha (and Anna) of yore. Has she not capitulated to housewifery, and de facto if not de jure matrimony, and submerged her subjectivity in the patriarchal paradigm? Lessing's implied answer is that she is *in* it but not *of* it. Martha is not an Olenka, trapped willingly, because unknowingly, in total self-effacement; nor a May Quest (Martha's mother), trapped unwillingly, but knowingly, yet endorsing hypocritically; nor a Marjorie, trapped knowingly, but honestly being critical; nor an Anna, trapped outside of it as a "free woman" (like the hapless Olenka between loves). In contrast, Martha has assumed the responsibility of a Mrs. Van, who flows with contingency, responding to others' needs from a place of empowerment because of the alternative resources of a dialogic self. Having the leverage of the transcendental observer enables Martha to be wherever she is provisionally, not just because of fate (although that, too), which frees her to attend to her role(s), rather than to expend useless energy passively resisting as a victim of fate. She reflects on her position as she goes about her business,

> calling Paul, Mark, Jill, Gwen, etc., etc., in a calm competent voice, the voice of the middle-aged woman who has every string in her hands. She had become that person who once she hated and feared more than any other—the matron. Well, what alternative was there? . . . (but luckily one never stayed in any stage long . . .) It was that thinking nine-tenths of one's time about other people, one acquired an insight into them that appalled even oneself. Power. Putting herself back fifteen years into Mrs. Van der Bylt's drawing- room, she was both the person who sat watching Mrs. Van, . . . wholly protective of her own privacy, . . . and Mrs. Van, who looked at Martha and knew, She will do this . . . If I do this then she will be saved. . . . Intolerable! (360)

Besides, entering into dialogue with others does not mean canceling out the self. On the contrary, it is expansion of self. The assumption that there is a self to be effaced is a throwback to the concept of an essential atomistic core that is somehow infringed upon by giving space to other's voices within its purview. Martha still lives as a host of transpersonal selves— Martha-Mark-Lynda, Martha-Francis, Martha-Paul, etc.[22] Even that quiet lit space that is the nearest thing to a solitary self is not an isolated single essence, but the absence of all essence,[23] and hence no positive entity that can be effaced, being the same in everyone. Yet every time Martha reaches the transcendental state she enters it at a different point in her process, so it is never experienced in quite the same way. That is, the timeless observer always surveys a different set of time-bound conditions, or always appears to arise out of different places, which is what makes it new, although, para-doxically, it is what one has always known.[24]

Having been newly discovered out of a particular set of conditions, any insights gained translate back into new time-bound conditions in the pro-cess of the situated self. Depending on the needs and desires of the situated self, there is, for example, the danger of "getting hooked on" transcendence itself and refusing all dialogue with the world, or worse, getting corrupted with power over others, as in Jack's case. In Martha's, she is enabled to relate in more varied and developing ways. Since any transcendental posi-tion is just one subjectivity among many, it is not a permanent self that can be effaced, but only another resting point with a new perspective along an endless way. Precisely because Martha entertains more vistas than an Olenka, she can afford to become involved with others without getting trapped in them. While Olenka's plasticity so completely shapes her into the mold of the current man in her life that she gets stuck in it, Martha's plasticity is engaged in breaking molds or making connections across them by flowing through transcendental self-narrators.

An example of Martha's ability to gain from her transcendental perspectives occurs precisely during a phase when she does perceive herself as effaced—after some of the worst times are over and there is a lull. Without some compelling challenge she becomes bored and drifts into the doldrums. Upstairs, Mark has been involved in Communist activity and an affair with a comrade; downstairs, Lynda and her inmate friend Dorothy have a new lease on life with a set of occultist friends and their coddling of Paul; both Paul and Francis are getting by with Martha's management. Her competence at organizing the household leaves her long hours alone, questioning her existence and purpose in life: "But what was she really doing? What ought she to be doing? She did not know . . . she was a person who watched other people in a turmoil of living . . . did they see a woman who watched and waited—passive?" (199). Although it is springtime, a

> lethargy like an invisible poison filled her. . . . Thoughts of death slowly filled the room. . . . she thought how strange it was; a few weeks ago . . . Lynda . . . talked of death, of suicide. . . . Now . . . the basement was alive again, and. . . . Death had moved up to Martha's room
>
> *It seemed as if her capacity to think this, see this, had the power to shift the fog in the room, to start a fresh current* .
>
> She had a glimpse . . . where the house and the people in it could be seen as a whole, making a whole. It was not a glimpse or insight which could be easily brought down into an ordinary air: it came late at night . . .
>
> Martha was suddenly, not easily, but after effort, able to look down into the house, achieve that viewpoint. *As she did so, the heavy atmosphere of death in her room cleared, thinned, and went.*
>
> There she was, . . . empty, at peace. She watched other people developing their lives. And she? In every life there is a curve of growth, or a falling away from it; there is a central pressure, like sap forcing up a trunk . . . and there, from a dead-looking eye, or knot, it bursts again in a new branch, in a shape that is inevitable but known only to itself until it becomes visible. (200–201; my italics)

The emptiness of boredom breeds a self-effacement that is suicidal, whereas the emptiness of peace, which is the state of the observer looking at boredom, not being *of* it any longer, becomes an invitation to new vitality, as new emotions pour through her—of sexual desire for Mark (and any other likely man), then anger at Mark and jealousy of his lover. In short, her inner life becomes as lively as ever, despite the outer appearance of stalemate.

While Martha's connection to others in the house is nested in their connections beyond the house, their relation to her opens up avenues to them. For example, Mark goes from notoriety as a Red to fame as an author by collaborating with Martha, who is more than a secretary. It seems that although Mark has written a novel about the inevitability of war, he intuits from her a latent sense of the four-gated city, which excites him into sharing her vision and abandoning his old resigned attitude. Over time he writes a story, then expands it into a novel, *The City in the Desert,* with her help. It brings him fame, and some kind of artistic satisfaction for her. It also brings her into the politics of the publishing and literary world. So Jouve is right, Martha is a writer. But self-effaced? Having collaborated is an expression of her old dream, therefore not *intrinsically* self-effacing; yet the prevailing notion that a novel is the work of a unitary author does efface public recognition of her collaboration, and is therefore *extrinsically* self-effacing. Since she has more interest in pursuing other aspects of herself than ambitions for literary success, however, she can afford to leave the recognition to Mark, who is, after all, the initiator and driving force behind the writing.

Martha contributes again to Mark's writing by allowing him access to Thomas's manuscript, which inspires yet another novel, one driven by Mark's guilt for the Jews, based on his neglect of Colin's Jewish wife and his guilt for his Jewish lover's breakdown because of his commitment to Lynda. During this period Martha catches and is reinfected by something of Thomas in him, as he becomes haunted by the madness of the Holocaust.

In traversing the upper storeys of herself at the Coldridge's, Martha has revisited the political through tending the personal, has met her youth through the eyes of maturity, and has reinterpreted her utopian vision—and her nightmare of violence—through art. Besides acknowledging these old issues through new eyes, she has been making up for the past error of abandoning her daughter by playing the role of mother. Even at Jack's house the thought of bearing his child reduced her to tears for the folly of "freeing" her daughter Caroline. Her need to fill that void tugged her toward the poignant, needy face of young Francis in spite of her not wanting such responsibilities then. When Francis is a young man, Martha advises him to be his own person—but only after working through old issues as she has been doing: "You start growing on your own account when you've worked through what you're landed with. Until then, you're paying off debts" (454).

But if all this yea-saying to past debts has been difficult, it has been relatively safe. So far she has kept her distance from frightening and alien states of madness like Thomas's and Lynda's, whose conditions are beyond any neuroses she is familiar with—until an event precipitates her into that region of the mind. That event is the threat of a visit from her mother.

Throughout these years Martha has kept a steady rein on her behavior, even when internally roiled in the crosscurrents of emotion in the house, but now she begins to crack as her competent matron self gives way to shaky confusion and the hysterical tears of her child-self pleading, "Mama, mama, why are you so cold, so unkind, why did you never love me?" (232) as she recalls that her mother always wished she were a son. Having avoided the pain of this issue for years of polite correspondence, she falls sick reading and rereading her mother's reproaches encased in letters of sentimental endearments. Alarmed, and alarming Mark, Martha reads voraciously in the psychoanalytic literature, as she has done at times of personal crisis in the past, only to find that all the great experts on mental illness disagree, as did her old psychology experts of the "normal." In her desperation, she descends to the basement for advice from the experts in the house, Lynda and Dorothy, who warn her against "them"—the psychiatric establishment. Their contempt for the profession is summed up in the phrase "Nothing-but"; every patient's disorder is labeled, preceded by "nothing but (depression, schizophrenia, etc.)," in spite of complex cases like that of Lynda, who has been diagnosed as "nothing but" every label there is at one time or another.

Nevertheless, Martha is propelled into the office of Lynda's psychiatrist Dr. Lamb by her repugnance for what seems to be a worse alternative—occultism. Unsolicited by her, Dorothy's occultist friend Rosa Mellendip (a name suggesting the "dottiness" attributed to that fringe of society)[25] comes upstairs to shore up shaky Martha with competent matronly advice. The only calming effect on her is Rosa's personal stability, not her ideas. Polarized by that mumbo-jumbo element, Martha has nowhere else to go but to the "scientific" establishment. But because of a fortunate postponement of her appointment with Dr. Lamb (and of her mother's impending visit), Martha is forced to confront her own fear, whereupon she rediscovers the observer.

Putting on a show of calm for Mark, she watches herself deteriorate into a "dishevelled panic-stricken creature biting its nails [like Lynda]" (225). Then she asks, "*Who* watched?" (225). The naming game goes into reverse, as her own name and words for things dissolve in a wave of bodily knowledge that bypasses the symbolic. This observer perceives the sycamore tree as a no-name, abiding presence, in an undeniable bond with nature that has a calming effect, like contact with the depths of the sea far beneath the waves (as Bernard perceives the willow tree in *The Waves*). And she perceives herself dually: "Watching, she smiled; reacting, she wallowed and panicked and wept" (229). Activated by her rediscovery of that deep silent witness, the watcher of herself, she finds out that Lynda, too, is a watcher of herself. This is the beginning of her solidarity with Lynda, who warns that such an admission to "them" would result in being labeled psycho or schizoid, and advises Martha not to let "them" know.

Martha then undertakes a program of inner work very much like psychoanalysis. She strenuously relives scenes of the past with all their emotional impact, except that now she is more the observer than she used to be.[26] She struggles to gain the high ground of *pity* for her mother, which she once felt as a young child, but suppressed out of self-defense (232). Unable to reach it on her own, she starts analysis with Dr. Lamb, but finds that their sessions are more like a cat-and-mouse game, and so draining that she has no energy left for the heavy-duty inner work. The greatest value of Dr. Lamb's sessions is her insight into the workings of power: "In approaching Dr. Lamb one approached power. It was hard to think of a power like it, in its inclusiveness, its arbitrariness, its freedom to behave as it wished, without checks from other places or powers" (321). She trembles before it as he manipulates her by the expert timing of his remarks—which do not help her gain pity for her mother.

If Martha achieves any pity for her mother, it is only revealed through her narrator, who abruptly leaves Martha's point of view and narrates from Mrs. Quest's, from the time leading up to her trip to England. (Lessing has done a similar shift in *Landlocked*, where the mother's point of view focuses on recalling herself as a young woman defying her own dead mother's memory.) This glimpse into Mrs. Quest is very sympathetic, for her racism has been tempered by a caring relationship with a black servant boy while living at her son's house. At the same time this section helps to clarify why she cannot get along with Martha when she arrives. The narrator is suspended between them both then, but while Martha is controlling herself and appeals to her mother to be tolerant, her mother keeps letting out her reproachful feelings, and biting her tongue with self-reproach at Martha's hurt responses. The truth is, the woman cannot help feeling that Martha leads a sinful life and cannot help interfering in the life of the household by not only rearranging everything in her daughter's room but by cleaning everyone else's as well. Dr. Lamb helps Martha best by seeing her mother and getting her to admit she is unhappy and should leave at last. The experience of her mother's visit has taught Martha that she cannot hope to make peace with her directly, since the old woman cannot change and grow to meet her.

While that interpersonal relationship is doomed, Martha has yet to deal with her intrapsychic "mother," the inner voice of the angry self-hater spawned originally by her mother's rejection, along with many other voices she is discovering through close observation of her thoughts. Among them are strange thoughts she can hardly attribute to herself—thoughts of passion for Lynda, in terms unlike her own. At first she assumes she has found a vein of lesbianism in herself, but then realizes these thoughts are Mark's, not hers, confirmed by his confiding his renewed passion for Lynda in the same terms (369). (This is one of the few examples of comic relief.) In addition to "hearing" others' voices and feelings, especially Paul's, who is the most violent in his emotions, she has "seen" in advance a scene of Dorothy slashing her wrists, which appeared too exact in certain details of the actual event for Martha to think it was merely her imagination or just general sensitivity to Dorothy's depression then. When she gingerly broaches that vision to Dr. Lamb, he dismisses it as déjà vu.

Martha's revealing to him all the strange mental phenomena Lynda has warned her not to reveal does not result in his labeling her psycho, which suggests that he is interpreting the same phenomena in Lynda differently because Lynda too easily loses touch with her rational, controlling powers, whereas Martha retains hers for the most part. This is to his credit. While Lessing generally discredits the psychiatric profession (through other characters' encounters with various practitioners), Dr. Lamb himself is shown to be more humble about his knowledge than society grants, although orthodox in his thinking. Lessing indicts the *system* that grants him power over people's lives but does not grant the resources for research and the proper care of mental patients.

Martha becomes her own researcher, self-consciously seeking her process in the laboratory of Lynda's basement, where she spends all her free time (since Dorothy's hospitalization after the wrist-slashing).[27] This is during one of Lynda's more lucid phases, when they can discuss their experiments in "listening" and becoming more receptive, as well as seek out literature that will provide some guidance or a discourse in which to frame their experience. While Martha finds no scientific literature on the subject, she does realize that imaginative literature is full of hints of the paranormal. Eventually, she succeeds in obtaining references from the assistant in the factory Mark owns and has managed for years (besides being a writer). This assistant, Jimmy Wood, is a technological whiz who writes science fiction and has researched the literature of the paranormal for his bizarre tales about altering the human mind. His place in Martha's story is to represent "the mad scientist" mentality, the completely amoral expert in love with technology—like the bomb—and to foreshadow the genre-switch to science-fiction fantasy that Martha's *Bildungsroman* undergoes in the appendix.

At the same time that Martha is "working" with Lynda secretly (so as not to alarm Mark and the youngsters about her sanity), she leads another life upstairs, which "outer" life gradually intertwines with the "inner" life of the basement as Martha's comprehensiveness of mind, her solidarity with a world in crisis, accelerates at both levels. While sensing the cacophony of the world through ESP with Lynda, she is also becoming increasingly aware of the breakdown of society and the environment through more objective means with Mark, who has become obsessed with covering the walls of his study with clippings of dire statistics and incidents, pinned to world maps. He even includes passages from Dorothy's journal documenting the deterioration of workmanship and service in ordinary life, as Martha has also been noting in her capacity of housekeeper. In society, being in analysis has become the "in" thing, as more and more people and marriages crack up, even in leftist circles, which never used to acknowledge such matters.

While the outer world is going mad, Lynda has been strengthened enough by her secret alliance with Martha to join in the upstairs life at times, though this alternates with periods of relapse when she overextends herself. Emerging from seclusion into society, she and Martha play the hostess for several months, getting in touch with all the trends "in the air" and documenting the conformity of the cult of uniqueness, until that merry-go-round palls on them. A more serious social scene takes place at the famous Aldermaston March protesting the bomb, where major characters in Martha's life come together (even one of the Cohen boys from Africa, and Jack scouting for women). Mark, Martha, and Lynda are participants and observers of "the spirit of the march, the wry gaiety, its gentle self-mockery" (413) in the carnival attitude of the youth, among whom they recognize younger counterparts of themselves. The scene of the march is pivotal in Martha's story in that it reverses the perception of madness from being a private, subjective condition to being a public condition that calls for action. But the overriding impression of the march that Lessing suggests is the futility of such demonstrations, although voices justify its consciousness-raising impact. Her point is that the inner work of consciousness-raising is the key to dealing with public issues.

On the other hand, a key to dealing with personal consciousness lies in public attitudes in both the collective conscious and unconscious mind. Martha and Lynda suffer from the secrecy that isolates them from public discourse, and they need to legitimate their experience more broadly. The only discourses that come near enough are various forms of occultism, which are little help to Lynda because they are as much at the fringe as she is, and which, as ancient orthodoxies, Martha finds as pat and complacent as the current ones. Martha's reading among the sources Jimmy has supplied to her and all the others she can get her hands on—readings in all the mystic traditions of world religions and esoteric orders like Rosicrucianism—reveal to her that they universally speak of the same kinds of experiences she and Lynda have had, and that she has been afraid to use many of their terms because of her own socially induced attitudes of rejection and fear:

> Words like "prana," "aura," "astral" were particularly [distasteful]—yet they were easily translatable into others from different systems which did not produce distaste (a form of fear). These reactions were identical with those she had experienced in politics. . . . hating and fearing the labels and attitudes "left-wing"; and then switching to "left," while the targets for what she hated and feared switched; so that ever since she had been able to put herself, at will, into these attitudes; . . . moving in and out of mental positions (but they were emotional, or emotionally reached). . . . The mechanisms were always exactly the same, whether political, religious, psychological, philosophic. Dragons guarded the entrances and exits of each layer in the spectrum of belief, or opinion, and the dragons were always the same dragon no matter what name they went under. The dragon was fear, fear of what other people might think; fear of being different; fear of being isolated; fear of the herd we belong to; fear of that section of the herd we belong to. (516)

Here is the crux of what builds and maintains barriers among people, the emotional difficulty preventing free dialogue among subject-positions. Martha must overcome not only the conventional modern and leftist distaste for the *para*normal, but even more frightening, for the *ab*normal. Indeed, there is a distinction to be made here that even Roberta Rubenstein confuses in her otherwise excellent discussion of consciousness in Lessing's work. Rubenstein uses "abnormal" for all areas of mind Lynda opens up to Martha, although the term "paranormal" is available to distinguish the supersensitivity of geniuses, mystics, and psychics from the "abnormal," i.e., pathological.[28] The confusion is abetted because many of those who are gifted with paranormal insights are so misunderstood, feared, and hated that they are mistreated and consequently turn violent or incoherent, as even a normal person who is abused might. Martha recognizes the overlapping regions of the paranormal and the abnormal:

> Perhaps . . . if society is so organised, or rather has so grown, that it will not admit what one knows to be true, will not admit it, that is, except as it comes out perverted, through madness, then it is through madness and its variants it must be sought after. (375)

This conclusion prepares Martha to dare enter a dialogue with Lynda during one of her lunatic spells, a dialogue in which Martha learns to speak Lynda's language—not of "sensible" talk, but the language of symbolic, though largely nonverbal, behavior and of intuited feelings and thoughts. By entering the region of the mind that Lynda inhabits, Martha not only attunes herself to Lynda's state, but recognizes that her old "self-hater" is the same archetype as Lynda's, as she acts out her own torment side by side with her. Telepathically, Martha comes to understand that the source of Lynda's illness is a social and "scientific" dragon that forced her to deny her paranormal perception in adolescence and that, with shock treatments and drugs, permanently damaged her ability to assume normal autonomy, leaving her walled up in helpless irrationality. Now she understands why Lynda behaves as if there is an invisible wall within the exterior walls of the basement, which she constantly "tests"; these walls are projections of the internalized barriers society has imposed that she is trying to break through, which duplicate Mark's visible walls covered with evidence of social breakdown.[29]

When Martha suffers alongside Lynda, they reverse roles as Lynda begins to feel compassion for her, guiding her, and warning her of pitfalls. For one, they plug into the "sound barrier" (498ff.), an ocean of unbearable static from the disharmonious thoughts of the human race, which Lynda urges her to resist with all her might. Then, after sharing an Edenic vision of heavenly gardens, they cannot bear the ugliness of ordinary life, as Martha remembers how as a child she sensed the discrepancy between people's sentimental pretenses and their hidden, ugly rejection, as Lynda did, and even most children do, secretly hating themselves for being programmed to "forget" or deny that intuition. The naysayer of the four-gated city returns with a vengeance when Martha decides to take a walk outside—which Lynda warns her against. On the street she is overcome by an aversion to people so strong that it resembles Gulliver's reaction to the Yahoos.[30] Only the sight of the sky restores her momentarily to her idyllic vision shared with Lynda. But then, her own reflection disgusts her as much as anyone's, and she returns (like Gulliver) to the hell of the self-hater. Martha nearly succumbs to the temptation of drugs and helplessness to avoid the hatred and restore the peace, but Lynda stops her.

After nearly a month their mutual support has strengthened them enough for the madness to have run its course. Martha resumes her normal control and Lynda is reprieved enough of madness to venture back into society. Martha has learned the danger of being dragged into Lynda's orbit without retaining enough of her own trajectory to get back on track, and then ironically, having to depend on Lynda's help. Lynda's strength has come from her weakness, her fear that if Martha, the stronger one, can't get back in control of herself, then she, Lynda, will not be able to count on her. Thus, their differences contribute to each other, and yet pose a risk. There is another danger of reinforcing the worst in Lynda as well as the best, for the forces they encounter, "[g]reat forces as impersonal as thunder or lightning . . . [that] swept through their bodies" (496), are easily channeled to good effects or bad. This responsibility is what enables Martha to struggle to regain her normal state of mind. It also warns her that any further work she does must be without the burden of responsibility for Lynda.

An opportunity to work alone occurs after the youngsters have snapped out of adolescence as if waking from a bad dream, and the old authority-defiance games between Martha and them (especially Paul) are over. What sustained her during those bad years were the occasional flashes of eye contact with their "permanent selves," between her observer and theirs, which almost made her smile at times behind the frown of her mask. What they could not acknowledge then, they now can freely: it is possible to relate sensibly, as adults. As young adults Francis and Paul still defy authority in that they lead unconventional lives. Francis refuses to take exams to go on to higher education, preferring to drop out and be his own person in the theatrical world, and he assumes the burden of his cousin's Jill's illegitimate children (not his), replaying his father's role of protector of a dysfunctional woman. Although Paul has become economically more conventional by turning his brilliance to being a wheeler-dealer instead of a thief, he lives on the fringes of society and is sexually dysfunctional. It is Paul who, as a rich owner of real estate, provides Martha an ideal place for her "retreat," another house where she sojourns for a few months. Paul's house is tenanted by social misfits who are prepared to tolerate her strangeness as some form of LSD tripping or, from a Catholic boy's point of view, as the grace of doing penance.

Martha now knows how to get into an altered state of mind through fasting and sleeplessness. Although she is unfamiliar with the Catholic ritual of the stations of the cross, she seems to have picked up a sense of it from the Catholic boy, for she undergoes that crucifying ordeal tormented by the self-hating devil (whom the boy identifies as God, when she tells him of her "penance," because his discourse of a loving God is dominated by the aspect that castigates in order to purify). She knows she is on dangerous ground and can easily succumb, because her devil, the self-hater, is very powerful. The self-hater becomes the hater of others, an inversion of her dearest values and convictions (the Jungian "shadow" self), as all the voices of a racist, an anti-Semite, and a sadist cry out in her.

But another voice, that of her instinct for survival, the guardian, keeps telling her to remember this and write it down as fast as she can, even if it is all a jumble like Thomas's manuscript. The record keeping, like the housekeeping, is a mechanism to open doorways of dialogue and keep them accessible to the neutral observer in Martha: "I've seen the underneath of myself. Which isn't me—any more than my surface is me. I am the watcher, the listener ... [original ellipsis]" (553). The survivor depends on the observer to teach Martha to distinguish between the voices of the self-hater, which are emotional, and all the other voices, including the "overheard" voices of others—all those she has contacted in her experience and reading who can help her with their example, rational advice, and warnings.[31]

Thus, the survivor, while working closely with the morally neutral observer, protects Martha from allowing that observer to get translated out into the situational world as a Jimmy Wood, whose innocent curiosity, can become amoral and capable of monstrous human (or animal) experimentation, unless checked by the caring voices. What is missing from Jimmy's neutral observer is the big sack of greasy tears—not slobbering emotionality, but compassion for suffering, which is the basis for active responsibility. Although she cannot always feel pity, Martha's greatest forte is responsibility, the one voice in the comprehensive dialogue that can reduce the devil from a "histrionic, flamboyant, accusing, violent" voice to "a silly little nagging voice, which became swallowed in a sea of sound— ... just one little voice among many. And soon, the thing was all over—finished. Her mind was her own" (556).

Martha returns to her sensible self out of responsibility for welcoming her old friend Maisie's daughter, Rita, a girl of straightforward, simple good nature, and self-respect, like her mother. Only her looks are like her father's side, the Maynards, Martha's old enemies, whom she meets briefly, acknowledging to herself a debt to them: she learned what her values are by contrast with theirs. The story proper ends as the Coldridge household breaks up—the house is sold and Mark enters into a May-December marriage with Rita, releasing Lynda from his protectiveness at last, although not from his heart. He has invited her and Martha to participate in his venture to build a community in North Africa, inspired by *The City in the Desert*, to rescue people from a catastrophic world. But both decline. Lynda decides to live in shaky independence with a new inmate friend. And Martha? Once again, all she knows is that she does not know: "I don't know what it is I'm waiting for—something" (453). It seems she has sunk back into opacity and forgotten to remember what the guardian had told her to, except that she knows her process will spin itself out one way or another, through dreams when she is too outwardly busy to do inner "work," or by suddenly becoming aware of what is "under her nose, of course. It always is—the next step, but she couldn't see it" (453).

Martha's story demonstrates survivorship beyond the usual endings for women.[32] She has resisted remarrying—becoming "the woman in love. ...

that hungry, never-to-be-fed, never-at-peace woman who needs and wants and must have. That creature. . . . of marriage and the 'serious' love" (301)[33]—by saying yea only to being Mark's spouse-surrogate. She has atoned for running away from motherhood by serving time as a den mother. She has resisted madness by going mad for awhile, and death by "dying" to old voices and being reborn again and again. She has not gone into a convent for life, by entering into the solitude of the observer from time to time. Instead of renouncing the world, she says yea to it, especially to sex, when she says of that aloof "person who watched and waited," namely her observer: "Oh God, if only she could kill that person, send her, it, him, away . . . to vanish entirely into this place of smooth warm bodies whose language was more beautiful, more intelligent than any other . . . [original ellipsis]" (239). She says yea to both passionate transcendence and to the cool observing kind, or in other words, to both "poetic" and "ironic" transcendence.[34] At one time or another, all her voices have their say, whether nay or yea, expressed or suppressed, and Martha has become the housekeeper opening doorways instead of keeping rooms separate, as the responsible mediator of the dialogue. Her job description at the Coldridge's has been that of a dialogic self.

Had Lessing left the ending on the note of Martha's rediscovery that her path now lies "Here, where else, you fool, . . . where else has it ever been, ever . . . [original ellipsis]" (591), the novel would have been completed by suggesting the incompletion of a process to be recycled.[35] But instead of ending realistically in a pregnant silence, Lessing goes beyond Martha's personal story into a dialogue with the visionary voice of her impersonal and transpersonal subjectivities, represented by the four-gated city. Her final "here" is not only the point the past has led to, but , as Hannah Arendt might put it, *"between past and future,"* that is, a point also determined by anticipation of the future.[36] Martha simply must address her greatest passion as a responsible survivor, her hopes and fears for her own future being bound up with the survival of all her other voices—of humanity, of life on earth.

Thus, Martha's personal story switches from the politics of the self to the politics of the planet, and from historically realistic narrative to a visionary genre like science fiction, or dystopias/utopias. That is the scale of the "house" where Martha's visionary self resides. She has not disappeared, but is tending many new rooms in a broader dialogue, although the narrator's voice does disappear into the direct voices of individual characters, including Martha's own characteristic voice, in documents, like a long letter from middle-aged Francis to one of his cousin Jill's daughter's. This letter largely carries the narrative burden of what happens to the Coldridge family and friends in a catastrophe that destroys England (among other world catastrophes).

He tells how in the years preceding the catastrophe he and his (and Paul's) friends—the "misfits" of society—retreat to the simple life of the country to live together. Their commune is the nearest thing to the four-gated city that is actualized in this time-bound world, but not because they have any ideology or principle to prove. Their "secret" harmony is based on everyone's willingness to pitch in to do what is necessary, and on living a more wholesome life than in the polluted city. They simply recognize they depend on one another to survive and are ready to contribute and negotiate their way along in an ad hoc, informal fashion. But they cannot isolate themselves from the forces tearing apart the larger society, nor, as Francis recognizes, can they go on indefinitely without dealing with their own inner demons and barriers, which correspond to those of the larger collective. There is no way to remain a "simple self" or group or City in the Desert without confronting the voices from hell within and without. The gates can never be closed against "them," but must be opened in all four directions, i.e., comprehensively, so that each can contribute rather than dominate, and so that distinctions can be made to clarify positions. A distinction to be made in this appendix is that it is premature to expect a four-gated society when people's minds are opaque and insulated from one another. Thus, Mark's project and Francis's commune are doomed.

Martha's best hope is in developing paranormal sensitivity, like Lynda, who becomes recognized as a "seer" by a secret network of dissenting psychiatrists (modeled on a Laingian psychopolitics) and by people like Francis, who is as skeptical as Mark at first but then realizes there is something to it. He relies on Lynda's prophecies to guide rescue missions he and Martha help organize. Not only do Francis, Martha, and greater numbers of people develop varying degrees of ESP, but the catastrophe has produced mutant children with superior mental powers (as well as nonviable monsters) among the survivors on the rugged island where Martha's rescue party finds refuge (narrated in her own letter to Francis). Although she is too old to leave it, and foresees her own death there, these supersurvivor children represent her reincarnation into the next stage of human evolution, where four-gated cities might be possible. Martha is not just Martha, but a "thought around," an echo of the common aspiration for progress or salvation.

This visionary extension of Martha's self might seem too much at odds with her practical frame of mind to form a unified work, but if the unity is conceived of as a comprehensive dialogue between disparate voices, then a form that is "shot to hell" makes more sense. This "future" has been integrated into the novel, and into the whole series all along.[37] A more realistic version of Martha's future might have bridged the abrupt schism between Martha's down-to-earth voice and her visionary one by being more along the lines of Anna Wulf's brief glimpse of herself as one of the "boulder pushers" who do the heavy work in bringing the masses of humanity to a more comprehensive view at the top of the mountain. Martha's fantasy of a shortcut through mutation seems like impatient wishful thinking and overlooks the potential already "here" in the human mind. And the implied belief in getting there someday also seems wishful when the devil can always push the boulder back down at any time.[38] "Here" is the only place to end—or begin.

In such a more realistic future back here Martha would still have some personal boulder pushing to do, for she still has some old debts to run through and to refine her observations and practice. She herself has not attained the level of pity for her mother that her wiser narrator has. And she has yet to discover a better way to gain the observer's metapositions than by abusing her body, which is related to her preference for sleeplessness and her naysaying to the dark, fallow phases of rest. While she has admitted tears more readily, for the loss of her mother and daughter, she could use a little more laughter.[39] Although Martha acknowledges laughter to be "a kind of balancing mechanism, a shock absorber" (510), it is merely the crude mechanism of a deficient creature—again, from the point of view of the unemotional Houyhnhnm toward the muddy Yahoo. Overall, as a child of violence, fear has made Martha's process hard-edged and full of internal friction from one voice to another. Ironically, as the desperate survivor, she is earnestly attached to the otherwise detached state. A little more laughter in the works might facilitate greater detachment because it would lubricate and loosen the flow of the dialogue, especially when the channels get jammed; perhaps it would quicken the interchange around a point of increasing equilibrium and deconstruct the dualisms. Margaret Atwood's *Lady Oracle* will be an antidote, with more laughter but no less seriousness, as an ironic voice that laughs at this fragmented world and lets the humor push the boulder.

Part Three

Margaret Atwood's *Lady Oracle:*
The Misplaced Self

5
The Concept of Self in
Margaret Atwood's Life and Work

Margaret Atwood implicitly endorses a dialogic concept of self in her definition: "The self is a place in which things happen . . . where experiences
intersect."[1] Her idea of self as an intersection of events corresponds to
Lessing's statement about Martha being the intersection of individual conscience and society, and to Hollway's dialogic self as the intersection between the axis of available social discourses and the axis of the individual's
intrapsychic history. Atwood's definition of self as located or situated in a
context seems to fit in with her activism as a Canadian nationalist. Lessing,
although speaking from her context as a white colonial from Africa, emphasizes a more international and cross-cultural archetypal consciousness.

Atwood's sense of self as place is an emphatic choice, judging by her
statement, "Canada is a place where you choose to live. . . . It's easy . . . to
leave" (*SW*, 112). Furthermore, "Refusing to acknowledge where you come
from . . . is an act of amputation: you may become free floating, a citizen of
the world . . . but only at the cost of arms, legs or heart" (113). Of course,
someone like Lessing is not necessarily amputating her place of origin, but
rather growing extra limbs, like a Buddha figure. Atwood might acknowledge this, judging by the following organic metaphor of self:

> I don't think you transcend region, anymore than a plant transcends earth.
> . . . you come out of something and you can then branch out in all kinds of
> different directions, but that doesn't mean cutting yourself off from your
> roots and from your earth. . . . an effective writer . . . can make what he or
> she is writing about understandable and moving to someone who has
> never been there. All good writing has that kind of transcendence. It doesn't
> mean becoming something called "international." There is no such thing.
> (*C*, 143)

This difference between a free-floating or a rooted orientation affects the scope of consciousness in Lessing's and Atwood's protagonists. Anna and Martha are far more inwardly mobile and cosmic than any of Atwood's heroines, who tend to be constrained by plot. However, both authors write with equally sharp observation of local detail (which is historically contextualized on a wider scale) and sense of the ahistorical archetypal patterns in which those details take shape.

Like Woolf's and Lessing's, Atwood's concept of self includes dimensions that intersect with nature as well as society and that transcend time and space. Of the three, Atwood is most at ease on terra firma. She roots herself in the local, hence her greater willingness to speak as a nationalist, whereas Woolf and Lessing, both antinationalists, seem to fear getting bogged down in identity politics as much as they fear the outer reaches of the chaotic night self. They locate themselves more easily at some intermediate level, like Bernard. From her diaries, Woolf seems the most ready to risk a "dialogue" with chaos in her acceptance of fallow states, while Lessing resists dark forgetfulness and Atwood explicitly singles out chaos as her greatest fear.[2]

Atwood, although ready to assume identity as a Canadian as opposed to an identity as international or cosmic, does so contingently and provisionally, without being bound to any essentialist core self of Canadianness. Her attitude is that her life just happens to be taking place in a Canadian context, and therefore her "events" are colored by that experience, which is itself constantly changing and being redefined. In her critical work *Survival: A Thematic Guide to Canadian Literature,* her attempt to define Canadianness in terms of its literature, Atwood clearly limits that definition to a few decades of the twentieth century and uses it for the purpose of making useful distinctions between the Canadian psyche and both the American and British psyches, but not for the purpose of fixing such a distinction in national self-image for all time. Indeed, the image of the "victim" mentality she finds in the Canadian literature she cites is posited not as some fixed state, but as a *relationship* between "victor and victim," and hence susceptible to change. She suggests that the very act of articulating Canadian identity becomes, in effect, a factor precipitating change, because only by first recognizing its own distinct voice in the relationship can an entity generate dialogue. It is the perception of difference that confers identity; without any significant differences from the United States, a separate identity for Canada would be meaningless.[3]

Although critics differ on the validity of Atwood's *Survival* thesis regarding Canadian literature, there is general agreement on the importance of her book as a statement of her personal credo, her moral and political position not just as a writer or as a Canadian but as a human being.[4] *Survival* is a key to understanding not only Atwood's sense of her situated Canadian self, but also her concept of self as a site of power negotiations among diverse voices. She is particularly concerned with the victor-victim or winner-loser discourse that splits the self into a destructive either-or polarity. Sherill Grace makes a distinction between polarity and duality in her study of Atwood's work, *Violent Duality*, in which she claims that Atwood is dismantling polarity—rigid, mutually exclusive, and hierarchical binary oppositions—in favor of a fluid interplay between dichotomous positions, a kind of turn taking with mutual recognition, as in a dialogue.[5] (Of course, Grace's emphasis on duality tends to obscure the multiplicity of positions that may include, but are not limited to, oppositions.) Since *Survival* is not an evaluative criticism of Canadian literature, but a theory of the formation of the Canadian self based on literary evidence, Atwood's thesis can be transposed to issues of the self in individuals and groups where the victor-victim mentality plays a crucial role. Shannon Hengen's study, *Margaret Atwood's Power*, for example, extends Atwood's argument on the Canadian-American (once British) power struggle to that between socialist feminism and capitalistic patriarchy.[6] Atwood's theory about Canada, therefore, demonstrates a theory of the self that is particularly relevant to feminist identity issues.

The dialogue Atwood has in mind is not a polarized chauvinism, a power struggle between national egos that concede only strategically in response to counterpower, but a genuine exchange, where Americans have something to learn from Canadian values and Canadians have something to learn from the United States—not just how to exploit. She recognizes that these values are common currency, not the sole property of any one country; they are, as Lessing would say, "a thought around" or "in the air," and hence Atwood would encourage alliances with Americans, for example, on environmental protection. (Indeed, the significant lobby in the United States for a Canadian-style health-care system is a recent example of such a validation of Canadian values across the border.) If the Canadian victim mentality has any use, it has been in its discovery of the advantages of a more collective and cooperative society in contrast to the American mentality of individualism, which, in striving for mastery of the frontier (or the "American Dream") divides the people against themselves.

The role of victim can be destructive by denying one's legitimate differences or by setting up a self-fulfilling prophecy of failure and capitulation to the victor, which in turn, encourages that victor to further predation without any checks and balances. Atwood distinguishes between "genuine" victimization, in which one justly feels violated, and the victim complex, which is a "loser" state of mind that places blame externally or feels essentially inferior, abdicating responsibility for changing the situation. Of course, one may be a genuine victim initially, but then develop a victim complex that perpetuates one's victimization unnecessarily or totalizes it. Atwood argues that in moving out of the victim role, the first two stages of which seem to be first denial and then resignation, one would have to become energized in a third stage of confronting one's oppression—not just in anger and defiance against the oppressor, but also in recognition of one's own vested interest in complicity. For Canadians, that complicity lies in a tradition of respecting authority for keeping order, even when it oppresses; thus she implies they might heed a kernel of wisdom in the American tradition of individualism, which values defiance of authority, as represented in rebels and heroes— although the Canadian version might be collective heroes.

Atwood herself is a rebel in the sense of an iconoclast, which, in a capitalist culture, means that she may be open to socialist forms, but not in a doctrinaire way. Like Lessing and Woolf, she tends to shun political labels and the platform in favor of personal eye- or I-witness accounts (Atwood's pun) in fiction, where moral and political positions emerge from the subjective experiences of believable characters, not as a message imposed on them as mere puppets of the author. When she does take a stand outside her fiction, as a Canadian nationalist or as a feminist, it is provisional and on the condition that she retain her critical independent voice.[7] That integrity is what she demands of her writing, which, as art, she feels should convey the complexity of life and character, not become merely propagandistic even if it has political implications. Indeed, she claims "[n]o writing is morally, politically neutral—but it doesn't have to be endorsing a label either" (*C*, 150). Her own political consciousness is an outgrowth of writing from a personal location: "I began as a profoundly apolitical writer, but then . . . I began to describe the world around me" (*SW*, 15). This is a statement of graduating from individualism to dialogism in the discovery of the self as an intersection between the private and the public.

Atwood's collectivism, a general and nondogmatic preference for the survival of the human race over the rat race, comes to her via a bottom-up local view rather than via a top-down, global discourse like Communism, which Lessing imposed on her intuitions at an early age.[8] In both authors there is a meeting of concrete lived experience with theory, but starting from a bottom-up direction of values instilled by practice instead of by theory, Atwood tends to be more pragmatic than idealistic. For example, she claims, partly tongue-in-cheek, to derive her antagonism to war from her family's Nova Scotia frugality, i.e., from their abhorrence of waste.[9] While writing, she focuses on her craft rather than on ideas, which can be analyzed later, as she remarks:

When I'm not teaching, I don't have to think of my own work in terms of ideas or large social things. . . . I get right down in the mud, which is what engagement with the page is. It's mud. (*C*, 197)

As a result, she is less prone to engage in utopian visions than Lessing. Indeed, in writing *The Handmaid's Tale* she might seem to prefer the portrayal of dystopia. While Lessing also depicts dystopias, beginning with the one in the appendix of *The Four-Gated City*, her focus is on carrying them into positive visions of alternative worlds. For example, although *Memoirs of a Survivor* is a dystopia depicting the breakdown of society into a state of anarchy, it is also a kind of dream vision (like the medieval poem *The Pearl*), in which the protagonist has a glimpse of a paradise or heaven beyond the barrier of this world, which is enough to sustain her as a survivor who can bear witness to it as a distant hope for humanity. In contrast, Atwood's Canadian survivors only bear witness to how they manage to escape immediate perils. The hope in Atwood's tales is not explicit, but implied mostly by way of cautionary emphasis. "Progress" for her protagonists is usually minimal or nonexistent, and ambiguous in any case. But they do survive—barely—closer to where Anna Wulf might be than to a Martha raising supermutants. Atwood's hope lies in "a new way of seeing" for the victim, the way of being a "creative non-victim" by imagining positions between the voices of power and victimization. She defends herself from charges of pessimism by justifying her writing as an act of faith, hope, and charity because it cannot deny that the world consists of

every place from Heaven to Hell. . . . It is the duty of the writer not to turn down a visit to any of them if it's offered. Some . . . only live in a couple of these places, but nobody lives in just one. . . . Writing is an act of faith that someone is listening, hope that things will be better, and charity to write without flinching or bitterness. (*SW*, 349)

While both Atwood and Lessing are naysayers to romanticism in their insistence on facing the hard facts, Lessing seems to resent human fallibility, whereas Atwood regards it as a springboard for compassion, the way a sense of mortality can give rise to respect for life in others as well as ourselves (*C*, 126). Thus Atwood finds hope even in the heart of darkness.

Another possible reason Atwood may be more willing to hold the mirror up to victimization relentlessly, to "tell it like it is," without projecting how it should or could be as Lessing has, is that, ironically, she herself has not been as much a victim, and hence is without the same impatience to short-cut tedious boulder pushing. Atwood's personal history has been that of a child of good nurturance rather than violence.[10] She was fortunate to have parents who allowed her great freedom by living an unconventional life that encouraged her to think for herself and become hardy in response to the demands of survival in nature out in the Quebec North Woods where they lived half the year. Both of Atwood's parents had a sense of humor that freed her playfulness, and they had a tradition of storytelling that was the soil for their daughter's located self. This is in contrast to Lessing's frustrated, displaced parents, whose plaintive story-harangues she may have endured, as Martha's story suggests. Because Atwood's parents respected her independence, she took it for granted without having to be polarized into defiance.

This autonomy did not conflict with any feminine role, but enabled her to accept herself fully as a woman through her family's attitudes to sex roles and sexuality. Atwood cites their Nova Scotia tradition of not wasting even a girl's mind, which enabled her to get past having to play dumb in school unscathed. (99).[11] Her mother was an exceptional woman who loved their solitary life in the wilderness, in contrast to Lessing's mother, who felt victimized by her loneliness on the farm. Instead of pushing her daughter to conform to a certain kind of sexist image as Lessing's did, or becoming a model self-sacrificing Angel in the House as Woolf's mother was, Atwood's mother, who was a tomboy as a girl, gave her daughter the example of a loved and loving woman who was tough and adaptable without any loss of femininity. In the forest she was self-sufficient when her husband was away for long periods, and in the city she passed as a lady. For young Peggy, putting on feminine garb in town may have been like assuming a form of camouflage—the survival mechanism of a creature adapting to urban terrain. Her father, too, toward whom she apparently suffered little of the ambivalence both Woolf and Lessing felt toward their fathers, was largely a positive contributor to her androgynous selfhood. She respected his competence as an entomologist and absorbed not only his scientific curiosity and regard for reason, but also an attitude of caring for all the creatures of the North Woods habitat where he worked. Since her parents in their agnosticism had somehow grown away from the WASPish sexual complexes of their tradition, sexuality for Atwood was part of a respect for nature, not something to be repressed or used as a badge of defiance. Finally, Atwood's older brother did not set up the same kind of sexist relationship in their outings in the woods that Lessing describes in regard to the brother-sister playmates in "The Story of Two Dogs." Instead, his difference was felt as a matter of seniority rather than gender. Not only was she *not* excluded, she was the only companion he had for his games, and she was expected to play by the same rules.

In addition to an unusually liberal family background, Atwood had the advantage of living in a stable, moderate—and even boring—country that had shunted its minority indigenous peoples, Native American Indians, out of sight instead of living in a country as Lessing did, where the majority population of blacks was oppressed in plain sight as a servant class and where racial tension and white paranoia were pervasive. (Of course, Canada and Southern Rhodesia were both under a cloud as British colonial backwaters.) She also had the advantage of coming of age in the postwar boom period, at a time and in a place removed from the immediate impact of the two World Wars, and thus she was not affected in the same ways Woolf and Lessing were. However, Atwood and Lessing have shared the Cold War era, and now the New World (Dis)Order.

It is not that Atwood is more complacent because more sheltered—her experience is no less keenly felt and examined—but that her writing is relieved of having to work out issues of her own self that the two other authors had to contend with, issues of swinging between poles of idealism and disillusion, self-assertion and self-hatred, or mania and depression. Nor did she have to work through family traumas like Woolf's or family estrangement like Lessing's. Thus her writing does not reflect her autobiography quite as much as theirs, but is made up mostly from her observations of others, that is, by imagining "[f]ictions [as] . . . possibilities" she expands into new territory.[12] She is autobiographical to the extent that she is concerned to describe *where she lives* rather than *who she is* and extends the idea of personal experience to "wherever it comes from—[w]hat you identify with, *imagine*, if you like, so that it becomes personal to you [original italics]" *(C,* 110; *SW,* 342).

She often objects to the idea of writing as "self-expression," preferring to think of it as a task of *evocation,* which includes the professional discipline of researching details of place accurately. She does not think of herself as "a writer," focusing on a static self-image, but as someone who *writes,* focusing on the process of doing a task. She asks, "How can you take part intensely . . . and still be thinking about yourself?" *(SW,* 344), and later answers: "[Writing] is not expressing yourself. It is opening yourself, discarding your *self* [original italics], so that the language and the world may be evoked through you. . . . for the reader " (347–48).

Dispelling the myth of self-expression for the writer is parallel to dispelling the same myth for women who might regard the self as an object (or some essential female subject) to be expressed rather than as a spectrum of continual subjectivities to be engaged in dialogue with the world. Of the three authors, Woolf probably had the hardest battle as a woman writer to overcome the self as object and to assert her subjectivities, and Atwood the easiest. Perhaps because of that, Atwood went further than her predecessors in assuming the stance of subject-surveyor gazing outward at the world, more like that of the traditional man than of the modern woman who is the object of her own identity quest.

Her greatest identity problem was choosing a vocation, a difficult choice, at age sixteen, in view of the economic price she thought she would have to pay as a writer who could not hope to earn a living by her craft, and in view of the personal and social price she had to pay in the 1950s and '60s when the pressure on a woman to marry forced her into the either-or position of giving up relationships with men who could not accept her commitment to writing. And in those days before the advent of sisterhood, even women were critical of her choice of career over marriage. She ruefully notes that she was one of the lonely "protofeminists," someone who would have broken away from the patriarchal mold with or without a feminist movement (at least the second wave of feminism in the mid-twentieth century). That her work is acclaimed by feminists for dealing with issues of the female self is ironic, because her unconventional upbringing helped her avoid the victim complex that she portrays in her female protagonists. Now, fulfilled with a family and economically independent through her writing,[13] she rightly resists being considered a "role model" as a successful woman because she realizes her course is unique and unlike that of most women.

That unique advantage, from her formative years of happy family solitude in nature, gives her an "outlandish" point of view on her own society, a kind of transcendental leverage enabling her to see it through fresh eyes. Indeed, she describes herself as being in perpetual "culture shock" at what she observes of others and at what she experiences firsthand (*C*, 121). Her advantage has not been a total immunity, for as Emerson observes, the self-reliant, nonconformist person must endure being misunderstood and "whip[ped] with [the world's] displeasure."[14] In addition to personal sacrifices for her career, she was appalled at such impositions as being excluded from a library at Harvard for being female, particularly since she had achieved the status of graduate student there. Having undergone genuine victimization as a serious woman writer and as a Canadian,[15] she nevertheless copes with it from a solid base of self-reliance (aided by the independence of her material success). She could not have had the insight in *Survival* to outline the stages of victimization that culminate in the fourth step of "creative nonvictimization" unless she had undergone enough of the process herself. Whether one can go as far as she has may depend on how deeply entrenched the source of the victimization is, as she well realizes, which is why her protagonists do not get very far.

She reserves a fifth stage for some level of mystical transcendence, which she does not analyze, not necessarily because it is outside her experience, but because it is not possible to explain in words. When she does approach those airy spaces in the upper canopy of the psyche in her work, it is from a sense of earthy rootedness. She describes herself as akin to a pantheist, finding spirit permeating the physical world, as Woolf did. Her sense of the eternal mystery pervading all forms is more often playful than heavy with reverence, but it is nonetheless serious. For her, laughter is an antidote to the terror of the abyss. One of the ironies of her work is that despite the victimization she depicts, her narratorial voices often sound like they are romping through the world, like a mischievous imp stomping on the underbrush her characters are tangled in, as if to release them from clinging to all the petty details down below. Then, perched on her own tree, laughing above them, she beckons to the reader to gain a view of the forest composed of the myths of the collective unconscious.

Her own tree is rooted in the literary sources of Canada, beginning with European fairy tales, especially the original horrifying versions of the Grimm brothers, which she avers were most influential on her young mind. The horrifying parts may account for her frequent images of dismemberment as metaphors for psychic disintegration and victimization, while the more sanguine parts have given her a basis for female empowerment in their portrayals of clever heroines with magic skills, unlike the passive substitutes of popularized versions.[16] She also imbibed North American Indian legends, popular literature like comic books and movies, and of course, white Canadian literature, all part of the local scene. In her undergraduate work she studied English and American literature at Victoria College, and in her graduate work at Harvard specialized in Victorian, gothic, and romance genres, in which the occult interested her as literary or psychological phenomena rather than as literal representations. The kind of ghost story that fascinates her is the Jamesian kind, "in which the ghost . . . is in fact a fragment of one's own self which has split off" (*C*, 18).

Beckoning to the reader to see the myths her characters are enacting, the impish narratorial voice leads a chase around and up and down the tree so that it seems to come from diverse points of view, the secular and the spiritual, the time-bound and the eternal, falsifying one after another, in a peek-a-boo game between illusion and reality. In debunking myth she does not claim a position outside of any myth, but only questions whatever seems out of place (or time). For example, in *Survival* she cites the mismatch between some European settlers' romantic assumptions of nature as a benevolent Mother and the harsh conditions that belied such a view. She remarks in an interview:

> I think most people have unconscious mythologies. . . . it's a question of
> making them conscious, getting them out . . . where they can be viewed.
> And I don't believe that people should divest themselves of all their my-
> thologies because . . . in a way, everybody needs one. It's just a question of
> getting one that is livable and not destructive to you. (32)

From that point of view, she even defends reading escapist literature as a
harmless indulgence in fantasy if taken lightly, not as a way to avoid examining one's serious beliefs for their "livability."

As to whether Atwood's impish voice unduly transcends the "mud" of
her texts with too distancing an irony, Ingersoll acknowledges that her work
has struck some as "icy detachment" (*C*, xi), and Valerie Miner notes that
Atwood has a controlling manner in conversation[17] (as Bertelsen claims
about Lessing in her interview with her), all of which suggests that there are
signs of defensiveness and a need to "get above it all." Atwood herself admits she developed sarcasm as a protective shell against culture shock and
has to be careful not to let it emerge inappropriately. And as a famous
writer, like Lessing, she ducks questions (and photos) that fix her self-image.
However, her engaging narrative style, strictly from a given character's point
of view and often in first person and present tense, does not intrude the
sense of a controlling and distant narrator as Lessing may at times. The
difference is that Lessing's ironic voices explain and analyze, whereas
Atwood's describe the mud itself. For example, a Lessing narrator or character will remark on the absurdity of a situation, whereas Atwood will jux-
tapose absurd details, leaving the remark to the reader.

While both may seem like alien anthropologists examining society, as
Atwood claims a good writer must be to some extent, she goes even further
than Lessing in noting material details—something like an archaeologist
cataloging the junk of a culture and accurately dating fashions, and even
knowing what underwear her characters would wear. She exposes the pre-
tentiousness of the culture by honing in on the faded and the fake artifacts
of nostalgia and phoniness. Her impish descriptions seem too funny, too
sad, and too grimy with the mud of the "dig" for any French feminists to
worry about distance and control. If anything, she might get carried away
by dwelling on such details, like Lessing, although if Lessing tends to *tell* too
much, Atwood tends to *show* too much. Atwood is something like her pale-
ontologist protagonist in *Life Before Man*, recording bits of dinosaur bones
with the detached passion of one trying to shore up fragments of a vanished
(or vanishing) form of life against our own ruin.

If there is any way not to make ourselves extinct, Atwood implies, it is
precisely not to get stuck in the tar pits of our own material and spiritual

debris, but to be adaptable. Her interest in plot revolves around the principle of change, of character renewal. Atwood's fascination with change in nature—particularly the metamorphoses of insect life cycles—and her avid reading of fairy tales in childhood, which attest to magical transformations, have all contributed to her readiness for self-alteration in herself and in her characters. One key to change is integrated multiplicity, not counterproductive fragmentation. An example is her versatility in professional as well as personal life, since she is one of the few writers who is as acclaimed for her volumes of poetry as for her prose (if not more). This versatility allows her to switch genres and projects if she runs dry, so that she has a way around writer's block. And when she switches genres, she switches personalities—not just "somewhat," she assures her interviewer, but adapting "an almost totally different personality" (C, 71). As a literary critic, she refers to herself in the plural "Margarets Atwood" to suggest the changing perspectives of her reviews in *Second Words*.[18]

In her portrait of Atwood, based on a visit to Atwood's farm in Ontario, Valerie Miner describes her as

the archetype of the elusive writer, used to submerging herself in her symbols and characters. A classic protean personality: woman, artist, academic, wild creature. A fairy tale princess running away from the wicked camera.

Miner impishly takes a few "snapshots" elaborating Atwood's many facets:

The satisfied rural Ontario farm woman. . . . Frenetic hippie in . . . blue jeans. . . . the recluse writer. . . . The trenchant scholar . . . English instructor. . . . respected literary critic . . . and staunch apologist for nationalism. . . . Sardonically cool and professional. . . . The mythically free animal of her imagination. . . . the teenage "nature girl" explaining frogs and toads to summer camp children. . . . Successful, independent person with a strong sense of herself as a woman.

Atwood tells her, "I don't mind playing roles—as long as I can determine [them]."[19] In refusing to live up to others' expectations—even her mother has remarked that she was not one to be guided—she is exceptionally self-determined.

To counter this freewheeling protean impression, Atwood cautions that versatility and transformation are limited to "the hand you are dealt." A caterpillar can only change into a butterfly—not a rhinoceros. Her attitude to fate is to give it its due, including the fated power of the mind to observe what is and to imagine alternatives, and thus to effect change by negotiating among the other factors of one's contingency—in short, to play one's hand to the best of one's ability. Her position is very much like Lessing's, except that she does not look too far into the future of the race, but rather gets down in the present mud—sometimes to sling it and sometimes to shape it playfully. Like Woolf, Atwood's cosmic perspective flows through immediate concrete experience without having to kick herself into remembering "Here, you fool," as Lessing's Martha does.

In another apparent contradiction to, and contraction from, the image of Atwood's abundance and multiplicity, as far as her writing is concerned, her frugal upbringing inclines her to conciseness, to the evocativeness of a single well-placed stroke. Her style seems almost clipped, with relatively simple sentences approaching those in the childhood sections of *The Waves*— often punctuated with a surprise punch line that may undermine a passage. Thus, complexity of thought and abundance of detail may go hand in hand with simplicity of style. Hengen points out that Atwood's preference for "plain talk," even as far as using vulgar language at times, is part of her concern to communicate frankly instead of experimenting with esoteric stylized effects. In this she resembles Lessing. However, like Woolf, Atwood respects the unsaid as much as the said, whereas Lessing seems to begrudge that it cannot all be said. For all its ordinariness, Atwood's style shows a poetic appreciation for the semiotic and semantic play between words. As a prose writer, her style is analogous to the poetic style of Emily Dickinson, who packs so much intensity and surprise into so few words.

While Atwood has seen more of the world than Dickinson, whose "circumference" to eternity was concentrated into a severely circumscribed life, and while Atwood has the liberty to include things Woolf had to leave out as a lady writing, she is content to explore the possibilities for change in protagonists not nearly as comprehensive as Anna and Martha, who add on rooms and paper walls with global clippings. Atwood realizes that even the narrowest existence is at an intersection with the infinite (although her characters may not be as conscious of it as Dickinson was) and that her protagonists have to be respected for where they are. That she deals her characters a limited hand may be part of the popular appeal of her novels; she writes to the experience of ordinary people. Her exaggerated or simplified characters may also be due to her consciously writing from the tradition of romance rather than heavy realism.

One might be tempted to link the relative simplicity of Atwood's protagonists to their author's claim to be "depressingly sane."[20] But even if simplified, some of her characters might still be judged insane; moreover, the biographical link is belied by the contrast between Atwood's happy and creative life and the bare survival of most of her heroines. In addition to debunking the biographical fallacy, Atwood cites her own life to counter the myth of the suffering, neurotic artist. Indeed, she claims that writers create in spite of, not because of, their suffering, that the act of writing is in itself a positive impulse, which Woolf's history would confirm. However, it is possible that experience at the extremes makes a difference, if only that the artist is more concerned about exploring those extremes in the work. For example, Woolf includes a Rhoda among an otherwise ordinary cast of characters. Yet the most ordinary people are capable of extreme states and one need not have been mad, suicidal, or criminal to write about altered states of mind or violence, if the writer is enough of a sensitive observer to extrapolate from experience.

Even in Atwood's most heavily realistic novel about the most middling people, *Life Before Man*—which she compares to George Eliot's *Middlemarch* because it is about the middle of everything: middle class, mid-century, and mid-country—one of the triple (middle-aged) protagonists, Elizabeth, the wife in a marital-infidelity triangle, for all her worldly and narrow maneuvering, realizes that just surviving in the status quo is a miracle. She is conscious of "the chasms that open at her feet. . . . the visible world as a transparent veil or a whirlwind" (*LBM*, 302); for underneath Elizabeth's hard-won facade of sensibleness lies a monstrous history of suffering. Perhaps survival is the acid test for the curbing of extremes, which is why Eliot's Dorothea ends up married instead of martyred as a saint and why moderation is a Canadian hallmark.[21] Still, *Middlemarch* has a moral range and a scope of action far broader than *Life Before Man's*.

Where Atwood achieves breadth is over the scope of her body of work, and where she reaches depth is in certain scenes and insightful remarks that erupt from the surface texture of ordinariness she creates with her descriptions of the banal, like "moments of being" jutting out of cotton wool. From the normalcy of her own life springs a surprising turn for the bizarre, the violent, and the paranormal, more concentrated in her poetry and short experimental prose pieces (prose poems and instant fiction) that defamiliarize the ordinary than in the novels.[22] An example of one of these pieces, followed by brief outlines of those of her novels that focus on the female subject, will illustrate her key metaphors for exploring the interplay between the multiple depths and facades of self.

Atwood writes of her confrontation with the terror of the void in "The Page," in her slim collection of micropieces, *Murder in the Dark*. This piece not only reveals the hazards of a writer facing the uncreated selves of her fiction on the blank page, but the human being facing the blank self upon which experience is inscribed. In this brief space, Atwood encapsulates some of her chief thematic concerns and stylistic figures on several levels of interpretation. From the first sentence the prevailing tone is of mock danger, its mystery and duplicity underscored by ironic humor: "The page waits, pretending to be blank. . . . What else is this terrifyingly innocent?" ("TP," 44). She compares it to an arid, lifeless place that people venture into as endurance tests, risking blindness from staring too long at its whiteness, or getting lost forever in its directionless space "without vistas and without sounds, without centres or edges," the only marks of direction being "what you yourself put there" (44). She notes that its whiteness is light containing the whole spectrum all at once, implying that its blankness is not only an illusion of nothingness, but that its awesome comprehensiveness would be blinding if stared at, like the face of God or the infinite potential of the self that cannot be seen all at once, only a little at a time in "marks of direction" put down in fragments of the Whole, which are constituted by and of "you yourself." Shuddering from the mere thought of disorientation in this primordial chaos of the void, she asks, "Have you never seen the look of gratitude, . . . of joy, on the faces of those who have managed to return from the page?" They "fall on their knees, . . . push their hands into the earth, . . .clasp the bodies of those they love, . . . with an urgency unknown to those who have never experienced the full horror of a journey into the page" (44).

To help those who venture into the page to get back to terra firma, she writes the next passage as if a set of "wilderness tips" (the title of a short story that gives its title to a volume of her stories) for survival, such as "something you can hold onto, and a prism to split the light and a talisman that works . . . for getting back" (45). The prism is for breaking that unbearable Wholeness into multiple subjectivities, the things to hold onto are their concrete observations, and the talismans are myths and symbols that create paths out of tracklessness. The latter are the formulae, the maps, for locating the self. (She and her brother loved to make maps on scouting expeditions.) Furthermore, she cautions, "You should never go into the page with gloves on" (45)—in order to be sensitive and receptive in feeling your way along. A frequent image of hers is the power of touch in hands, as an extension of the brain and as a way to connect to others (*C*, 229).

Warning against the danger of narcissism, the next paragraph in this part also suggests an alternative to it:

> There are those, of course, who enter the page without deciding, without meaning to. Some of these have charmed lives and no difficulty, but most never make it out at all. For them the page appears as a well, a lovely pool in which they catch sight of a face, their own but better. These

unfortunates do not jump: rather they fall, and the page closes over their heads without a sound, without a seam, and is immediately as whole and empty, as glassy, as enticing as before. ("TP," 45)

The charmed alternative is for those who might be writers unconcerned with "self expression" or mystics who reach some exalted state of bliss that contains no objects, not even self as an object. For an eternal moment they exist in a cleared state of readiness, like a supersaturated solution trembling before the moment of precipitation. When they do precipitate into form, it is with a sense of humility and gratitude, perceiving others not as objects, but as subjectivities fragmented out of the selfsame consciousness as their own, looking back at them. That state resembles the lack of self-consciousness in children and simple souls like Olenka, who, however, have yet to acquire selfhood and cannot know the bliss of losing it.

In contrast, the unfortunates are those who "fall" in love with themselves as objects, fascinated by a limited self-image that excludes any other subjectivities in the world. For them, the page/pool turns out to be, not the consciousness of the Whole, but the consciousness of Nada. By thinking they are everything, rather than that everything simply is, the contemplation of self becomes a vacuum that sucks them beneath the deceptive surface. The glassiness and enticement of that surface illustrate Atwood's frequent mirror and water imagery, in which, for example, the viewer ought to see "behind his own image in the foreground, a reflection of the world he lives in" (S, 15), if the page, i.e., literature, is to mirror the self as contextualized rather than isolated. In the case of water, reflecting surfaces also have deceptive depths.

This leads to a metaphysical inquiry into the nature of the surfaces and depths of self and art. "The question about the page is: what is beneath it?," she asks, tricking the unwary reader into thinking of the page as only two-dimensional with nothing "on the back," instead of looking "beneath. Beneath the page is another story [original italics]. Beneath the page is a story. Beneath the page is everything that ever happened, most of which you would rather not hear about" ("TP," 45). Once you go beneath the looking glass, everything is reversed as you discover your own subjective sensitivity in the page itself: "[T]he page is not a pool, but a skin . . . and it can feel you touching it" (45). The ability to feel gives rise to suffering, and so you "[t]ouch the page at your peril: it is you who are blank and innocent, not the page" (45). But if like the naive Adam and Eve tempted by curiosity "[y]ou touch the page, it's as if you've drawn a knife across it, the page has been hurt now, a sinuous wound opens. . . . Darkness wells through" (45).

Atwood plays on the dualism of light and dark, reversing the binary oppositions from that of Genesis, as she posits Light in the beginning, with a limited self precipitated out on the power of the words "Let there be Darkness" —i.e., marks, directions, a story, many stories, a mapped location, and a dialogue among many locations—as the self inscribes *life* on its page, transforming its white sterility, like that of a Canadian winter, into survival by taking root in the dark earth underneath. Atwood's idea of wholeness seems to be not a blank page of consciousness like a "vegetable" in primordial union with nature, but the inscribed *human* page, an integration between the words that fragment us and the spaces between them (*C*, 16).

Atwood's adventure into the page is a metaphor for her protagonists' survival in spirit, if not body. The only novel in which there is some doubt of the physical survival of the heroine is *Bodily Harm*. Rennie's spiritual survival requires her to enlarge her comprehensiveness—from being preoccupied with immediate personal concern only for her health and attractiveness after a mastectomy, to being personally concerned with political justice in the larger world. As a writer of travel pieces, she goes to a Caribbean island hoping for anonymity in the sun, but, when she is inadvertently involved in an aborted revolution, ends up imprisoned by the local dictator. There, after realizing her solidarity with other victims of the regime, Rennie defines herself no longer as escapist narcissist but as responsible citizen. As she languishes in her cell dreaming of freedom (or as she is being freed), the implication is that she would become a political reporter instead of trivia writer and would expose to innocent "sweet Canadians" (like her former self) the darkness welling through from the corrupt dictatorships they blindly support. The other novels dealing with the encounter of a female protagonist with the pages of herself are *The Edible Woman, Surfacing, Lady Oracle*, and *Cat's Eye*.[23] In each the heroine is something of a blank page to herself, but by going through a redefining experience as Rennie does, manages to inscribe something meaningful that at least gives her enough direction not to become totally lost.

Marian in *The Edible Woman*, having been defined as "sensible" by her conventional fiancé, Peter, increasingly feels herself to be merely an object of consumption, symbolized by his capturing her in the static photographs he takes. But she is not to be fixed and pinned down in his images of her. Drifting along in subconscious rebellion, estranged from the sensible Marian she now speaks of in third person instead of first, she resists eating one food after another in sympathy with other animal—and even vegetable—victims, who are consumed by predatory humans like Peter (who hunts with a gun as well as a camera). By drifting into a relationship with a sardonic graduate student, Duncan, who looks as anorexic as she gets to be, Marian is enabled to see Peter from a countercultural perspective. She finally bakes a cake in her own image to offer Peter as a substitute for herself. After he leaves in disgust, her appetite returns to being sensible—as she becomes a consumer again herself.

T. D. MacLulich argues that Duncan, who has also "had" her (symbolically eating some of the cake-woman with gusto), has victimized her like the deceptive fox who gets the gingerbread boy after it runs away from sensible human predators.[24] However, Duncan, the character who represents Atwood's metafictional playfulness, is always ironically undermining his own lies and admitting his tricks to her, as when he tells her, "Peter wasn't trying to destroy you. Thats't [sic] just something you made up. Actually, you were trying to destroy him." After he has caused her to question herself, he follows this up with, "But the real truth is that it wasn't Peter at all. It was me. I was trying to destroy you"—which MacLulich quotes, missing the point that one should not take this fox too literally.[25] It is his humorous postmodern consciousness about the fictions he creates that helps Marian break through the thralldom of facades. This anticomedy comedy (only "anti" because it defies the convention of marrying off the heroine at the end) is comic in that she is saved from a bad end, i.e., marriage with Peter (reflecting Atwood's own fear of marriage then) and anorexia. But having gotten out of the predicament of that particular page in her life, she does not seem to have integrated any of Duncan's ironic play into herself and is hardly more self-aware or socially aroused than she was at the beginning, except to be less consumable herself, perhaps—or as MacLulich argues, more accepting of her female body, if assimilating the cake represents psychic integration of her biological needs.

Perhaps Atwood's best novel of this genre is *Surfacing*, in which the unnamed (blank) protagonist returns to the Quebec North Woods, the scene of her childhood, in search of her father who has disappeared. In searching for him, she recovers that part of herself that has been numbed by the trauma of an abortion, which she was passively coerced into by a past lover. Due to that shameful experience, she denied herself contact with her parents and lost her ability to feel. Her numbness also manifests as denial, or rather unreliability of memory. She relies on pseudo-innocence to hide from her guilt and to abdicate responsibility, shunning power as if it would corrupt her, as Atwood claims many sweet, helpless people do (*C*, 14–15).

Returning to the scenes of her happy childhood, she is awakened to stirrings of past love for the country and for her parents, becoming more estranged from her city companions—a couple, David and Anna, trapped in the torment of a victor-victim relationship, and her present lover, Joe, an inarticulate and clumsy, but well-intentioned, fellow. As feeling wells up, like dark knowledge from beneath her deceptively glassy page of memory,

she realizes she must pursue her quest for her father and for herself in solitude. Alone, diving deep into the lake, she thinks she discovers his drowned
body weighted down beneath the surface by a camera—that device that
weighs us down to a rigid rather than fluid account of history—pinning his
body against a rock of prehistoric drawings he sought to capture in it.

She, however, "surfaces" and destroys the paraphernalia holding *her*
down to a deadening job as a commercial artist and to the objects that
falsified memories in her parental cabin—discarding even her clothes. She
symbolically turns the cabin mirror to the wall so that she cannot fix her
image in her mind; she hopes to free herself to flow into a silent dialogue
with her roots in nature. Bare of clothes and of the civilized trappings of the
mind, she then dives down into the lake of her self, a descent into a state of
madness (to a modern interloper), but to the ancient Indian keepers of the
place, a state of sacred trance, in attunement with the spirits of her de-
parted parents, who assume totem-animal shapes. It is a Jamesian kind of
ghost story. Atwood's secular debunking voice, the one that zooms in on the
banal and ugly details that mar the landscape of our society, is suspended at
this climactic scene in the novel, and a visionary voice takes over, in keeping with the protagonist's trance. Here Atwood chooses to bow to myth
with a degree of reverence she reserves for such "moments of being" in her
work. But the protagonist cannot survive in that state and must surface
from submergence in primeval timelessness back into the time-bound world
of her present situation, connected to her future by the new life she had
gotten Joe to impregnate in her before her Jungian descent, as a kind of
rebirth of her aborted child corresponding to her own rebirth. Determined
to be a victim no longer, she seeks a simple complement in Joe, whose silence—like a fresh blank page—is what she needs to inscribe, together with
him, a new language of survival upon.[26]

Another one of those scenes of magical entrancement occurs in *Cat's
Eye*, the story of another homeward journey into the past by a heroine. Like
Surfacing, *Cat's Eye* contains several autobiographical elements, such as a
scientist father who brings his wife, son, and daughter into the Quebec
North Woods. It is also a nostalgia trip for Atwood to record the schoolgirl
life in town of the protagonist Elaine, particularly her victimization at the
playground for being a greenhorn. Here Atwood may dismay feminists
who sentimentalize sisterhood, since she depicts the aggressors as female;
she claims no special virtue for being female, because the victim of one kind
of relationship may be the aggressor of another. The aggressors here are
Elaine's "best friends," particularly the one she admires most, their leader
Cordelia, and also the formidable matriarchal mother of one of the girls,
Mrs. Smeath, who has been a recurring subject of Elaine's art work as a

professional painter, perhaps in her compulsive attempt to exorcise that old demon's past influence. Elaine is the closest alter ego for Atwood of any of her characters, being a middle-aged serious artist who is professionally successful and happily settled with a family.[27]

Returning to her girlhood scene in Toronto for an opening of her art show, Elaine delves into her memory for some clue to her unresolved relationship with Cordelia, another missing person, a blank page, an alter ego in the victor-victim game they played in childhood. Cordelia's sadistic baiting of Elaine culminates in a scene in which Elaine is abandoned by her pals and nearly freezes to death. Unlike Andersen's little match girl, she has a saving vision of the Virgin Mary, the only female figure of compassion she knows (even her mother, probably not realizing the seriousness of the problem, has not come to her aid when she is in the hands of her secret tormentors). The other saving grace she carries with her is a talisman against the blank page of nonentityhood and disempowerment—a "cat's eye," the prize marble of playground competition, which she keeps secret from them, reserving it as if it were a part of herself that they cannot command.

Elaine's physical survival leads to her spiritual survival in a pivotal scene following her visionary near-death experience. When her tormenters have the nerve to approach her to reestablish the old relationship, she, recognizing clearly their hypocrisy, turns her back on them. That is the decisive moment of her empowerment and the dissolution of their hold over her. Elaine's new ability to simply walk away from them demonstrates Atwood's cryptic claim that "[p]ower after all is not real, not really there, people give it to each other."[28] Elaine later befriends Cordelia from a position of power, not so much in revenge but simply as holding her own. Cordelia, however, caught in the either-or net, cannot reconstruct the loss of her power creatively, and undergoes her own downward spiral of victimization. Back in the present time frame of the novel, Elaine hopes to meet Cordelia, partly to assuage any guilt for having neglected her over the years, fearing for her possible madness or death, and partly to understand the source of Cordelia's victor-victim complex. However, Cordelia, like her nearly silent namesake in *King Lear*, remains a blank; her role has been to focus attention on the development of the protagonist. In the process of remembering, Elaine has made some peace with the ghosts of old female antagonists and more consciously incorporated their spirit into herself (Hengen).

Atwood develops this theme of the power struggle among women exclusively in her recent novel, *The Robber Bride*. As in *Life Before Man*, there are three protagonists, but here they are all women and all friends, who may be regarded as not only a composite self but as a collective whose survival depends upon their dialogue with each other in their confrontation with their common enemy, the beautiful and perfidious Zenia. Each protagonist represents an important aspect of the human mind—Tony the intellectual, Charis the spiritual, and Roz the material—and their friendship represents the balancing of these aspects in an idealized whole mind, just as in *The Waves*. The story is structured around the return of their old antagonist, who was supposed to have died a few years back. In flashbacks of their isolated struggles against Zenia, they each recall the humiliation of defeat by her skillful manipulation of their weak points. Now that they have become friends and allies, respecting each other's strengths and availing themselves of each other's support and knowledge, each is strengthened in her single combat with the adversary. This alliance is made explicit in the scene in which Charis summons the strengths of her two friends to sustain her, in a ritual of psychic preparation for her coming encounter with Zenia.

But Zenia is not just an outer enemy, a robber of their men, money, and power, she is the incarnation of their own dark impulses, a shadow alter ego for each of them. In realizing this, they learn to acknowledge and even respect her as a member of their dialogue. In psychological terms, instead of splitting and projecting their evil onto her, they recognize her in themselves. In Nietzschean terms, Zenia might be their best friend who is their best enemy, the one whose opposition will either make or break them by forcing them to overcome their weaknesses and to take their own dark feelings into account in the process.[29] Atwood creates a strong current of validation for the power struggle that refines and strengthens the self through the necessity to marshal all its resources—material, intellectual and spiritual.

The Robber Bride illustrates the Nietzschean reversal of the good-evil discourse of the world's religions that gives homage to the meek (i.e., weak, helpless, and pseudoinnocent people, not merely modest ones): it exposes the vulnerability of intellectual, spiritual, and materialistic pride that Zenia exploits in each of the protagonists. Implicitly supporting this Nietzschean ethic—but in a kinder, gentler tone than Zenia's final contemptuous tirades—are the third-person narratorial voice that mocks the protagonists with humor and the protagonists themselves who criticize but tolerate each other's foibles graciously. The narrator retains a fine balance between creating empathy for the protagonists' points of view and a distancing mockery of them. The only times the balance swings entirely into sympathy with a character's state of mind is during deep pain and agonizing soul-searching. At such moments, irony, mockery, and the flip humor of the banal that Atwood excels in elsewhere would blunt the compassion the situation requires. Here, as in *Surfacing* and *Cat's Eye*, Atwood turns to enthrallment (with the character's point of view) at the right moment, and does not maintain a narrator trapped in the ironic mode. Thus, the narrative in its content and tone operates both to support and to undermine the ethic of competitiveness. All three are undone by their impulse to do good—to Zenia—and saved by that same impulse toward each other. The existence of Zenia creates the need for cooperation and dialogue, rallying the weak to become strong.

Love and compassion are the key to undermining the Nietzschean code. For all the admiration of Zenia's powers of beauty, cunning, and resilience, for all her adaptability to circumstances by playing fictitious personae skillfully, which the text conveys, she is nevertheless an isolated and narrow creature. Atwood once said, "The exercise of power is the opposite of the practice of love,"[30] which power refers only to a certain kind of power *over* others, not the power of love *for* others that Zenia deprives herself of. If love is redefined as a form of power rather than vulnerability, and power as a form of love rather than domination, then Atwood's original polarized statement can be revised to imply an interchangeable and enhancing duality rather than a violent one.

Unlike the three protagonists, who are both respectful and critical of each other (and of Zenia), Zenia is incapable of respect for others, being under the compulsion of the superwoman to succeed "over all" by regarding others as mere objects for her purposes. She exhibits the "regressive narcissism" Hengen discusses. Such a drive for success is a sign that her weakness is the fear of weakness. Her self-image as a superior manipulator is an image she is trapped in, like Milton's Satan who is himself hell; it is not just one mask among others she is free to put on or take off, but compulsory. The protagonists, in contrast, are free to experience tenderness, the price of which may be vulnerability, but their options are greater, because they can learn success too, not as exploiters of others, but for the sake of their own "creative or progressive narcissism."

But the importance of *The Robber Bride* is not to understand Zenia as a situated self, for she is left a mystery, an archetype of the demonic power that reincarnates in various guises from within and from without. She, like Cordelia (and Percival in *The Waves*), is present mostly through absence and is seen only from the point of view of the protagonists. She is a device to develop their self-knowledge, although she represents the self's nemesis (not its ideal, as Percival does). It is significant that the traditionally masculine discourse of power is conducted among women who revise the meaning of power (as Hengen notes of Atwood's prior work). But here the antagonist is neither a patriarchal male nor a woman complicitous with patriarchy (like Mrs. Smeath in *Cat's Eye*), but a robber-rapist in her own right. In this power struggle between women, Atwood demolishes gender distinctions, showing that a struggle between women is as dangerous as one between men, although the methods and the turf may be different. Here the booty is the man instead of the woman, and the weapon is female seductiveness toward that booty instead of physical combat between the adversaries. Of course, the booty can also include gender-neutral money and the weapons gender-neutral cunning or deception.

Atwood further breaks down gender distinctions in her protagonists' portraits. Tony is a brilliant academician who has invaded the male domain of military history, and whose cold analyses subscribe to the might-makes-right ethic on the grounds that historical impartiality boils all the "right" down to who won and why, and all the "wrong" to who lost and why. In such a hard-nosed view, war is as moral as a game of chess. The only "feminine" touch Tony adds to her method of study is to construct a sand-table model of the battlefields using the contents of her spice rack as soldiers. Tony's obsession with contemplating military power is a kind of Napoleonic complex due to her extreme shortness of stature (even for a woman) and as an escape mechanism for her unhappiness as an unwanted child. By her professional code, Tony salutes the power and success of Zenia as her imaginary shadow twin.

Charis is much more traditionally feminine in her "spaced out" New Age spiritualism and her reliance on intuitive insights and psychic power, which is inarticulate but uncanny. Typical of Atwood's matrilineal theme (Hengen) and fairy-tale parodying style (Wilson), Charis's healing power is bequeathed to her by a potent fairy godmother—in this case, a maternal grandmother with healing, and killing, hands. However, Charis has undergone a personality and name split, from child-victim Karen into transcendental Charis, the cool, detached, above-pain alter ego. The scene of this transformation has that reverential visionary power of Atwood's, set off by the ironic frame. The Charis persona, in keeping Karen suppressed in order to survive the otherwise intolerable pain of neglect, rejection, and violence, also allows Karen to fester subconsciously into an avenging demon resembling Zenia. In Karen-Charis we can recognize Martha-Doris (or Rhoda-Virginia), all children of violence, who are plagued by the self-hater and driven to seek refuge in a transcendental or astral state. They survive in this world through visions of utopia or heaven, a better world somewhere or sometime else.

Of the three, Roz is the most category-defying hybrid—a cross between an impoverished Catholic Cinderella and a rich Jewish princess, and between a worldly wise capitalist boss-lady greedy for money and a love-foolish wife who lavishes affection and money on her handsome but unfaithful prince. With her sense of humor she can afford to acknowledge her appetites, her neediness, greediness, and envy, and with her humble background can find the inner and outer means to do without and survive her losses. She ruefully respects Zenia as her archcompetitor without denying her own strengths. Like the other two, hating Zenia is double-edged sword against the self and the destroyer of the self.

What Atwood does with good and evil in *Robber Bride* is different from what Lessing does in *The Four-Gated City*, in that Lessing draws a sharper polarity. Martha confronts her own demon almost as if it were a mission assigned by the guardian self to explore the territory of hell and report back. She knows she cannot split off the devil and locate it only in others, and her integrity drives her to hunt down the enemy right in the backyard of the self. But after having risked that descent, she returns to a position of "goodness" residing in her evolutionary vision, which is still polarized with respect to the evil, stupid, and apathetic, i.e., alien, world that is externalized in the symbol of the boulder that has to be pushed by the wise few. Atwood's heroines in *Robber Bride* (and *Cat's Eye*), however, respect and even value the devil in addition to battling her. Atwood's dealings with the demon self in her work in general are not limited to an occasional foray into enemy territory for the strategic purposes of the good self, but entail a more continuous awareness of the shifting values that can attach to all positions. Hence, Atwood's transcendence is a kind of cosmic laughter, a mockery of *all* positions, including the "goody-goody" and "bleeding-heart" liberal ones that can be blind and foolish and therefore vulnerable. Goodness, too, needs to be alerted to its weaknesses when encountering power politics. This respect for power does not deter Atwood from commitment to causes of nonviolence, as in her support of Amnesty International and PEN, organized for politically imprisoned writers. Her commitment is to counterpower.

Thus she can imagine victimized heroines who learn how to defend the survivor self, just as Martha does. But even more. By actually honoring the dark impulses as springing from some legitimate source—while keeping them from overpowering the dialogue—compassion becomes possible, not only toward fellow victims, but toward the enemy, which is a much harder kind of compassion to achieve, with respect to both the intrapsychic dialogue and the transpersonal dialogue. Satire that is laced with compassion has a different quality of laughter, a humorous kind, as opposed to the scathing kind of satire in which the subject assumes an utterly alienated position from that of the target. Instead of extreme subject-target polarization, humor becomes possible when their distance is balanced by a sense of their connection and oscillating interchangeability. While Atwood has a strong tendency to satire, it is often with the humor that senses the interchangeability of positions, the vulnerability of the mocker as well as the mocked. In contrast, while Lessing's characters' subjectivities may switch positions with their targets, each new subject position retains the severity of distance toward the new target, as if their reversibility were forgotten.

Believers in absolute right and wrong have difficulty with how one can develop moral positions and values if everything is questioned and nothing is sacred. They forget that in the process the devil's positions are also undermined in *Robber Bride*, where Zenia is exiled from love and exposed as ridiculous in her own complex web of lies as her opponents compare notes (or in *Cat's Eye* when Cordelia seems to collapse without the domineering kind of power). On one hand, Zenia destroys herself in her machinations, and on the other, is immortalized in their memories as a formidable power to be ever vigilant about. In recognizing the power of evil as goodness gone amok, as part of one's very self, it can the better be curbed rather than complied with under a new disguise of self-righteousness.

Of all Atwood's novels dealing with the female self, only *Lady Oracle* focuses squarely on the postmodern problem of the decentered subject in the heroine, Joan Foster, who is consciously concerned with an "identity crisis." Her problem is a protean multiplicity gone wild. Like Olenka, she fashions herself into a new image to suit each relationship and is stricken by the angst of her own blankness between them. But Joan is not as simpleminded as Olenka, who forgets a former image as soon as a new one replaces it, for Joan remembers and carries around all her old images like excess baggage. She explicitly entertains the question of how to relate to her multiple personas—or to put it another way, how they relate to each other. However, instead of an earnest and comprehensive quest for self like Martha's, Joan drifts along in more of a quandary than a quest, in a game of hide-and-seek between romantic escapism and ironic self-mockery. Hers is a parody of the quest for self in which she is as victimized by her selves as by anyone else. As a parody of a woman's postmodern identity crisis, the matter of the *fictionality* of any single self-image or of any paradigm of the self—such as the dialogic one—is brought into focus. The next chapter will sharpen the case for the paradigm of a dialogic self versus that of an essentialist core self, using the least likely example, the fragmented Joan.

6

Lady Oracle:
Herself A-mazed in a Funhouse Mirror

Joan Foster, alias ethereal poet Lady Oracle, alias Louisa K. Delacourt, author of trashy gothic romances, alias various other personas, including the romantic heroines she creates in her fiction, meanders through her own life as through a labyrinth of dead ends, panicked by a sense of no exit. This existential angst of self-alienation arises from her perception of the fictitiousness of her personas. Indeed, Joan's autobiographical personas are invented to fit the perceived plots of her situations, much as in her written fictions. The culmination of her final identity crisis is intertwined with the characters of her latest novel in a scene of gothic horror set in a castle-garden maze. The maze is the central metaphor of both the embedded fiction and of the framing story of her own life, suggesting a bridge between art and reality.[1] The main question that concerns us here is whether the lack of an essential unified self necessarily leads to a maze like Joan's, and whether her plight illustrates the danger of the dialogic paradigm—that is, of feeling lost or having misplaced one's sense of self.

The narrative begins with Joan in a state of limbo between fiction and reality as she tells of her faked suicide and all the events of her life leading up to her present predicament of being identityless—which to a Canadian is something like being out of place,[2] in this case, a Canadian hiding out in a small Italian town. Joan has planned this escape to Italy like one of her costume-gothic romance plots, for, as she says, "All my life I'd been hooked on plots" (*LO*, 310). Her comment reveals that, superimposed on the theme of serious alienation, there is a wryly ironic and very funny voice coming out of Joan, who narrates her story in first and foremost person (whoever that may be) in a satiric tone that mocks chiefly her sel(f/ves) as a buffoon, a ridiculous "fool-heroine."[3] Yet Joan's self-satire operates as a key that seems to both unlock her from the maze as well as lock her into it.

Those readers who share Joan's angst about the hydra-headed specter of fragmentation assume that those multiple selves are obscuring her "true" self. For example, Clara Thomas maintains that Joan's "essential kindness, warmth and decency are discernible throughout her story as the rock-solid foundations of a personality that has veered off in mad tangents from them."[4] Yet Joan herself points out that the strong, compassionate "core" supposedly underlying her ineptness is just a myth (92). That she realizes she is not the soul of kindness is to her credit; it prevents her from falling into self-righteous complacency. Thus, not being fixed in any core self-image may actually be an advantage for her as a means to gain distance through self-critique. However, if that critique is fixed in self-mockery, it can also be self-defeating, a sign of a pathological victim complex. Only insofar as it gives her an ironic distance from that part of herself which would be immersed in a monologue of self-pity might self-mockery serve as a possible opening wedge to self-enhancement. Indeed, the distancing move of satire implies superior insight and thus works to empower part of the self to prevail, even as it condemns another part. The problem is that in the polarization of superior and inferior positions, they tend to cancel each other out—unless, like Martha, one were to question *who* is mocking *whom* to get off the tail-chasing merry-go-round.

If Joan does not seem to escape her maze, it is not because she is flexible, but, on the contrary, not flexible enough. As inventive as she may be in constructing personas, something seems to inhibit her resourcefulness in outmaneuvering the victor-victim bind itself. Her versatility seems to be covering up a *fixation* on something that is blocking her. That something might very well be the paradox that the more creative she is in constructing personas, the more she fears she does not know who she really is—or the more she suspects she is *really* something she must avoid confronting at all costs. How does she know that her "rock-solid foundation" is as benign as Thomas reads her to be? It is this fear that entraps her.

Joan's fear is derived from the very imperative of having to be essentially this or that, which society dictates by virtue of its power to determine identities in the practical world. Joan's self-mockery is often some internalized voice of society, as she assumes positions others would take against her. On the other hand, she is equally capable of turning her satiric voice against others. The complex satirical relationship between self and society in this novel is comparable to that of *Gulliver's Travels*, as Susan Maclean has observed when she calls Joan a "modern-day Gulliver" whose "wry detachment" is the stance of a "disillusioned but bemused spectator."[5] However, she argues that Joan is not primarily a vehicle for commenting on the social scene, as Gulliver the anthropological observer is in his first travels; "the social commentary represents only peripheral concerns" and the emphasis is on Joan's psychological state and personal (mis)fortunes.[6] Implicit in this view of Maclean's is an individual-society split rather than intersection. In the example of Gulliver, the individual-society intersection becomes evident in his final voyage and return home, when an increasing emphasis on self-satire distills the social satire into himself and reaches its culmination in his mad self-hatred of the Yahoo he thinks he is. If the assumed definition of satire as an attack on the (social) "other" is expanded to include the self-as-other, then the psychological drama of Joan's predicament becomes inextricable from the social commentary.

Molly Hite, one of the commentators who discuss Joan's satiric voice, claims that it reveals her internalized patriarchal values that cause her to victimize and marginalize herself on behalf of the dominant powers.[7] Part of the terror of the inner Yahoo is that it is excessive, chaotic, and does not fit into the rational orders that try to contain her. Chaos also implies void, the absence of positive form, so that Joan suspects her inner "essence" is a blank page of nothingness; hence her panic about her lack of "real" identity and consequent rush to construct ad hoc selves that only reinforce her dilemma by contradicting the social pressure for a unified self-image. Joan's plight is an extreme version of Everywoman's, according to Hite.

And Joan suffers from one of the chief issues of female entrapment in social attitudes—entrapment in the body, which for her is obesity during youth. Although her gross body is primarily a personal attack upon her mother in retaliation for her rejecting and controlling attitude toward Joan, it is also, indirectly, a form of social protest against her mother's patriarchal values that equate slimness with feminine success. However, while her personal vengeance against her mother succeeds, Joan can't overcome the general social opprobrium that eventually turns her into her own target as the Fat Lady, whose grotesque image haunts her even after she loses weight. The social price she pays in childhood is to be ridiculed and excluded, a butt to her peers' cruelty, as when her Brownie friends tie her up and leave her in a ravine (an earlier version of Elaine's freezing trauma). Joan's response is to target herself for being duped by the hypocrisy of Girl Scout honor. While she at least does not deny her victimization, she still falls short of Elaine's ability to opt out of the victor-victim game, for this episode only deepens Joan's fear of betrayal and abandonment and hence reinforces her desperation to please powerful others at the expense of herself.

Dancing school poses another critical trauma when she is rejected by her teacher Miss Flegg from dancing the role of a butterfly in a recital, which means so much to her because of the symbolic beauty of self-metamorphosis and the desire to take flight. Instead, she is coerced into playing the oddball mothball whose steps she has to improvise: " I made it up as I went along. I swung my arms and stamped my feet as hard as I could. . . . I bumped into the butterflies. . . . it was a dance of rage and destruction, tears rolled down my cheeks behind the fur, the butterflies would die; my feet hurt for days afterwards" (50). This passage illustrates how Joan's private testimony of pain is overlaid by a distancing and mocking adult voice echoing the social view of herself as a ridiculous clown bumping into the pretty butterflies. Even the self-gratification of having vented her rage onstage is deflated to an anticlimactic crack about aching feet.

Banal remarks like this are a frequent satiric marker of Joan's (and Atwood's) style as she punctures any billowing self-pity from developing into exalted philosophical angst. This satiric tactic operates to protect, to keep her down to earth, and ultimately sane and nonsuicidal. Who would kill herself over aching feet? The use of comic trivia changes this from potential tragedy to humor much as Jewish "gallows laughter" aided survival in the face of tragic history. Indeed, laughter is now acknowledged to be physiologically healing as well as psychologically restorative. Further, the release of hostile feelings through laughter may decrease the internal pressure to commit violent acts, and thus act as a safety valve. When the hostile aggressor and the target are recognized to be the "same" by a consciousness that negotiates between both, the laughter may be as "with" as it is "at," as sustaining as it is destructive. Through such laughter the reader who empathizes with Joan takes a position between the mocker and the mocked, which is neither superior nor inferior, but compassionate.[8]

But if the reader is disarmed by Joan's wry laughter, Joan herself does not quite attain self-compassion like Bernard, who can reach points of transcendence beyond his self-mockery. For her the flip humor only lubricates the otherwise harsh grinding of gears while she remains shifting uneasily between the poles of condemnation and guilt. Moreover, were she to achieve a transcending position beyond the victor-victim polarity, it would still not be the compassionate core Thomas credits her with, but simply a new location, a different viewpoint that does not obliterate the polarized positions by some synthetic fusion, but only alternates with them in the spotlight of her attention as yet another position to place herself in, one that is more empowering than the either-or trap. Positing a constant core is only an attempt to attain some kind of eternal guarantee of stability that is not possible in the constantly changing time-bound process of situated experience. Transcendence of the victor-victim and superior-inferior discourses must be constantly reattained. The closest thing to a guarantee would be eternal vigilance.

Joan does not discover an alternative view because of her addiction to paranoid plots—in her real life as well as in her fiction—which her sense of humor just barely keeps from overwhelming her. For example, when she has become a media celebrity as the entranced poet dubbed by her publisher "Lady Oracle," she appears estranged to herself as

> my dark twin, my funhouse-mirror reflection. She was taller than I was, more threatening. She wanted to kill me and take my place, and by the time she did this no one would notice the difference because the media were in on the plot. (251)

Though this is insanely funny, Joan is not mad but fantasizing (out of gothic-romance habit), because she is carrying on separate lives in secret from her husband, Arthur, and from her publishers, and fears being found out. Beyond the practical need for secrecy, she is afraid others will discover her to be a phony (thus "killing" her), but she is most afraid to find that out herself. She might have ended in tragedy, and Atwood originally intended to have her commit a real suicide as the natural counterpart to her faked suicide at the beginning, but in the mysterious writing process, Atwood ends the novel with Joan continuing to live (*C*, 45). It is Joan's mocking voice that saves her. Her view of how the media have blown up and distorted her is as savage as satire gets—murderous—but it attains a humorous perspective by being objectified in the framework of a funhouse mirror. Her ability to reflect (in every sense) on her image and achieve some distance from her panicked self enables her to survive—"Pull yourself together, I told myself. You've got to get out" (*LO*, 251)—even if it is in her usual willy-nilly fashion.

Hite astutely observes that Atwood rescues her heroine from the madness and suicide that otherwise might befall a life hopelessly entangled in and blocked by the rational pieties of the dominant culture that can't contain her: "It is precisely the tone of *Lady Oracle*—its familiarity, its banality, its flakiness—that precludes such a grim resolution. . . . The emphasis shifts to the character and to the character's act of storytelling and away from the threatened ending of the story. The model for the narrative . . . shifts . . . to therapy: self-revelation or talking cure."[9] One question is, does this satiric self-narrative work as a "cure"? It is possible to see some progress in the course of her retrospective psychoanalysis. Joan's frank revelation of her childhood mothball trauma is one key to her lifelong strategies of self-defense. "'This isn't me,' I kept saying to myself, 'they're making me do it' . . . I felt naked and exposed, *as if* this ridiculous dance was *the truth* about me and everyone could see it [my italics]" (50). Even then, as a child she is rejecting society's judgment and affirming her "self" by negating *that* particular self-image (i.e., the mothball as her then Yahoo), while having to paradoxically accept the cultural assumption of some positive "real core" self that is vulnerable to such an exposure. She wants that real core to be a pretty butterfly, but half-suspects she is nothing but a grub, which, in her struggle to deny, forces her into a limbo of self-nondefinition unable to fix on either. Thus, (to turn our psychoanalytic framework back on itself) she is in the same kind of bind that Freudian psychology imposes on women in general, having to define herself ontologically as *lack* of any core self that "exposure" presupposes the existence of!

Thus, Joan's flip humor, a kind of whistling in the dark, may serve to protect her from confronting something even more unthinkable than being a grub: self-annihilation at the core, the Yahoo as imageless blank page (replicating the putatively imageless Yaho-veh). She graphically describes this Yahoo, overwhelming her like a formless ghost of her old Fat Self: "It would have no features, it would be smooth as a potato, . . . it would look like a big thigh, it would have a face like a breast minus a nipple. . . . Within my former body, I gasped for air. . . . Obliterated" (321). The choice between the twin horrors of self-annihilation and forced fixation on a single self-image are conflated in this description of an indeterminate fat self.

This dilemma can only be a threat if one assumes that everyone must have an essential unitary core. Joan would not be threatened by this fear of nothingness if she could afford to recognize that in having no single determinate essence, *she is just like everyone else* (as we shall see subsequently), instead of feeling alienated on account of it. Thomas's way of conceiving Joan's problem as "being off on a mad tangent" from her "true" self is not as helpful as seeing the part social expectation of a core self plays in her struggle to conform. Thus, behind Joan's self-satire, one senses that the novel as whole is Atwood's satire on the prevailing fiction of a unified core self.

But Joan does not have her author's insight. The only lesson Joan learns from the mothball experience—thanks to Miss Flegg's improvised solution, which made Joan the hit of the show—is to turn seeming disaster into seeming success by appearing to choose and accept "what you are." By "accepting what you are" as if it weren't also *unacceptable* as a core-self concept, Joan is forced into denial, into a life of pretense. The next stage for her is to play the buffoon deliberately and become the popular class clown and good sport, somewhat like Martha's "Matty" persona—but unlike Matty, one who "accepts" herself as sexually undesirable in adolescence. She mockingly describes her neutered persona as a great pal to her slim "feminine" girlfriends, cheerfully interposing her mass between them and unwanted boys' attentions like "a fat duenna" or a "private tank" (94); or alternatively, discreetly acting as a foil to set her friends off to advantage for the attentions of the boys they want. She comments ironically, "Though immersed in flesh, I was regarded as being above its desires, which of course was not true" (94).

A dubious advantage of this stratagem is that her fat becomes a heavy mask to protect her from the male gaze, so that she is not "reduced" to being merely a sex object. Joan retrospectively acknowledges—and this is one measure of her progress—that outer seeming success was a cover up for inner failure, that to please others she had to denigrate herself in some sense. The desperate need to please others that society encourages in women is clearly under attack here, not incidentally, but as a major factor in Joan's behavior. Torn between the conventional acceptance of jolly, wise obesity and the conventional rejection of unsexy fatness, Joan's mind-body is split between the two norms and is a reproach to both. By internalizing, accepting and rejecting herself from both points of view, Joan's chief target is herself, for whichever way she turns in the maze a distorted mirror-image confronts her. Atwood is right to point out that there is no single moral position from which to aim the satire in *Lady Oracle*, since every position is itself mocked (*C*, 55). Thus the satire, otherwise an enabling device, becomes itself part of the trap when she becomes locked into it with no further key.

If transcendence of polarized thinking is a way out, the next question is whether it might take some form of mystical or occult state rather than a talking cure. At the same time that the novel suggests occult possibilities it also casts doubt on them. Altered states do not seem very liberating for Joan, because instead of expanding her mind beyond self-conscious discourses her experiments just turn into exercises in narcissism, signaled, for example, by her use of a mirror to initiate the trance state in which she writes as Lady Oracle. She does not transcend what she needs to, but only invokes yet another self-image—that powerful dark twin, who turns into a victor-self against her victim-self. All that her ethereal trance does transcend, with its "automatic writing" as pure inspiration, is the 99 percent of earthly perspiration the task of writing usually requires. Thus Atwood is debunking the kind of occultism that is in the persona-forging business, that is, creating power through self-images as opposed to the business of attending to the task at hand through the power of dialogic engagement.

That Joan even attempts the feat of automatic writing is due to her encounter with the dubious medium Leda Sprott (the counterpart of Martha's Rosa Mellendip for matronly dottiness). However, Atwood, like Lessing, while poking fun at the fakery of occultism, leaves open a respectful possibility. After all, Leda Sprott, in her later guise as the justice of the peace who marries Joan to Arthur, confesses frankly to Joan the phony contrivances she falls back on when her genuine powers fail her. Whether this is just a ploy is itself doubtful, because Atwood allows Leda some uncanny insights and positive representation, at least from Joan's point of view as narrator, which might itself be unreliable. In any case, Leda does act as a nurturing fairy-godmother figure like Charis's grandmother by recognizing in Joan, or by passing on to her through the power of suggestion, enough ability to achieve at least a semblance of serious writing in her trances (as opposed to her popular romance stuff), and to hoodwink the establishment media and publishers into believing she is following in her mentor's footsteps. Atwood implies that this hoodwinking is deserved, along the same lines as Anna Wulf's pranks on publishers and Lessing's own Jane Somers hoax. Of course, Joan also hoodwinks herself and is not at the level of deliberate manipulativeness as Anna or even Leda. The importance of Leda Sprott has been as an encouraging mother figure for Joan rather than as a serious conduit to the occult. Since Joan's oracular powers are not a significant recourse for her, but are themselves suspect, Leda's influence is equivocal.

Two other women much more influential on Joan's life than Leda also seem equivocal in that they both empower and disempower her. The primary one is her own mother. Whether Joan can ever be liberated from feeling trapped in self-mockery may depend on whether the strong formative influence of her mother can be overcome, or as Hengen argues, turned into a positive contribution if she absorbs the virtues of her maternal adversary.[10] Going back to her early years, Joan tells that she is an only child whose ambitious but frustrated mother, feeling burdened with an unwanted child, treated Joan like an object to be molded, denying her both a sense of autonomous selfhood and a feeling of being loved. Having to live up to another's image of what one should be in order to be loved is a fundamental condition for that angst of self-alienation, of feeling unfree to be *whatever* may spontaneously develop. Lacking the unconditional kind of love that affirms one's existence *without having to define it,* Joan starts off with the need to affirm her existence by defining it in some way. Joan reveals that part of her reason for gaining weight was to increase her sense of being solidly real as a bulwark against nonentityhood: "Sometimes I was afraid I wasn't really there . . . I'd heard her call me an accident" (*LO,* 78). Her bulk is a massive hedge against nonexistence.

Obesity also fits into becoming whatever is *not* what her mother is or wants her to be. Her survival strategy is to reject being rejected, that is, to accept what her mother rejects, in the same way that Martha relates to her mother. In Joan's case, not only does she reject slimness, she rejects her mother's persnickety neatness and conservative dress style by becoming defiantly untidy and flamboyant in her choice of clothes. She develops clumsiness to a fine art, almost as if she were consciously fashioning herself as a buffoon by repeating her programmed mantra of how inept she is. However, her excessiveness may also be attributed to positive sources as well as negative or reactive ones. The sheer energy of a sensitive and artistic temperament has to burst through the rigid seams of her mother's corsetting mentality.

At the same time that she is asserting her separateness, she estranges her mother more than ever, but Joan is intuitive enough to realize that winning her mother's approval would not win her any self-confirmation, so she develops a tough satirical attitude toward her mother and keeps a clearly drawn battle line from a young age. She develops an acute observation of others, which might yield the insight that they are as fragmented and phony as she. One of the most striking images of her mother is that of her sitting before her triple-mirrored vanity table, creating the illusion of a three-headed monster, a Cerberus from hell. Joan's gothic imagination colors this vision, but her eye for satiric detail, which detects her mother's exaggerated lipstick application through which the shadow of her real lip line shows, deflects horror into laughter. The triple-mirror and real-illusory lips call attention to the multiplicity and duplicity of everyone, including the most seemingly rigidly defined conventional character, the mother (who, incidentally but significantly, also keeps her family background secret).

However, Joan fails to use her insight into others' fragmentation as a way to close the gap of her alienation from them in this respect. Her satire is just a double-edged blade against both self and others. While it works to keep her going, it isn't any positive cure.

The only potential counteraction of her mother's destructive influence is the constructive one of Aunt Lou (the namesake of Joan's Louisa K. Delacourt pseudonym as a romance writer), who not only thrives on her multiple-faceted personality from a base of undefined self-confidence, but conveys to Joan something of her spirit. Aunt Lou is an independent and unconventional woman with secret lives that Joan gradually discovers: she is not the old maid she appears to be, being married to a man who deserted her but whom she never divorced; she is carrying on a discreet long-term affair with a married man; and she is also the ghostwriter of a pamphlet for menstrual products, an occupation one would have to speak sotto voce in polite society. Aunt Lou is quirky, but cares for Joan as a human being without imposing any particular image on her. However, even Aunt Lou comes in for some satiric jabs—perhaps because she is also an oddball and Joan can mock her from society's point of view just as she mocks herself; perhaps also because her aunt contributes some share towards Joan's self-abnegating profile. It is Aunt Lou who indulges in and acculturates her niece to escapist movies, reliving old hurts in melodramatic and romantic sob stories. Joan wryly observes that they rated movies by how many packs of Kleenex they used up—and how much candy they consumed. Aunt Lou did not limit or nag Joan about her food intake. However, eventually she felt some obligation to get her niece out of a self-defeating obesity problem when she made Joan's reducing a condition in her will for receiving an inheritance.

That Aunt Lou is herself a large woman who feels successful in a love relationship with a man suggests that it is possible to be heavy and still feel attractive. But she could not have been a role model in that respect for Joan, who was fat for perverse psychological reasons, unlike Aunt Lou who was naturally inclined to be big. Aunt Lou not only bequeaths to Joan more natural measurements, but perhaps some spirit of hardy resilience beyond all that escapism. She endows Joan with enough of that fundamental self-worth, evinced in her attitude toward herself and toward Joan, to enable Joan to have the necessary inner capital to afford to laugh at herself without destroying herself. Thus, her contribution to Joan might be stated as a re-writing of the trite injunction to "accept yourself for what you are" as: "Accept your (undefined) self, regardless of whatever condition(s) may attend you." Self-satire might then be directed against the *conditions* of one's existence, not against that existence per se. By valuing Joan, and not the layer of fat that Aunt Lou regards as not "essentially" Joan, she helps release Joan from it . Although Aunt Lou pressures her to reduce as a condition of her inheritance, it is not her *love* for Joan that is conditional by that time, but merely a small sum of money. This matter-of-fact level of conditionality comes close to the terms of a "contract" such as the proponents of "tough love" would advocate.

In Hengen's approval of Atwood's protagonists' reclamation of powerful female forebears, she acknowledges the influence of Joan's mother and Aunt Lou, but interprets the mother's as empowering and Aunt Lou's as disempowering to Joan in the final analysis. She claims that by "relinquishing [Joan's] Aunt Lou persona [i.e., giving up writing costume gothics] and then accepting as invaluably useful her mother's strong will" at the end, Joan progresses from Aunt Lou's pattern of romantic escapism and "fatalist emotional vulnerability" to her mother's strong resolve.[11] Whether, indeed, Joan does finally demonstrate such strong resolve is an issue that will be addressed later. At this point, it is more interesting to examine the way Hengen interprets the contrast between Aunt Lou and Joan's mother. In view of Hengen's acknowledgment of the mother's setting an example of "duplicity and self-denial" in adhering to the conventional patriarchal order, and of Aunt Lou's contrasting unconventionality, it is surprising that

Hengen values the mother's legacy over Aunt Lou's. If Hengen is intent on finding dramatic reversals in which the heroine finds strength by reclaiming her matrilineage after being victimized by men, it would explain her reading that Joan has been victimized by her husband and finds strength at last in her formerly vilified mother.

However, Atwood confounds this straight feminist reading by interposing Aunt Lou as an alternate mother figure who happens to have a conspicuous weakness for escapist romance that obscures her quiet strength. Indeed, for Aunt Lou that very weakness might be a resource in Atwood's value system, a harmless release she pragmatically allows herself because she is otherwise quite down-to-earth about accepting the hand she has been dealt (which Hengen reads as "fatalistic"). One could even say Aunt Lou unabashedly allows her "big sack of greasy tears" to flow freely, accepting the needy child in herself and in Joan without trying to suppress it beneath a facade of "strength" like Joan's mother, precisely because she has enough self-confidence to afford this self-indulgence, whereas the mother cannot allow her vulnerability to intrude on her unitary fortitude. In judging Aunt Lou harshly for this, Hengen is joining the same patriarchal value system that delegitimatizes the admission of vulnerability without recognizing that it has its place alongside fortitude. One might go so far as to say that fortitude is important only because it protects a precious sensitivity that must not be crushed or devalued—certainly not by its own defense mechanisms.

But if romantic escapism is kept in its place as an occasional outlet for Aunt Lou, in Joan's case it dominates her whole way of life and is excessive to the point of caricature, precisely because she has been deeply oppressed by her mother's wonderful resolve—to dominate her. The great maternal strength Hengen hails is the very "regressive narcissism" she condemns when it is exhibited by the men in Joan's life who treat her as an object to be molded into an image. Again, Atwood shows the power game is available to both sexes.

That Joan longs to appease her mother's spirit near the end is not her repossession of the mother through a reversal of hatred, as Hengen claims, but rather a return to the original narcissistic stance of neediness behind her defiance (like Martha's inner plea to her mother "Why did you never love me!"). Joan is taking the position of capitulation to the mother's power when she blurts "I would do what she wanted" (329), even though she wants to be loving and consoling to her mother's weeping ghost out of a moment of pity for her.[12] The mere reversal is not enough as long as it remains on victor-victim terms, as long as Joan is willing to sacrifice herself even momentarily to the mother goddess in the name of "love," i.e., that mutual clutching neediness between victor and victim called "codependence" (as distinct from a healthy interdependence) in the jargon of current pop psychology. This inability to break through the power-game barrier is symbolized by the glass door between them as Joan realizes, "I loved her but the glass was between us, I would have to go through it" (329). The only way to reach a truly loving repossession of the mother's spirit would be to shatter the need to be her victim, to love her mother without appeasement and without any expectation of love in return, which would be difficult. For even if her mother were still alive, in maintaining her rigid standards she would be afraid to be shattered by "capitulating" to Joan's needs. Neither Joan's nor Martha's mothers could respect their daughters' differences because they could not face their own dualities and multiplicities the way Aunt Lou could. And each daughter could not succeed in a dialogue with a mother intent on monologue.

Hengen's discussion of the contrast between Joan's two mother figures is particularly valuable in underscoring the point that it is not some abstract quality, essence, or image that is empowering as a general core attribute, but rather the way that a quality is collocated with other factors in concrete situations. In this case the mother's "strength" without love is self-defeating because of Joan's defiance. Indeed, if measured by the counterforce of her defiance, Joan has had her mother's strength all along, and in that victory over her mother she, too, only defeats herself. On the other hand, because Joan absorbs Aunt Lou's "weakness" for escapism in a context of relaxed and loving acceptance, she develops an aptitude for romance writing that is at least a material asset.

But more importantly, being a writer of fiction gives her enough perspective on the fictions of her own life to escape from escapism itself—or nearly. Combined with a satiric eye for mundane detail that counterbalances her romanticism, her writer's perspective gives her the advantage of a dual consciousness that can deconstruct as well as construct her escapes. As an artist of her own life, her stance might be regarded as "romantic-ironic." On one hand, she constructs her story from a place of serious or sentimental emotional involvement, but in the process of telling it, she gains enough ironic distance to attain a metafictional perspective on it. As Maclean succinctly puts it, "Joan moves between insight and hysteria."[13] Joan's running comments often show how much she can be the aware artificer, as when she remarks, "I got a reputation for being absent-minded, which Arthur's friends found endearing. Soon it was expected of me, *and I added it to my repertoire of deficiencies* [my italics]" (217). That she actively regards her "deficiency" as an addition to her repertoire, rather than passively absorbing others' judgments of her *being* deficient, is the beginning of detachment from deficiency as essence. Absentmindedness is not Joan but merely a constructed stance of hers. A conscious (though not controlling) artist of her life and fiction, Joan realizes how closely parallel the process is of creating roles for real-life plots and creating characters for make-believe plots, giving her an advantage over other wives in Arthur's circle who expect real husbands to fulfill their media-induced fantasies (the very type Joan writes under her pseudonym). She, however, knows where to draw the line: "I kept Arthur in our apartment and the strangers in their castles and mansions where they belonged" (216).

Joan's capacity for this much detachment from at least some of her deficiencies may hold some hope for a good prognosis, except that she is still nurturing these deficiencies to gain approval, especially from the men in her life. In all Joan's relations to men, once she has reduced herself to the level of an acceptably slim sex object, she plays along with appearing essentially deficient in order to curry favor. When the new slim Joan uses Aunt Lou's legacy as her ticket to get away from home and the whole gestalt of fatness, she relocates in England, where she begins to deal with the issue of the male gaze, which she managed to avoid during her school years. It is more threatening than she thought. She stumbles (literally) into an affair with a Polish count, Paul, who treats her possessively. Having contrived a false autobiography to hide her shameful fat past from him, Joan develops further the paranoid mind-set she gained in childhood persecution, now with a combined fear of his jealousy (he keeps a gun) and of having her background found out. She chimes in to support his notions of her on the flip premise that his fictions are more plausible than the facts of her story as she perceives them. The desire to please and fit oneself into a dependence on male versions of reality are clearly being mocked even as she feels she has no choice but to go along. With her integrity compromised, driven to lie and accede to lies, it is no wonder a woman will denigrate herself.

Not only that, she becomes confused herself about that line she seems to draw between fiction and reality. What confuses her is the expectation that there must be an objectively correct version, one that she too-readily concedes others may have better access to than she. She does not realize that doubting one's own account does not necessarily grant the correctness of some authoritative-sounding other's. It is not a question of whose version of reality is the "truth," but rather whether all available versions are taken into account, including her own. But Joan discounts her view of things, especially when judged by conventional expectations of what "sounds convincing." Somehow her untidy life does not fit into the plots she is familiar with. However, unlike Olenka who is unable to even articulate her views to herself, Joan at least articulates her own account in her narrative, allowing the reader to figure out, by examining the internal logic of her story, how reliable she may be despite her confusion.

Joan's confusion can also be attributed to the sheer complexity of her story, which is a maze of secrecy that intensifies her paranoia and alienates her from open dialogue with others. When she meanders into a relationship with Arthur, a fellow Canadian who introduces her to his kooky radical friends, she concocts a story about being a political refugee in order to hide from Paul by moving in with Arthur. By this time she has already become a pseudonymous romance writer and thinks she must also keep her occupation secret from Arthur, who would disapprove. She easily manages this because Arthur & Co. are so full of abstract theory and vague plans that they are out of touch with what's actually going on. After she has been married to Arthur for some time, she further complicates her life by having an affair that is another secret to be kept from him. Keeping Arthur out of touch with her hidden life tends to put Joan out of touch with him as well.

One of the most revealing instances of her confusion between fiction and reality is her account of her suspicions that Arthur is trying to kill her, which is part of the reason she engineers her faked suicide with the help of two of Arthur's coterie, Sam and Marlene. Ironically enough, she dare not tell them her paranoid imaginings about Arthur for fear they will think she is imagining it! This is an example of her sacrificing her account in order to tell something more plausible—at least to them—since in their phony plotting as radical saboteurs, they readily believe she is endangered by undercover agents who are onto her, and will soon be onto them as her accomplices. She also claims vaguely to the more skeptical Sam that she is being blackmailed for personal reasons. Meanwhile, she presents no evidence in support of Arthur's homicidal intent, but does provide the reader with convincing details of a professional blackmailer, who, in threatening to tell Arthur she is having an affair and to expose her past to him and to the public, establishes a more logical basis for her wanting to flee. Adding to her overdetermined motivation is the sudden reappearance of Paul, who threatens to rescue her from Arthur by abducting her. As a result of all this intrigue, the reader is left with the impression that her paranoia about her husband is literally unfounded, but may have its truth on other levels.

The complexity of her plots is further complicated by others' duplicity and confusion as well as her own. Joan's satiric comments on the major players in Arthur's circle reveals their sincere phoniness, which is a jab at radicals who want to reform the world without knowing what they're doing and without a deep practical commitment (Arthur switches causes almost as easily as socks). Switching causes also becomes another metaphor for changing identities, and Arthur & Co. appear to be as multiple as Joan, confirming the pervasiveness of duplicitous selves in society. Even Paul has a secret career as a writer of popular nurse romances. Indeed, as Robert Lecker and Sherrill Grace argue, every character in Joan's life is leading at least a double life. Significantly, Grace points out that Atwood places a positive value on the kind of duplicity that acknowledges we are all mirrors of each other.[14] Joan's satiric comments are an attack on the social pressures that induce people to assume various facades while still maintaining the fiction of a unified encapsulated self to themselves as much as to others, causing the common feeling of alienation among competing egos. Her predicament becomes a caricature of the general human comedy of masks.[15]

Another significant character who carries out this theme of general duplicity is Joan's extramarital lover, Chuck Brewer, whom she first meets in his self-styled guise as "The Royal Porcupine." The man is the spirit of carnival literalized. His escapist romancing of Joan is what intrigues her. Only when he reverts to his straight self and seriously proposes she leave Arthur and marry him does Joan balk, thinking that "For him, reality and fantasy were the same thing, which meant that for him there was no reality. But for me it would mean there was no fantasy, and therefore no escape" (270). Again, her ability to draw that line is crucial to taking a satiric stance and to retaining whatever detachment she has. When he moves out of the playful mode into taking their relationship seriously and destroys his get-up as the Royal Porcupine, she finds that instead of his dashing beard "he had the chin of a junior accountant" (271), dashing the illusion she loved. But even her sharp satiric eye for telling detail becomes its own target: "I hated myself for thinking this. I felt like a monster, a large, blundering monster, irredeemably shallow. How could I care about his chin at a time like this?" (271). Such a judgment of shallowness points out that Joan's detachment from a sense of essential deficiency is rather shaky.

If Joan blames herself for being unloving and shallow, the satire is aimed, through her, at society. She explodes the social pieties relating love to the need to please (injuring herself in the fallout) when she realizes from her old Brownie slogan " 'There's magic in love and smiles' [that] love was merely a tool, smiles were another tool . . . just tools for accomplishing certain ends. . . . I'd polished [Paul, Chuck, even Arthur] with my love and expected them to shine brightly enough to return my own reflection, enhanced, sparkling" (282). In this respect she is different from Olenka who has not even enough ego to make the pleasing of a man an instrumental strategy. Chekhov's "darling" Olenka simply empathizes so completely that her own

legitimate narcissistic interests become congruent with his. It is this innocent and selfless love that Tolstoy admires in contrast to the narcissistic type
of instrumental love Joan recognizes in herself.

Thus, her budding detachment from the feeling of essential deficiency
is undermined by the practical necessity of catering to men for a kind of
love conditional upon expectations she can't meet, replicating the original
conditional love of her mother, whose ghost haunts her throughout. And
because Joan's love for them is also largely conditional, like that of a per-
forming seal who expects a reward, and less a genuine empathy and concern for the beloved, she easily succumbs to a feeling of victimization, for
the romantic promise of noble, enduring love retains its hold on her: "Why
had I been closed out from that impossible . . . paradise where love was as
final as death?" (284). Her lament is the general one of those who would
cling to fairy tales even when they know better. She can't help but sense that
her very dependence on conditional love is a more fundamental deficiency
than her made-up ones, and hence it operates as an undertow tending to
suck her back down into the quicksand of essentialist female lack.

Because Joan is maintaining facades of deficiency (as the lovable bun-
gler) and has the more deep-seated fear of essentialist lack, she almost overlooks her actual competence, e.g., her faked suicide and escape, which she
carries out according to plan, although not as neatly as Zenia arranges her
own phony death. Although the cunning required to perpetrate a fraud
may be successful, it nevertheless is a deficiency on another level—it constitutes a denial of others' truths and interests, which Joan does care about, in
contrast to Zenia. Joan may not be as loved and loving as she would like,
but she is not indifferent about causing harm. The consequences of her
actions precipitate her toward a crisis in which she must confront her self-
hating fears as well as her responsibilities, for as an escape artist, she has
become so a-mazed in complications that she can no longer escape without
paying too high a price.

The end of the novel raises questions as to whether Joan is "saved" in
some sense, in the tradition of the fall/salvation theme. Those who find her
problem resolved might attribute it to a form of the talking cure (Hite), or to
a Jungian rite of passage (Pratt), or to a socialist-feminist redemption through
reclamation of mother power and Canadian social conscience (Hengen).[16]
The climax of Joan's narrative occurs when she fuses her own life story with
the gothic novel she has been struggling to complete in Italy to earn money
under her pseudonym. Excerpts of her nested novel are alternated with her
comments as her reality is interwoven with her fiction. In writing the ending of her novel, Joan rejects any clear identification with her pale, victimized heroine Charlotte and comes closer to the evil wife Felicia, only to find

her a female menace (her own self-mocking, self-murdering aspect, per-haps, or her mother's), then nearly succumbs to being rescued from the female maze by her strong male hero Lord Redmond, until she realizes he is her duplicitous husband Arthur with the face of death. Now it is clear that her paranoia about Arthur is founded on this mythological level of reality. He has been killing her by not relating to whoever she happens to be, but to a mirage of his own construction. Her insight is a Laingian vindi-cation of her paranoia.

At this point she escapes her passive clinging to a male rescuer, and indeed, her whole gothic romance collapses like Alice's Wonderland of cards. All the people of her past have shuffled through her novelistic writing trance; instead of her writing being an escape from life, it has escaped her and taken on a life of its own as the characters act out her inner dialogue despite her efforts to stick to the genre. She comes out of it decided never to write gothic romances again. It looks like a form of talking, or rather narrating, cure combined perhaps with a Jungian (w)rite of passage, something like that of *Surfacing*'s protagonist,[17] although Joan's is a descent into the symbolic trance-world of her novel rather than into nature. The oracular implications of the title would support such an interpretation of mystical initiation—unless it were to be taken as satirically here as it is in her automatic writing experiments as Lady Oracle.

Not only does Joan go through some kind of self-revelation in her struggle with her writing, but external events make her realize that her staying in hiding is as untenable and absurd as the situation she fled in Canada. For one thing, she has a moral obligation to free Sam and Marlene, who are accused of her "murder." For another, she has become a suspicious charac-ter in her Italian hideaway, having had her old clothes that she buried un-der the house "resurrected" by the locals (a satire on the rebirth theme), and otherwise attracted attention to herself as an odd (single as well as weird) woman. She seems to realize that this escapade is as foolish a con-trivance as any in her past, and that she is strong enough to confront the fallout from her charades and stop trying to placate her mother's ghost and please Arthur. It seems the only way she can put her past behind her is to acknowledge it rather than escape it, and move on. Symbolically, she de-cides to leave "Terremoto" Italy as if she is leaving a place of "shifting/shaky ground" presumably to find a more solid basis for carrying on her existence.

Joan's apparent resolve to return to Canada to "face the music" sup-ports Hengen's view of Joan as incorporating some of her mother's firmness and uprightness and acknowledging her Canadian social conscience in her mother's voice when she remarks, "I keep thinking I should learn some lesson from all of this, as my mother would have said" (345). However, concluding that her return to Canada is symbolic of an "essential" Canadian identity, as we might suppose when she rejects the idea of becoming one of the fat Italian housewives, is problematical. She may just be rejecting the idea of settling down in a pasta culture that will pressure her back to obesity. Reducing Canadianness to the place itself as symbol obscures Joan's unsymbolic multiplicity at more concrete levels. She would obviously not have to reside in Canada to be culturally Canadian and could transplant whatever Canadian voices may be rooted in her, just as the English who settled Canada transplanted their Englishness. Regardless of which set of traits of hers might be considered Canadian, she will always exceed them or have traits that are contradictory. For example, if being orderly is Canadian, then Joan, admitting she will never be a tidy person right to the end, could be regarded as un-Canadian, although the implied valorization of order behind her statement would be Canadian. In any case, she would probably be creative and adaptable enough to add un-Canadian traits to her repertoire. When looked at nonsymbolically, the issue of her Canadianness is beside the point, because Joan is not going back to assume an identity, but to perform a morally right action that would be consistent with the moral values of many cultures.

Atwood herself seems to ascribe some degree of resolution to Joan's breakthrough in Terremoto—three quarters of an inch of progress, to be exact (compared to one inch of progress for the protagonist of *Surfacing*)— and claims, "[Joan] is taking the parts of her life which she has kept very separate. They will finally be together and she will be able to say 'O.K., that's who I really am'" (*C*, 66). She goes on to say Joan is willing to come out of hiding and not be afraid of rejection by others, with an attitude of "I am who I am—take it or leave it" (66). This would seem to solve her anxiety about having some unacceptable identity or a lack at her core. However, Joan intimates that her future might not be so very different. Now she is contemplating writing science fiction instead of gothic romances, and is probably going to have one affair after another with men who capture her romantic imagination, like the young reporter following her trail whom she conks on the head with a Cinzano bottle in her panic in Terremoto, and who, lying in a hospital bed in Rome, brings out a bit of the nurse-romance feeling in Joan that might have been the stuff of Paul's novels.

That she surprises herself by not telling the reporter any lies (or at least "not very many" about her faked suicide) and by not escaping from him in the terror of being found out (*LO*, 344), indicates that the nature of her progress is something like Rennie's, i.e., she realizes she cannot escape because she is bound up in responsibility to others—to him for injuring him, and to her friends in Canada—not just to her own narrow survival. This development only indicates that her moral decency is being tested as never before and that she has passed to another level of comprehensiveness, but it may still not address her central problem. Even her newfound courage to be responsible to her friends in Canada and face Arthur may not be enough to overcome her lifetime addiction to romance and ad hoc facades. She can always fabricate new personas and flee the "core" issue.

In carrying on her charades, Joan is somewhat reminiscent of Jinny in *The Waves*, who flows from affair to affair, adopting whatever persona suits the new man's fictions. But Joan is more ironic about her role-playing than Jinny, who throws herself into her affairs with the involvement of an Olenka, except that (unlike Olenka) Jinny retains her continuity with a consciousness something like that of a "method" actress. While Joan also retains her continuity and consciousness of creating personas, she fabricates them defensively, as a victim who barely survives by her wit, thus turning herself into an object of self-mockery and creating ironic distance from her involvement. If Joan ever reaches Jinny's triumphant sense of going up in flames in abandonment to the passion of the moment, it might be in those fantastic interludes with the Royal Porcupine—except that the satiric "voice-over" of her narrative does not allow such a mythopoetic state to be kindled. Judging by her continuing self-mockery, Joan may still have the tendency to create roles as a cover-up rather than as an affirmation of life's vitality, as Jinny does in her willingness to burn any "true identity" bridges behind her.

While Joan has had some kind of insightful experience, the ending is ambiguous, as Lecker would agree. He observes that Joan has not discovered any "true" self, such as a "victor" to replace her "victim," but more importantly, that any resolution of identity would be as much a construct as any of her facades.[18] To reverse Joan's original statement that "hidden depths should remain hidden; facades [are] at least as truthful" (197), Lecker might say, "The hidden depths are as *un*true as the facades." One problem with Lecker's (and Gergen's) postmodern view of the fictionality of all positions is that by dismantling the distinction between "deep" and "superficial," all positions appear to have equal weight in determining behavior. However, a distinction can be made between those that have been reinforced, such as through close dialogue with the body, and hence made into more powerful, i.e., "deep," positions, and those that are assumed for a limited purpose and taken up or dropped like a garment. Thus, Joan's personas are more easily altered than her lifelong patterns, and she has enough insight to draw the line between fantasy and reality, despite her lapses into confusion when pressured by fear. Unlike Chuck, the Royal Porcupine, who lives either in total fantasy or total reality (reality being a more deeply and dialogically established fantasy, perhaps), Joan needs one level to offset the other. What keeps her from getting stuck in the romantic monologue is her ironic voice counteracting it.

But if she escapes such a unity, she is still stuck in a polarized duality, like Gulliver, signaled by the constancy of the satiric voice right to the very end. Joan is, after all, bound to the genre(s) she has created for herself: the caricature of a romantic. Atwood acknowledges Joan's story developed into a parody, not serious realism. Once Atwood caught onto the right "voice," she ran with it all the way *(C,* 54–55, 229). However, that voice works against the resolution one might expect of a novel of realistic development and tends to reinforce the hint that Joan's story is episodic, in the picaresque tradition. Lecker, too, recognizes *Lady Oracle* is a parody on the quest-for-self genres and claims the irresolute ending is a satire on their illusory clear resolutions. *Lady Oracle,* like Lessing's *The Four-Gated City,* obscures easy generic classifications, approximating the unclassifiable protean quality of life by being a hybrid genre. On one hand, events stand out as turning points and moments of realization, which we endow with meaning as "resolutions" of some sort in the story of our life; on the other hand, we rarely reach ultimate resolutions, having to rediscover insights as they keep breaking through old habits that carry on, as in episodic forms. Just because Joan has gained some insight does not mean it is consolidated; like Martha, Joan is already forgetting and slipping back to old thought habits.

Thus, the irresolution of her situation, reflected in a somewhat mixed-genre ending, works to undermine a reading of Joan's accession to any true identity. The absurdity of her story also mocks serious conclusions about Joan's "true" self. Despite that, this novel has serious implications and is realistic about the way we construct our self-images in response to social pressures that force us to deny our multiplicity in the need for orderly containment in a unified self-image. If Joan were capable of writing herself out of this endless maze, she might develop a polyphony of voices, *including* the satirical and the romantic, but not be limited to them.

Indeed, Joan's creativity has been misplaced by not being dialogic enough. Instead of trying to become more stable by settling on some core identity, which would always be contradicted, forcing denial of those contradictions in the vain effort to maintain unity, Joan needs to cultivate reliance on an integrity that *validates* contradictions instead of merely mocking them. Again we see the problem with the postmodern view of the world as illusion: everything has its truth as well as its fiction, and one can only act on the basis of belief, not disbelief, wherever one is at. Integrity is an affirmation of belief. Taking a stand is a result of weighing the relative merits of all available positions in the light of how the situation appears. Thus, the integrity of the observer that transcends, that is, escapes, any given position or set of polarized positions is, paradoxically, the most reliable and stable as well as fluid. If integrity operates as a center or core, then it is the kind of center that is mobile, capable of centering itself on any position and breaking deadlocked dualities by moving to any number of alternative positions. The beauty of being such an escape artist as the mobile observer with integrity is that one does not deny any truth, but faces it along with all the other truths (or readings) that present themselves.

This means taking others' realities into account in transpersonal and environmental relations as well as within one's intrapsychic space, and modifying one's positions if necessary. The reassessment process alternates with action, which can only occur when assuming a position provisionally for a particular purpose. The danger of so much potential for mobility may be great uncertainty and paralysis of action, but that is more likely if one assumes there is only one right way and, undecided which it is, becomes paralyzed from fear of risk taking. However, it is quite possible to act fully in the moment on one's best assessment of the situation (intuitively as well as analytically) with a strategic unity, like Jinny, who plays each part with complete concentration, in contrast to Joan, who is divided against herself. Although her self-critique is justified because she is acting without either integrity or courage, the result is an action bungled by the blur between making a judgment and executing it. In contrast, Jinny's actions burn cleanly. Neither Joan nor Jinny is as comprehensive as Martha, of course, although both develop somewhat more of a collective consciousness in confronting mortality, but at least Jinny succeeds in her limited circle of action by taking responsibility and accepting the ashes between loves, whereas Joan is driven desperately from that center of bold integrity toward untenable positions in passive victimization.

The dialogic model may be difficult, but in its apparent maze of choices there are ways out, not just dead ends. It is the easy-seeming model of a unitary self that leads to Joan's difficulties. Her maze is only a mirror image of the dialogic process in that her assumption of herself as an objective center that can be located (identified) and gazed at not only falsifies all other centers, but turns that fixed core into an object instead of a subject. Thus she misplaces herself. Instead of locating herself *wherever* she happens to be as a vital center gazing out provisionally so that it can expand out to new subject-positions when necessary, she locates herself as an object, an unacceptable one in her case, which she tries to avoid by expanding into decentered and distorted *object*-positions (i.e., persona identities) that accumulate around that dead center. Atwood cannot blame Joan for not wanting to stare at the *sterile* blank page of the self, but if she were to elevate Joan to her own level of dialogic self-narrativity, Joan would realize she is a *fertile* blank page staring at a world that stares back at her in the infinite reflexivity of subject-object interplay, which would empower her to inscribe something she herself values.

Conclusion: Sustaining Self-Reconstruction through Dialogue

As a theoretical tool, the dialogic paradigm has been in a reciprocal relationship with the authors examined here. Not only has the lens of dialogism produced "a new way of seeing" their texts, but through this discussion of them, a new way of seeing dialogism emerges. This intersection of dialogism with the literary selves in Woolf, Lessing, and Atwood is more than a study of how their texts construct subjectivity formally; it contributes to a wider discourse of *sustainability,* which posits balancing diverse interests and recycling resources to address our ecological, economic, and cultural interdependence at every level of a compressed world.[1] As an art of self-renewal, the dialogic paradigm has shown its own sustainability for many years by lending itself to interdisciplinary uses, beginning with Bakhtin's original theory of novelistic discourse, which was extended to a theory of subjectivity as inner speech, and then enriched with gendered and multicultural discourses Bakhtin himself never thought of, such as those that have contributed to this discussion.[2] For example, using a dialogic approach among conflicting claims of contemporary feminists has shed new insights on Woolf's concept of androgyny, recasting it from a static model of "wholeness" to a dynamic one that both affirms and deconstructs gender categories according to context. Indeed, the success of dialogism lies in its *contextualization* of the process, which is why this analysis of the authors' lives and the contexts of their works emphasizes the content as well as the formal configuration of their discourses. By probing contexts in depth, the possibilities—and problems—of dialogism may be grasped not only theoretically, but concretely.

For, as successful as dialogism has been, it is not unproblematical. The very advantage of contextualization in theorizing subjectivity has its "situation-ethics" underside in that a dialogic self may appear too shifting or

unprincipled, suggesting either debilitating self-doubt, as in Atwood's fragmented Joan in *Lady Oracle*, or opportunism, as in her multifaced Zenia in
Robber Bride. Every chapter answers both these charges by showing that dialogue can only take place when one *believes* in a position taken, even if for a
day, not assuming it cynically or vacillating in doubt. While postmodern
doubt like Bernard's in *The Waves* has its place, at some point action must
be taken as if it were unproblematical and the self were taken for granted.
That is, something of Percival's self-assurance is required. Insofar as the self
acts (including thinking and speaking) in linear space-time, its positions can
be decisive and appear unified to sustain a given trajectory as long as that is
viable, but insofar as the self is part of a multidimensional network, its actions must be fluidly responsive, i.e., "fitting," to be sustained in changing
contexts. Thus, a self-narrative may value its rootedness, as Atwood emphasizes, while being capable of branching out globally, even cosmically, as
Lessing and Woolf emphasize. As our authors and their protagonists demonstrate through their successes and failures, one can be alert to contradictions and negotiate among conflicting discourses and still be committed to
causes and relationships. That is, one can be truer to oneself and others by
being flexible.

A related ethical problem, one observed by Bauer in *Feminist Dialogics*, is
that Bakhtin contradicts himself in holding a utopian ideal of the *equalizing*
of voices and a pragmatic theory of the power struggle among *unequal* voices.[3]
That contradiction, however, is only in the abstract. In concrete situations
such as those discussed here, dominant voices may win provisionally at times,
as the merits and powers of positions vary. Bakhtin contends that dialogism
consists of making choices among voices, not just airing them. Equality is
the ideal of achieving a rough balance *over time* so that authority does not
become entrenched, for Bakhtin recognizes the centripetal tendency for
power to consolidate itself and become corrupt through inertia and loss of
vitality, which, however, is no excuse for refusing to assume the responsibility of exercising it. Once we do, the risk requires us to be alert to our own
corruptibility, like Lessing searching out the devil in her mirror. A dialogic
subjectivity allows for both the resistance to authority and the assumption
of authority to balance conflicting interests.

Bakhtin's dialogic paradigm is under fire for an even more fundamen-
tally ethical contradiction, in the view of Jeffrey T. Nealon, who criticizes
his dialogic imagination for its self-centeredness. He compares Bakhtin's
version of dialogism with the ethical philosophy of Emmanuel Levinas, which
is very similar in that it also admits the construction of a self through others.[4] The important distinction Nealon makes, however, is that Bakhtin con-
ceals an authorial self that is ultimately an end in itself, with others' voices

merely instrumental to its sovereign permissiveness, whereas Levinas puts
the ball in the court of others who, by taking the initiative put the self in a
position of being nothing but responsive. Nealon claims that Bakhtin's dialogic self is just an insidious variation on the bourgeois self exploiting or
cannibalizing others, whereas Levinas's idea of self must always defer to the
priority of others.

Indeed, Nealon rightly points out the danger of a self as an end containing, and therefore "beyond," others. While Nealon acknowledges that
the "I" may be a necessary mechanism to locate response in the feedback
loop of "schemata" in the mind,[5] he seems to conflate this ego with the
blank subjective space just slightly ahead of such constructs as the ego. Although he seems to accept the open-endedness of the Bakhtinian subject
intersecting indefinitely with others, he claims Bakhtin reduces that infinite
process to an ultimate private self beyond the objective world, retaining the
old split between subject and object. To do this, the Bakhtinian subjective
gaze would have to reverse from moving outward toward the external world
to moving inward toward self-as-object in a closed narcissistic loop of an
ego that supposes it is beyond, and therefore able to contain, others. Such a
split would be between the object-self's ego, masquerading as the transcendental subject, and the rest of the object world. Zenia, for example, appears
to be dialogic only to ensnare others in her monologic purposes, but she
fails because she does not reckon with and honor the dialogue that escapes
her. They, in turn, are "beyond" *her*, which is the point. If self-narrative goes
beyond others, then no one can completely contain other selves, since each
exceeds the other. That is, we all both contain and exceed others because
there is no final state of containment for anyone. In fairness to Bakhtin,
how could a self be enriched by intersecting with others who didn't bring to
the relationship their own capacity to go "beyond"? To posit a subjectivity
that exceeds others, e.g., Woolf's night self, does not necessarily collapse
the world into a central black hole of an ego, but rather, as Woolf and
Atwood prefer, unself-consciously focuses the subjective gaze toward others, such as on the object of writing, rather than on the lady doing it. Then,
even when the object is the self, as Martha is to Lessing, the narrator cannot succeed in controlling or containing, only in observing and responding
to her, which is what Bakhtin maintains about the relationship between the
author and his (or her) characters.

Furthermore, while we can agree with Nealon that subjectivities arise
out of prior social inscriptions, and even as response to the immediacy of
the other's bodily presence, he doesn't explain how its "*re*marking or
*re*inscription of existing socio-linguistic codes [original italics]"[6] becomes
agency. He hesitates to locate responsibility totally in the other, which would

invert the subject from the classic active agent to a passive tabula rasa, like Olenka or even Joan, who, in contrast to Zenia, play the victim rather than the victor, with an object-self so beholden to others that they abdicate responsibility. Worse, if the others are also merely the effects of still others, the buck of responsibility stops nowhere. By acknowledging that the subject is not totally determined by others, Nealon might mean that *cumulative* prior input exceeds any given other's immediate influence upon subjective response. If so, he might concede that the cumulative effects of subjective history could be "beyond" any given other's immediate presence. Moreover, if we accept the premise that immediate input is multidimensional and global, subjectivity becomes a unique process of integrating it into the unconscious and selecting elements into manageable linear consciousness. Without that unique process, nothing new could be made out of the old and nothing different made out of the same. It becomes necessary to posit a self that, because of its specific history, is responsible for contributing uniquely to relationships, since it is always "other"—that is, prior—to the others' selves.

Nealon's polarization of dialogism between Bakhtin, representing a masculinized, egocentric pole, and Levinas's feminized ego-empty pole, a pseudo-Taoism,[7] is neither sustainable nor sustaining. If there is any ethic in dialogism, it is the affirmation of what is "beyond" in one another. Nothing less than a shared responsibility will do. Our authors show pragmatically how dialogic theory can steer between such abstract polarities as Nealon's—even by reviving bourgeois selves at times for purposes such as empowering female subjectivity.

While the above criticisms of Bakhtin's dialogism can be answered by close examination, thus sustaining it, a major premise of his original theory has been revised here, namely, by extending dialogic self-narrative from only the sociolinguistic and ideological constructs of literary texts to include their evocation of nonverbal or preverbal constructs as well. These range from the "higher" spiritual or mystical insights that suspend space-time categories of knowledge to the "lower" insights of semiotic bodily, cultural, and ecological knowledge. While such dimensions of experience are traditionally associated with feminine intuition, as essentialist feminists may claim, a dialogic approach does not simply oppose them to rational, linear thinking, but engages them with it *a*ppositionally, to use Judy Little's term.[8] Our three authors demonstrate this: Woolf, in the linguistic precision with which she articulates a semiotic style that foregrounds the minute materiality of spiritual connectedness; Lessing, in her admission of the body, emotions, and altered states into the dialogue without excluding her formerly privileged rational voices; Atwood, in her respect for inarticulateness and uncanniness even as she dispels her awe with ironic laughter. Since we do not know how anyone's process works, or whether it is by free will, chance, determinism, or all of the above, we can only marvel at its workings from a place where dialogue meets silence.

Respect for semiotic silence opens up the necessary distance to acknowledge the multiplicity and contradictions of linguistic discourses, thus enabling resistance and engendering creativity. A sense of humor or irony may also loosen up the space around thetic discourses, as Joan's self-satire shows. Every voice participates by becoming also an *ear* receptive to other voices in formulating a response. The process entails going within to that blank but active margin of the page where an unseen hand inscribes the next mark, as all these authors maintain in their different ways: Woolf, in the fluid metaphor of waves oscillating to find equilibrium through lifetimes of Day and Night against oceanic timelessness; Lessing, in the task of renovating the rooms where identities reside, unblocking passageways, adding on new rooms, and altering plans to suit contingencies in collaboration with collective resident voices; and Atwood, in marking the pages of self-narrative with the nonviolent duality of humorous iconoclasm on one hand and serious counterpower on the other.

In all their narratives, a sustainable dialogic process is associated with recycling old forms into new, which is the most difficult part, because giving up familiar notions, even when they are oppressive, is threatening. While breaking deeply encrusted shells of self-images may be painful, it is sometimes necessary for an even deeper sustainability. A dialogic self has to be ready to retire whatever has outlived its usefulness, to notice the signs of decay and watch for new sources of being. Thus, the dialogic process suggests a kind of immortality by accepting mortality. Bernard discovers this when, confronted by the death of his body, he feels the wave of a new dawn propel him courageously into the unknown. Although this looks a great deal like salvation, as preached by various religions, it is different in that no specific predictions can be made, or dogmatic explanations given, or knowledge of an afterworld claimed. It depends on open-mindedness and inclusiveness rather than excluding sinful others by an elect, and it depends on valuing this world as much as any other.[9]

Having been constituted by the world, the dialogic self may reconstitute the world, in turn. Transformations of society into more sustainable modes would depend upon individuals internalizing a dialogic process that contributes to the continual reconstruction of relationships as part of the self. Locating responsibility for transforming society has become the latest response to postmodern uncertainty. If responsibility is conceived primarily as *inner*, the province of the individual, then civil liberties appear paramount, and the government or majority must be restrained to safeguard them. If conceived as *outer*, as in cultures that consider private thoughts to be woven into the common fabric (or, as Lessing would put it, her thought is not hers, but "a thought around"), then the community becomes paramount, and the individual must be restrained to keep from tearing that web. The challenge is to balance these approaches, for violations either way destroy both the individual and the society: if society is too heavy-handed on the individual, it destroys the social web because it destroys its websites. This is Bauer's thesis of failed communities who suppress voices from that precious margin between the stable center of the known (tradition) and the infinite possibilities of the human mind to revitalize it.[10] On the other hand, when individuals impose their "rights" or causes on others without it being reciprocal, they damage themselves as well and make it more difficult to maintain the very liberties they supposedly cherish. From the dialogic view, responsibility is distributed at every level of human interaction, from private to public, from local to global. The relations among every sector of society—government, business, academe, nonprofit organizations, neighborhoods, families, and so on—are now being renegotiated to solve the problems that beset us. The call is out for more civil debate, with less partisan acrimony and attachment to ideological formulas, in order to encourage maximum participation and creative thinking. We are publicly beginning to dismantle the dichotomy between individualism and social responsibility.

Negotiating that dichotomy, however, has pitfalls that may require historical perspective, as in the case of the oppressed, who, when first liberated, seem self-centered because they carry the baggage of past deprivation. For example, the feminist and multicultural movements, which have been opening up the process to those who have been too long denied their due, have a streak that is becoming problematical even to their adherents. We are in a stage where pent-up repression stridently preaches resistance to the dominant other—a necessary first step, but only one in a series of liberating responses, as Atwood suggests in *Survival*. At the same time, the postmodern dismantling of the subject seems to be at cross-purposes with identity politics. For instance, the study of literature is now fraught with uncertainty about the role of a teacher or scholar in opening up dialogue with noncanonical work and with readers from different backgrounds. The politically correct assumption that one can only speak from an identifiable cultural position, a kind of ethnic, gender, racial, or class essentialism, is muddied by the postmodern injunction to perform a position that doubts all identities and authorities. Yet many thinkers are finding innovative ways of navigating through the clashing waves of postmodernism and feminist or multicultural-identity politics.[11]

Indeed, the practice of interpreting literature has always entailed meeting another in a space that is neither wholly determined by the text nor wholly by the reader, where every reading intersects with the world beyond the text as an appositional misreading because the experience of the writer is never exactly recreated in the reader's mind. As we frankly acknowledge that we are always outsiders to the text and to the experience of other readers, and even to our own text at some levels, all that we can legitimately sustain is the process of contacting other minds, thereby realizing the multiplicity of all our positions and increasing the likelihood of transforming everyone involved to some extent. That includes the continued cross-fertilization between literary studies and other fields. When finding common ground is uppermost, we can overlook differences and create unities; but when differences make a difference, we can overlook commonalities to draw important distinctions. The way out of either-or positions is to value differences as contributions to the joint creative process.

In practice, dialogue and monologue are in a deconstructive dance with each other; every "voice" of the dialogue is a limited monologue, while every monologue grows out of past dialogues. Monologue becomes dangerous only when it destroys the relational balance by stepping on its partners' toes or going beyond its time and place to try to circumscribe the music. Our tendency when enthralled with our own power or "truth" to lose sight of our limitations, or when enthralled by helplessness to lose sight of our power and truth, must be resisted at first, but more than that. If a dialogic sense of self were available as a "thought around," it might facilitate the release of a monologic trance, like Martha's transcendent view arising from time to time to snap her out of immersion in conditionality, and in turn, her conditionality arising to land her back from outer space. As a technology of self that resists systemization, a dialogic view can be no more than just "in the air," for institutionalizing it would be its undoing. The telling of dialogic stories, such as those retold in these pages, may be the best way to keep it afloat. One by one, each of us will have to test whether the dialogic self has validity and to what extent it can be realized, recognizing that there is no formula, no ideal configuration of monologic and dialogic forces, in one's unique path. Only if we discover how the dialogic principle may be operational in our lives will it be self-sustaining.

Notes

INTRODUCTION

1. Michel Foucault, *The History of Sexuality*, trans. Robert Hurley, 3 vols. (New York: Pantheon, 1978) and *Technologies of the Self: A Seminar with Michel Foucault*, ed. Luther H. Hartin et al. (Amherst: University of Massachusetts Press, 1988). A good example of Foucault's method of tracing the genealogy of power discourses is in his *History of Sexuality*. In *Technologies of Self*, his analyses rely upon tracing power discourses in various contexts of self-formulation.

2. Kenneth Gergen, *The Saturated Self: Dilemmas of Identity in Contemporary Life* (New York: Basic Books, 1991).

3. See for example, Christopher Lasch, *The Culture of Narcissism* (New York: Warner, 1979). In this popular book, Lasch decries the loss of community and civic values in the deterioration of twentieth-century individualism.

4. Gergen, *Saturated Self*, 224; Alasdair MacIntyre, *After Virtue*, 2d ed. (Notre Dame, Ind.: University of Notre Dame Press, 1984).

5. The term *individual* will only designate the unique single member of a species or category (such as a human being), without attributing to it a unified essence as the romantic notion of *individualism* implies. *Transpersonal* or *interpersonal* will refer to the relationship between individuals as opposed to *intrapsychic*, which will refer to the relationships and discourses the individual assimilates into the self-narrative.

6. Mikhail Bakhtin, "Discourse in the Novel," in *The Dialogic Imagination: Four Essays*, ed. Michael Holquist, trans. Caryl Emerson and Michael Holquist (Austin: University of Texas Press, 1981).

7. Simone de Beauvoir, *The Second Sex*, trans. and ed. H. M. Parshley (New York: Bantam, 1961).

8. By this definition even a matriarchy could be "patriarchal" except for a masculine-feminine reversal.

9. See Leo Tolstoy, "Tolstoy's Criticism on 'The Darling'" (from "Readings for Every Day in the Year"), in "TD," 23–28.

10. The term *subject* is used in this sentence to mean one dominated by, *subjected* to, the rule of another, as distinct from the sense it is generally used in this discussion. See below.

11. The term *subjectivity* will be used here to designate a single point of view, attitude, position, or discourse that is perceived or conceived, allowing for multiple and even contradictory subjectivities to be maintained at different levels of consciousness within an indi-

vidual person or group relationship. The term "mobile subjectivities," coined by Kathy Ferguson, suggests the ability to switch subject-positions in one's self-narrative. Seminar in "Genealogy and Gender," International Summer Institute for Semiotic and Structural Studies, University of Hawaii, June 1991. Thus, subjectivity is not defined here as some single irreducible solipsistic observer like the Cartesian subject split between itself and the world as its object, or, expanding upon that, the metaphysical Kantian construct of a universal ground or presence that can never itself be apprehended. Such transcendental subjectivities appear to arise because a relationship of difference always seems to exist between what is and what is not, which the linearity of subject-object grammar enforces. Hence a knower, experiencer, observer, or subject outside what is perceived can always be postulated. In this discussion the term *subjectivity* will *combine* the idea of the observer and the observed for every conceivable position. Thus, *what* Olenka is aware of (the observed) also serves to locate her subject-position as an observer. It is only for the sake of analysis, especially in connection with "transcendental" states of mind that are constructed as experiential, that *subjectivity* will be used provisionally as if split from its object.

12. Jacques Derrida, *Dissemination*, trans. Barbara Johnson (Chicago: University of Chicago Press, 1981).

13. Gergen refers to James P. Carse, *Finite and Infinite Games* (New York: Macmillan, 1986), in which a finite game is defined as playing by conventional rules and boundaries seriously to win, while the infinite game is defined as playing only in order to continue playing, and is thus free to alter rules and boundaries. He quotes Carse: "Finite players play *within* boundaries; infinite players play *with* boundaries [my italics]." *Saturated Self*, 197.

14. Barbara Herrnstein Smith, *Contingencies of Value: Alternative Perspectives for Critical Theory* (Cambridge: Harvard University Press, 1988), 150–56.

15. See, for example, Toril Moi, *Sexual/Textual Politics: Feminist Literary Theory* (New York: Methuen, 1985), 13.

16. Ibid.

17. Carol Gilligan, "In a Different Voice: Women's Conceptions of Self and Morality," in *The Future of Difference*, ed. Hester Eisenstein and Alice Jardine, Barnard College Women's Center (Boston: G. K. Hall, 1980), 274–317.

18. Robin Tolmach Lakoff, *Language and Woman's Place* (New York: Harper, 1975); Deborah Tannen, *You Just Don't Understand: Women and Men in Conversation* (New York: Morrow, 1990). Tannen's project seems to be directed not to demonstrating a kind of cultural essentialism, but rather to exposing the hidden assumptions of both men and women that judge the other sex by their own cultural attitudes without recognizing that they have differences. While bringing those differences to public attention may seem to be neutral as to which sex's attitudes are preferable, her purpose is to promote intersex dialogue and understanding, which will probably cause shifts in values on both sides.

19. Eileen Schlee, "The Subject is Dead, Long Live the Female Subject!" *Feminist Issues* 13, no. 2 (fall 1993): 70–79.

20. Rita Felski, *Beyond Feminist Aesthetics* (Cambridge: Harvard University Press, 1989), 73.

21. Feminists who explicitly theorize subjectivity as dialogic include Dale M. Bauer, who shows the price society pays in disregarding women's divergent voices. *Feminist Dialogics: A Theory of Failed Community* (Albany: State University of New York Press, 1988). Bauer also edited a collection with Susan Jaret McKinstry, in which most articles focus on resisting patriarchal authority. *Feminism, Bakhtin and the Dialogic*, Feminist Criticism and Theory Series (Albany: State University of New York Press, 1991). Going beyond resistance, Judy Little

shows how her women authors engage traditional forms and discourses, not in opposition to them, but in *apposition*, as she puts it, to create new hybrids. *The Experimental Self: Dialogic Subjectivity in Woolf, Pym and Brooke-Rose* (Carbondale: Southern Illinois University Press, 1996). In a similar vein, Mae Gwendolyn Henderson supports Felski's insight of taking advantage of tensions within and among cultural discourses to form innovative alliances for provisional purposes. "Speaking in Tongues: Dialogics, Dialectics, and the Black Woman Writer's Literary Tradition," in *Feminists Theorize the Political,* ed. Judith Butler and Joan W. Scott (New York: Routledge, 1992).

22.   Diana Fuss, *Essentially Speaking: Feminism, Nature and Difference* (New York: Routledge, 1989); Gayatari Chakravorty Spivak, *Interviews, Strategies, Dialogues,* ed. Sarah Harasym (New York: Routledge, 1990), 51.

23.   Sigmund Freud, *The Basic Writings of Sigmund Freud,* trans. A. A. Brill (New York: Modern Library, 1938).

24.   See, for example, Arnold Mindell, *Working with the Dreaming Body* (Boston: Routledge & Kegan Paul, 1985). Mindell's approach, closer to the Jungian than the Freudian school, incorporates shamanistic elements in a "process" or "dreambody" method whereby patients are encouraged to articulate their own imagery and meanings without being interpreted through the analyst's preconceived theory or having to "adjust" to any agenda of normalcy.

25.   Jacques Lacan, *Ecrits: A Selection,* trans. A. Sheridan (New York: Norton, 1977).

26.   Carl G. Jung, *The Portable Jung,* ed. Joseph Campbell (New York: Viking, 1971).

27.   Wendy Hollway, *Subjectivity and Method in Psychology: Gender, Meaning and Science* (London: Sage, 1989).

28.   Francis Jacques, *Difference and Subjectivity: Dialogue and Personal Identity,* trans. Andrew Rothwell (New Haven: Yale University Press, 1991).

29.   For a comparative study of Mead and Jewish philosopher Martin Buber, who propounded a social, dialogic self that also included a relationship to God, in contrast to Mead's secular theory, see Paul E. Pfuetze, *The Social Self* (New York: Bookman, 1954). Pfuetze's treatment is illuminating because he presents the strengths and weaknesses of both fairly.

30.   Ibid., 239–42.

31.   Paul Smith, *Discerning the Subject* (Minneapolis: University of Minnesota Press, 1988), 16. Smith takes the term "interpellation" from Louis Althusser, "Ideology and State Apparatus," in *Lenin and Philosophy* (New York: Monthly Review Press, 1971).

32.   Charles Taylor, *Sources of the Self: The Making of the Modern Identity* (Cambridge: Harvard University Press, 1989).

33.   Smith, *Contingencies of Value,* 101–2, 152ff.

34.   Spivak, *Interviews, Strategies, Dialogues,* 44.

35.   See MacIntyre, *After Virtue,* 154. This virtue may also correspond to the idea of right action in Confucian and Zen Buddhist practices, where spontaneity of action is emphasized rather than exercise of intellect and judgment, although it is a spontaneity that occurs only after long discipline. See Thomas P. Kasulis, *Zen Action / Zen Person* (Honolulu: University Press of Hawaii, 1981) and Wei-Ming Tu, *Confucian Thought: Selfhood and Creative Transformation* (Albany: State University of New York Press, 1985).

36.   Smith, *Contingencies of Value,* 148.

37.   Ibid., 119.

38.   Mikhail Bakhtin, *Problems of Dostoevsky's Poetics,* ed. and trans. Caryl Emerson (Minneapolis: University of Minnesota Press, 1984).

39.   John Keats, "To George and Thomas Keats," in *Critical Theory Since Plato,* ed. Hazard

Adams (San Diego: Harcourt Brace Jovanovich, 1971), 474; Anne K. Mellor, *English Romantic Irony* (Cambridge: Harvard University Press, 1980), 77, 86.

40. Mellor, *English Romantic Irony*, 7ff.; Lillian R. Furst, *Fictions of Romantic Irony* (Cambridge: Harvard University Press, 1984), 24ff.

41. Furst, *Fictions of Romantic Irony*, 34–35.

42. David J. Gouwens, *Kierkegaard's Dialectic of the Imagination* (New York: Peter Lang, 1989), 73–74; idem, *Kierkegaard as Religious Thinker* (New York: Cambridge University Press, 1996), 75–121.

43. See Gabriele Schwab, *Subjects without Selves: Transitional Texts in Modern Fiction* (Cambridge: Harvard University Press, 1994). Schwab claims that (post)modernist literature legitimizes unconscious scanning as a mode of knowledge, enabling readers to more readily enter the "transitional" state between linear and global modes. Her thesis seems to be corroborated in the popular media by news reporter Jack Wheat, who cites University of Florida professor Gregory Ulmer's claim that people who "channel surf" have an MTV kind of literacy that enables them to process information from visual and audio texts much more efficiently than from print. Wheat also reports that according to Roger Drury, an English teacher at Georgia Tech, students who regularly watch MTV were more receptive to T. S. Eliot's "The Waste Land" than previous generations. "Prof: MTV Rekindling Intellectual Growth," *Honolulu Advertiser*, 18 September 1994.

44. Julia Kristeva, *The Kristeva Reader*, ed. Toril Moi (New York: Columbia University Press, 1987).

45. Judith Butler, *Gender Trouble: Feminism and the Subversion of Identity* (New York: Routledge, 1990).

46. For example, *smoke* can be a sign of *fire*, which, in turn, can be a sign of destruction and pain or usefulness and pleasure, depending on the context rather than on any one meaning.

47. Of course, in any given local situation the negotiation may result in one side prevailing if no different alternative emerges, but this is the distinction between a finite game and an infinite one. A dialogic paradigm allows both.

CHAPTER 1. THE CONCEPT OF SELF IN VIRGINIA WOOLF'S LIFE AND WORK

1. Nancy Chodorow, *The Reproduction of Mothering: Psychoanalysis and the Sociology of Gender* (Berkeley: University of California Press, 1978). As Roberta Rubenstein observes in referring to Chodorow, female territory can be conceived as outside patriarchy, inside its own sphere, or borderline, capable of either including or excluding—or all of the above, depending on attitude. *Boundaries of the Self: Gender, Culture, Fiction* (Urbana: University of Illinois Press, 1987), 238.

2. Moi rightly takes issue with Woolf critics such as Herbert Marder, who glorify Mrs. Ramsay for being an androgynous ideal, while she agrees with Carolyn Heilbrun, who considers Mrs. Ramsay to be as one-sided as her husband. Moi, *Sexual/Textual Politics*, 14–15; Herbert Marder, *Feminism and Art: A Study of Virginia Woolf* (Chicago: University of Chicago Press, 1968); Carolyn Heilbrun, *Toward a Recognition of Androgyny* (New York: Knopf, 1973).

3. Frances Restuccia, "'Untying the Mother Tongue': Female Difference in Virginia Woolf's *A Room of One's Own*," *Tulsa Studies in Women's Literature* 4 (fall 1985): 262–63.

4. Butler, *Gender Trouble*. Like Foucault, Butler sees no way out of discourses and the power games they entail. She criticizes Wittig for returning to a universal Kantian subject for women as well as men, as if the "subject" existed outside of discourse, and Irigaray for positing a "female sexuality" that existed outside of discourse. In regarding sex as a social construct rather than a biological given that precedes discourse, Butler would go further than Woolf, who accepted a biological sex identity as prior to discourse, but only objected to culturally gendered attributes. My position is that the construction of sex is itself the product of a "dialogue" between the semiotic and the symbolic.

5. Ibid., 127.

6. As an example of the arbitrariness of gendered traits, Nancy Topping Bazin relates the feminine in Woolf's work with solidity, that is, what is eternal, and the masculine with the shifting fluidity of time, reversing the gendered traits from the ego-boundary theory discussed here. Yet Bazin contradicts these gender traits in her quotes from *To the Lighthouse* that show Mrs. Ramsay's feminine idea of the lighthouse is "a silvery misty-looking tower" (fluid?) in contrast to Mr. Ramsay's masculine idea of it as "the tower, stark and straight" (solid?). *Virginia Woolf and the Androgynous Vision* (New Brunswick, N.J.: Rutgers University Press, 1973), 46.

7. Virginia Woolf, "Women and Fiction," in *Collected Essays* (London: Hogarth, 1966), 2:141–48. In that essay Woolf uses "personal" to mean private rather than public, pertaining to the particular individual, especially the ego.

8. Quentin Bell and Roger Poole attribute her problems to early psychological trauma, the former accepting her diagnosis as "insane," while the latter rejecting it in favor of a kind of Laingian "sanity." Bell, *Virginia Woolf: A Biography* (London: Hogarth, 1972); Poole, *The Unknown Virginia Woolf* (Cambridge: Cambridge University Press, 1978); R. D. Laing, *The Politics of Experience* and *The Bird of Paradise* (Harmondsworth, U.K.: Penguin, 1967). Thomas Caramagno, however, argues convincingly for a primary diagnosis of clinical manic-depression (a genetic affliction), compounded by psychological trauma, and claims she was both sane and insane in her multiplicity. *The Flight of the Mind: Virginia Woolf's Art and Manic-Depressive Illness* (Berkeley: University of California Press, 1992).

9. Woolf does not use "being" here in contrast to "non-being" the way "self" might contrast to "not-self" as an inclusion-exclusion concept. Instead, she means *being* as a state of mind in touch with that underlying reality glimpsed in the moment as opposed to the dull "cotton wool" state of not being in touch with it.

10. Charles Taylor calls for such an art when he advocates "order through personal resonance"; that is, instead of the enunciation of a cosmic order as an official public ideology, the modern self would be the locus for experiencing and articulating a personal vision of order. *Sources of the Self*, 511.

11. Little's claim that Woolf was "unsuccessfully socialized" by not accommodating to patriarchal demands on a woman's ego (*Experimental Self*, 21, 31–32) resonates with Bauer's thesis in *Feminist Dialogics* of failed societies that do not allow divergent women's voices into a dialogue with dominant discourses. Yet Little recognizes that Woolf embraced the male literary tradition and thought back through the fathers as much as the mothers without, however, sharing the "anxiety of influence" of male writers (*Experimental Self*, 37). Without the imperative to "find her own voice," Woolf was free to interact with traditional discourses impersonally to produce dialogic outcomes rather than an egocentric style. (See introduction, n. 21.)

12. Bell, *Biography*. The death of her mother from what Woolf felt was too much self-sacrifice precipitated her first major breakdown; other family deaths—her half-sister Stella,

who was a young bride, her brother Thoby in his prime, and her father from cancer—precipitated some degree of imbalance, although she also showed remarkable strength during some of those times.

13. She expresses a similar view of illness in her essay "On Being Ill" in *The Moment and Other Essays* (New York: Harcourt, 1948).

14. Septimus's case is an example of how Woolf tried to work out in fiction her understanding of "madness" as she herself experienced it. Poole's thesis is that her symptoms were compounded by the misunderstanding of those closest to her, especially of her caring and caretaking husband Leonard, and of the medical practitioners attending her. She was not "mentally ill," Poole claims, but only repressed by Victorian morality and rationalist thinking that exacerbated her problems as she battled for her integrity as "sane." *Unknown Virginia Woolf.* While Woolf herself adopts the dominant discourse of "when I was mad" in referring to her aberrant states (*WD,* 169), her fiction bears out an intuitive striving to reach what is recognizably a Laingian position.

15. Woolf, "Modern Fiction," in *Collected Essays,* 2:103–10; "Mr. Bennett and Mrs. Brown," in *The Essays of Virginia Woolf,* vol. 3: *1919–1924* (London: Hogarth, 1988), 384–89.

16. A collection of essays relating the new scientific fields of "chaotics" to the humanities is N. Katherine Hayles, ed., *Chaos and Order: Complex Dynamics in Literature and Science* (Chicago: University of Chicago Press, 1991). One of the principles in chaotics is that local, marginal events may produce large-scale effects.

17. Although I agree with Rita Felski in *Beyond Feminist Aesthetics* that the formal properties of narrative have no direct connection to their political content or with whether they may be used to support or subvert a given ideology, I would still argue that any form that strikes the mind with fresh insight has the power of a fine match between form and content. In this case, the fresh form is the child's-eye view and what undermines authority is not this form per se but its perfect suitability to the absurd *content* of exactly what feet of clay one's idols have. As in Swift's *Gulliver's Travels,* the device of altering size and/or level lends itself to satire here.

18. Bazin comments on the cubist influence on Woolf's style, rather than the impressionist, because of the multifaceted treatment of content. *Androgynous Vision,* 144.

19. Woolf's poetic fiction, for example in the rhythmic quality of *The Waves,* illustrates Kristeva's theory of the sensory, preoedipal "semiotic" dimension of language as concurrent with the symbolic dimension.

20. Poole cites an empirical study of Woolf's style and concludes, "[W]hen the references [to water] are counted, they do empirically predominate over all other images from the natural world taken together." *Unknown Virginia Woolf,* 260.

21. Woolf would not have considered herself Shakespeare's equal in actual accomplishment, however, according to a diary entry while writing *The Waves,* which she felt to be her most challenging and visionary novel to date: "[compared to Shakespeare] This is not 'writing' at all" (*WD,* 157).

22. Rubenstein, *Boundaries of the Self,* 238.

CHAPTER 2. *THE WAVES*

1. In trying to finish *The Waves,* Woolf notes in her diary that she needs "a tremendous discussion, in which every life shall have its voice—a mosaic: the difficulty is . . . I have not yet mastered the speaking voice" (*WD,* 156).

2. Jean O. Love, *Worlds in Consciousness: Mythopoetic Thought in the Novels of Virginia Woolf* (Berkeley: University of California Press, 1970).

3. In a diary entry Woolf tells her intention in the interludes: "I hope to have kept the sound of the sea and the birds, dawn and garden subconsciously present, doing their work underground" (*WD*, 169).

4. Makiko Minow-Pinkney has a somewhat different angle on the tensions between unity and diversity in the style of *The Waves*, using Kristeva's theory of the features of language that counter one another: the thetic tendency toward unity, coherence, and completion, and the semiotic tendency toward open-ended, multiple evocativeness. *Virginia Woolf and the Problem of the Subject* (Brighton, U.K.: Harvester Press, 1987).

5. Perhaps her friend, the socialite Lady Ottoline Morrell, had some of this quality of extravagant flaunting of her "person" (in the old-fashioned sense of body). Bell, *Biography*.

6. Woolf acknowledges some people take her for a "sapphist" from her writing (WD, 148); perhaps, for example, from Clarissa Dalloway's appreciation of women the way men might (*MD*, 46–47), and from Lily Briscoe's infatuation with Mrs. Ramsay *(TTL)*. Bell, Poole, and Caramagno discuss her infatuation with various women in her life, especially speculating on her relationship with Vita Sackville-West, on whom her fictitious biography of *Orlando* is based. Caramagno credits her with probably knowing sexual passion even though repulsed by male power. *Flight of the Mind*, 144–45.

7. Woolf was captivated by Greek and studied it assiduously with tutors and on her own. Bell, *Biography*.

8. Woolf may not have had much patience with infants, but she loved children and envied her sister Vanessa's maternal fulfillment. Bell, *Biography*. Poole claims that she felt cheated of the chance to have children because of the diagnosis of mental illness and unfitness. *Unknown Virginia Woolf*.

9. Woolf and her full siblings formed the core of a group of intellectuals who became increasingly avant-garde and sexually liberated in their views (and even behavior, with adulterous flirtations and even affairs, or little escapades like Woolf's skinny-dipping with a male friend), shocking all their conventional relatives, including their half-brothers George and Gerald Duckworth, who preserved rigid moralistic facades. Their circle included a number of homosexuals, including Lytton Strachey, who stumbled into a brief engagement with Woolf when they both were thinking of marriage as a way to consolidate their friendship and gain the cover of a conventional status without having heterosexual demands put on them. Bell, *Biography*.

10. Neville's delight in simple things might be compared by Judy Little to Barbara Pym's discourse of the ordinary. Little, *Experimental Self*. Little might agree that Neville can better *feminize* his poetry, to use her term, in contrast to Louis's patriarchal construction of his poetic ambitions in the grand "master narrative" tradition.

11. This is not the only place in the text where Woolf associates a tree with eternity. Later Bernard observes that a tree represents something lasting, the only living thing that is stable (*W*, 349). The eternity of a tree therefore only emphasizes human mortality, accounting for Neville's "moment of being," which is almost exactly like Woolf's account of what she herself experienced with a tree after hearing of the suicide of a neighbor (*MB*, 71). The puddle Rhoda cannot cross is another one of Woolf's experiences (*MB*, 78).

12. Ruth Porritt, "Surpassing Derrida's Deconstructed Self: Virginia Woolf's Poetic Disarticulation of the Self," *Women's Studies* 2 (1992): 323–38.

13. Here Woolf reverses the real-life situation in that Percival, like Jacob, who is based on her brother Thoby, is the outsider brought home rather than being the "brother" who does the bringing. Thoby died in his prime as Percival and Jacob do. Bell, *Biography*.

14. Kathy J. Phillips, *Virginia Woolf Against Empire* (Knoxville: University of Tennessee Press, 1994); Minow-Pinkney, *Problem of the Subject*; Maria diBattista, *Virginia Woolf's Major Novels: The Fables of Anon* (New Haven: Yale University Press, 1980).

15. As an example of Thoby's high spirits, Bell recounts how Woolf joined Thoby and a group of friends in a bold prank on the British Navy in which they dressed up as Abyssinian emissaries—and got away with it. *Biography*, 157–61. Perhaps Woolf had that adventure in mind when Bernard speculates that Percival would have "shocked the authorities."

16. Schwab endorses an orderly process within the global unconscious, rather than equating the semiotic with chaos, to account for the communicative power of poetry. She draws upon the aesthetic theory of Anton Ehrenzweig (*The Hidden Order of Art* [Berkeley: University of California Press, 1967]), which posits a creative order of the unconscious that scans chaos more efficiently than linear consciousness, yet is always interacting with linearity to give poetry both symbolic (thetic) and semiotic power. Schwab, *Subjects without Selves*, 11–16.

This theorizes my point that Percival conveys semiotic as well as patriarchal power by representing an order beyond conventional linear thinking, which comes close to Schwab's view of him in her chapter 4 entitled "Interior Dialogue in *The Waves*."

17. Bazin notes that Woolf's experiences of cosmic wholeness seem to be related to her manic states, while her experiences of cosmic anarchy seem related to her depressed states; presumably, between the two lie states of ordinariness, or cotton wool. *Androgynous Vision*.

18. James Naremore, *The World Without a Self* (New Haven: Yale University Press, 1973), 182.

19. Amélie Rorty defines "presences" as literary entities distinct from "characters," "figures," "persons," and so forth in that "Presences . . . are evoked rather than represented." "A Literary Postscript: Characters, Persons, Selves, Individuals," in *The Identities of Persons*, ed. Amélie Oksenberg Rorty (Berkeley: University of California Press, 1976), 79. She goes on to define them as "a mode of attending, being present to their experiences, without dominating or controlling them. It is precisely the absence of wilfulness, or choice of roles . . . that makes [one] present, with immense gravity and density, to his experiences . . . their lives are not revealed on any surface. Their powers are always magnetic, always at service, but never centered. . . . Though others respond strongly to the quality . . . of the mood they induce, they are not agents" (93–94). They cannot be imitated because they are endowed by "a grace . . . beyond striving" (94). Her models are the great "Russian souls" whom Woolf also admired. Percival seems to be a hybrid between Rorty's concepts of a "presence" and an epic "figure."

20. Diane Price Herndl, "The Dilemmas of a Feminist Dialogic," in *Feminism, Bakhtin and the Dialogic*, ed. Dale M. Bauer and Susan Jaret McKinstry (Albany: State University of New York Press, 1991), 20.

21. Charles Taylor argues against "neo-Nietzschean" theories such as Derrida's and Foucault's since they take a metaposition of no-position, i.e., nothing is true, only "constructed" by language or power, which metaposition is untenable for a situated self. He claims deconstructionists overlook their own positive valorization of their disengaged outlook in contrast to Nietzsche's boldly inconsistent yea-saying to the will to power. While Taylor also acknowledges the constructed self, he affirms the search for constructs that mold the self according to the "Best [moral] Account" (the "BA principle"), to be arrived at genealogically and dialogically. However, while he criticizes modern moral theorists for suppressing or denying conflicting accounts that remain in the collective (un)conscious, he himself does not explicitly acknowledge that deconstruction has contributed to his own *process* of arriving at his BA by being a conflicting account to wrest it from. Indeed, his search for the

"highest" moral constructs to live by as "substantive" values rather than "procedural" values (e.g., utilitarian, instrumental values) turns his BA principle into a static ideal that obscures it as a dynamic process. He seems to prefer a modern identity arrested in static terms of what one *is* (having principles) rather than what one *does* (acting on them in complex contexts). Taylor, *Sources of Self.*

22. Butler reiterates that the grammar of the cogito produces the effect of an originary and substantial subject. *Gender Trouble,* 20–21.

23. Caramagno, *Flight of the Mind,* 152. Thomas Moore would agree, since he defines the "soul" as a multidimensional dialogic construct that goes far beyond the ego to include the rest of the mundane and spiritual world in an artful interplay. *Care of the Soul* (New York: Harper, 1992).

24. In accordance with my position, Butler advocates suspending the articulation of identity until a specific context arises that allows it to emerge spontaneously. *Gender Trouble.* This would be the "procedural" response to Taylor's "substantive" values forming identity. *Sources of Self.* Not that such a procedure necessarily denies substantive values, or even a hierarchy of values like Aristotle's, but rather, like Aristotle, holds all substantive goods in a state of reserved readiness. Indeed, Aristotle's supergood of *phronesis* is the "substantive" valorization of a "procedure," the science (or art) of selecting values commensurate with the occasion.

25. The anonymous medieval poem Louis quotes can be found in *The Norton Anthology of English Literature,* 5th ed. (New York: Norton, 1986), 1:311.

26. Friedrich Nietzsche, "The Genealogy of Morals," in *Basic Writings of Nietzsche,* trans. and ed. Walter Kaufmann (New York: Modern Library, 1968).

27. Woolf, "Professions for Women," in *Collected Essays,* 2:288.

28. Anne Herrmann, *The Dialogic and Difference: "An/Other Woman" in Virginia Woolf and Christa Wolf* (New York: Columbia University Press, 1989).

CHAPTER 3. THE CONCEPT OF SELF IN DORIS LESSING'S LIFE AND WORK

1. Florence Howe, "A Conversation with Doris Lessing (1966)," in *Doris Lessing: Critical Studies,* ed. Annis Pratt and L. S. Dembo (Madison: University of Wisconsin Press, 1974), 3.

2. Ellen Goodman attributes Lessing's "hoax" on the publishing world to a need to confirm her own talent without riding on her fame, rather than to her stated motive of exposing those publishers who would have accepted the work as Doris Lessing's, but not as an unknown's. (Soon after, she published both novels as *The Diaries of Jane Somers* under her own name.) Lessing herself admits her incognito authorship was for redefining herself, not so much to confirm her talent, but to try to deviate from her tone as Doris Lessing. Yet Lessing aficionados like Carey Kaplan somehow recognized Lessing in "Jane Somers's" work. Ellen Goodman, "The Doris Lessing Hoax," *Doris Lessing Newsletter* (hereafter *DLN*) 9 (spring 1985): 3; Lessing's talk on Jane Somers, *DLN* 10 (spring 1986): 3–5; Carey Kaplan, review of *The Diaries of Jane Somers, Diary of a Good Neighbor* and *If the Old Could. . .* [original italics] by Jane Somers [Doris Lessing], *DLN* 9 (spring 1985): 4.

3. Carey Kaplan and Ellen Cronan Rose, eds., *Doris Lessing: The Alchemy of Survival* (Athens: Ohio University Press, 1988), 3. The ellipses are in the original.

4. In addition to Lessing's own autobiographical books and essays, such as *In Pursuit of the English, Going Home,* and *Under My Skin,* which are reflected in her fiction, nearly every

commentator on Lessing makes this point in biographical sketches of her. See Mona Knapp, *Doris Lessing* (New York: Ungar, 1984); Jean Pickering, *Understanding Doris Lessing* (Columbia: University of South Carolina Press, 1990); Ruth Whitaker, *Doris Lessing*, Modern Novelists (New York: St. Martin's, 1988). Also, Claudia Dee Seligman documents the autobiographical facts in Lessing's work in "The Autobiographical Novels of Doris Lessing" (Ph.D. dissertation, Tufts University, 1976), abstract in *Dissertation Abstracts International* 37 (1976): 1544A. Claire Sprague emphasizes how the doubling of Lessing's characters is signaled by her giving them names with the same initial letters as her family, so that her own middle name *May* becomes Martha, Mark, Molly; her father's name *Alfred* becomes Anna, Anton, etc. *Rereading Doris Lessing: Narrative Patterns of Doubling and Repetition* (Chapel Hill: University of North Carolina Press, 1987).

5. Ingrid Holmquist makes the point that unity with nature becomes a defense against the conventional thinking of society, or in other words, the *im*personal can counteract the *trans*personal (which point is itself in keeping with the conventional nature-society dichotomy). *From Society to Nature: A Study of Doris Lessing's "Children of Violence,"* Gothenburg Studies in English, no. 47 (Göteborg, Sweden: Acta Universitatus Gothoburgensis, 1980).

6. Ibid.

7. Victoria Middleton quotes this from Lessing's introduction to Olive Schreiner's *The Story of an African Farm*, which greatly influenced Lessing in her own articulation of her African experience as a white woman. "Doris Lessing's 'Debt' to Olive Schreiner," in Kaplan and Rose, *Alchemy of Survival*, 145.

8. Lessing is quoted by Nancy Joyner, "I find Virginia Woolf too much of a lady.... I feel that her experience must have been too limited, because there is always a point in her novels when I think, 'Fine, but look what you've left out.'" "The Underside of the Butterfly: Lessing's Debt to Woolf," *Journal of Narrative Technique* 5 (1974): 204–5.

9. Lynn Sukenick, "Feeling and Reason in Doris Lessing's Fiction," *Contemporary Literature* 14 (1973): 515–35.

10. Katherine Fishburn, "Teaching Doris Lessing as a Subversive Activity: A Response to the Preface to *The Golden Notebook*," in Kaplan and Rose, *Alchemy of Survival*, 81–92. Fishburn puts a positive Socratic spin on Lessing's gadfly didacticism.

11. Rotraut Spiegel, *Doris Lessing: The Problem of Alienation and the Form of the Novel* (Frankfort: Peter Lang, 1980), 49.

12. Frederick C. Stern, "Doris Lessing: The Politics of Radical Humanism," in Kaplan and Rose, *Alchemy of Survival* , 43. Stern charges Lessing and most world Communists and leftists (except Brecht) with having misunderstood Marx, leading to the mistakes of Communism and subsequent disillusionment. The turn to other ideologies, he implies, would be unnecessary with true Marxism.

13. That individual-collective relation corresponds to Hollway's intersecting axes of socially available discourses and the individual's particular history. *Subjectivity and Method.* Jeanne Murray Walker also uses the same analogy of two intersecting axes in her literary analysis of Lessing's work. "Memory and Culture within the Individual: The Breakdown of Social Exchange in *Memoirs of a Survivor*," in Kaplan and Rose, *Alchemy of Survival*, 93–114.

14. Lorna Sage, *Doris Lessing* (London: Methuen, 1983), 71.

15. Jonah Raskin, "Doris Lessing at Stony Brook: An Interview," *New American Review* 8 (1970): 170.

16. See Nancy Shields Hardin, "Doris Lessing and the Sufi Way," in *Doris Lessing: Critical Studies*, ed. Annis Pratt and L. S. Dembo (Madison: University of Wisconsin Press, 1974), 148–64; and idem, "The Sufi Teaching Story and Doris Lessing," *Twentieth Century*

Literature 23 (October 1977): 314–25. See also Ann Scott, "The More Recent Writings: Sufism, Mysticism and Politics," in *Notebooks/Memoirs/Archives: Reading and Rereading Doris Lessing*, ed. Jenny Taylor (Boston: Routledge, 1982), 164–90.

17. Bernd Dietz, and Fernando Galvan, "Entrevista: A Conversation with Doris Lessing," *DLN* 9 (spring 1985): 5–6, 13. The interview took place at Clare College, Cambridge, in July 1982.

18. Raskin interview. Italics in original.

19. See Lessing's essay "In the World, Not of It," in *A Small Personal Voice*.

20. Sprague, *Rereading Doris Lessing*.

21. Nicole Ward Jouve, "Of Mud and Other Matter—The *Children of Violence*," in Taylor, ed., *Notebooks/Memoirs/Archives*, 75–134.

22. To simulate the discourse of madness, Lessing has experimented, in her mythic "inner space" narrative *Briefing for a Descent into Hell* with a mixture of a poetic style (even metered in places), a dramatic-present tense, and a play format closer to *The Waves*. However, the "method" in her male protagonist's madness still lapses back (or perhaps is "elevated" by authorial intent) into a highly coherent and time-bound style in the preterite that turns him into an omniscient and didactic authorial mouthpiece in the midst of his visionary state.

23. Kaplan and Rose, *Alchemy of Survival*, 7, 7, 8.

24. For a similar view see Elaine Showalter, *A Literature of Their Own: British Women Novelists from Brontë to Lessing* (Princeton: Princeton University Press, 1977); and Jean Pickering, "Martha Quest and 'The Anguish of Feminine Fragmentation,'" in *Critical Essays on Doris Lessing*, ed. Claire Sprague and Virginia Tiger (Boston: G. K. Hall, 1986), 94–100.

25. Lessing, like many authors, feels her books are a lie because they omit so much and distort the experience she wants to convey. Howe, "Conversation."

26. Joan Didion, review of *Briefing for a Descent into Hell*, in Sprague and Tiger, eds., *Critical Essays on Doris Lessing*, 192–96.

27. Sprague and Tiger, eds., *Critical Essays on Doris Lessing*, introduction.

28. Pickering, "'Anguish of Feminine Fragmentation.'"

29. Kaplan and Rose, *Alchemy of Survival*, 10ff.

30. Eve Bertelsen, "Who is It Who Says 'I'?: The Persona of a Doris Lessing Interview," in Kaplan and Rose, *Alchemy of Survival*, 169–82.

31. Molly Hite, "Subverting the Ideology of Coherence: *The Golden Notebook* and *The Four-Gated City*," in Kaplan and Rose, *Alchemy of Survival*, 61–69.

CHAPTER 4. *CHILDREN OF VIOLENCE*

1. Mary Ann Singleton, *The City and the Veld: The Fiction of Doris Lessing* (Lewisburg, Pa.: Bucknell University Press, 1977).

2. Lessing did give up the two children (a boy and a girl) of her first marriage, but raised the son of her second marriage as a single mother.

3. For current popular psychology theories of the (wounded) "inner child," see John Bradshaw, *Homecoming: Reclaiming and Championing Your Inner Child* (New York: Bantam, 1990) and Alice Miller, *The Drama of the Gifted Child: The Search for the True Self* (New York: Basic Books, 1994).

4. Holmquist, *Society to Nature*.

5. Hollway notes how it is often through interpersonal dialogue that formerly sup-

pressed content becomes expressed (or vice versa), as speakers polarize each other taking positions, much as Martha also does with her mother, out of reverse psychology. *Subjectivity and Method.*

6. Sprague and Tiger, eds., *Critical Essays of Doris Lessing*, introduction.

7. Sally Robinson, *Engendering the Subject: Gender and Self-Representation*, Feminist Criticism and Theory Series (Albany: State University of New York Press, 1991). Since Robinson only deals with the nay-saying phases, she does not anticipate Martha's later yea-saying to formerly rejected "unreasonable selves." Gayle Greene comes closer to my view, claiming that Martha's nay-saying to conventional thinking (even while being held in its power) supports Lessing's position that the self can be distanced from social discourses through subjectivities beyond them, such as through a "universal consciousness" arising from communion with nature in "moments of being" on the veld. Such subjectivities seem "truer" and more reliable than those derived from social convention. *Doris Lessing: The Poetics of Change* (Ann Arbor: University of Michigan Press, 1994), chapter 4 on *Landlocked.*

8. For a discussion of Lessing's short stories being constructed by discourses of the subject's gaze, see Margaret Atack, "Towards a Narrative Analysis of *A Man and Two Women*," in Taylor, ed., *Notebooks/Memoirs/Archives*, 135–63.

9. Dagmar Barnouw, "Disorderly Company: From *The Golden Notebook* to *The Four-Gated City*," in Pratt and Dembo, eds., *Doris Lessing: Critical Studies*, 74–97.

10. The name "Anton Hesse" closely resembles Lessing's second husband's name, Gottfried Anton Lessing, while the name "Doug Knowell" is a semantic play on Lessing's first husband's name, Frank Wisdom (itself a play on the very qualities Lessing aspires to).

11. Howe, "Conversation."

12. Lorelei Cederstrom, *Fine-Tuning the Feminine Psyche: Jungian Patterns in the Novels of Doris Lessing*, vol. 99 of English Language and Literature, American University Studies, series 4 (New York: Peter Lang, 1990).

13. Spiegel, *The Problem of Alienation;* Robinson, *Engendering the Subject.*

14. It was not until Lessing wrote these passages that she gave the title to the whole series.

15. Scott points out that Sufism does not advocate falsifying the historical, as some mystical traditions do, but acknowledges the validity of both historical and ahistorical (mythic) modes. Scott, "The More Recent Writings."

16. I suspect that "Thomas Stern" is Lessing's allusion to T. S. Eliot—for the fragments he provided to shore her up against ruin, symbolized in Martha's returning to the roots of her tradition in England with Thomas's fragmented manuscript as a keepsake. The same intuition is implied in Greene's comment, "Thomas Stern ends—like the speaker in Thomas Stearns Eliot's *Waste Land*—able to 'connect / Nothing with Nothing.'" *Poetics of Change*, 60. Greene credits *Landlocked* as being a mythopoetic work about the destruction of an old, sterile order for Martha, with a hint of change in the coming of rain, as in *The Waste Land.*

17. Cederstrom, *Fine-Tuning the Feminine Psyche.*

18. Kaplan and Rose, *Alchemy of Survival*, introduction; Barnouw, "Disorderly Company." Seligman claims Lessing coalesces with Martha beginning in *Landlocked*, but is more detached in the first three volumes. "Autobiographical Novels."

19. Sprague, *Rereading Doris Lessing*, 100.

20. Roberta Rubenstein, *The Novelistic Vision of Doris Lessing: Breaking the Forms of Consciousness* (Urbana: University of Illinois Press, 1979). Rubenstein analyzes the self as three-storeyed: the public (society), the interpersonal (primary contacts), and the intrapsychic (within the individual).

21. Scott, "The More Recent Writings."

22. Sprague, concerned with women's self-effacement in *Rereading Doris Lessing*, nevertheless finds the multiple transpersonal selves of Martha in *Four-Gated City* a fascinating play of possibilities, not an effacement. Sprague, *Rereading Doris Lessing*. Similarly, Greene regards Martha's self-effacement as exemplifying the feminine "fluid boundary" theory of Chodorow in *Reproduction of Mothering*, and positively celebrates it as a necessary change—from the "outstanding" woman that writer Anna Wulf represents to the Everywoman Martha now represents, and from the self-/mother hater to the self-accepting matron. Greene maintains that Martha is now affirming feminine qualities required to transform society as well as self. That is, instead of traditional feminine virtues of endurance, renunciation, and compassion merely upholding the patriarchal status quo, such qualities need to be encouraged in men as well as women to sustain us through the hardships of change toward a better society. *Poetics of Change*, 24–28.

23. Scott speaks of a mystical trinity in "The More Recent Writings" where Absence is "the cloud of unknowing" in which not even the conscious observer is awake, that is, the utterly dark night self of complete forgetting, as in dreamless sleep, which Martha still keeps fighting, until her death.

24. Atack uses the term "surprise" to describe the subject's gaze upon the object-self in "Towards a Narrative Analysis."

25. Hite notes that Lessing has cleverly familiarized the discourse on the paranormal with Martha's pejorative labels like "dottiness" to enable the reader to overcome "the distaste factor" later when she herself breaks out of conventional thinking with her own experiences. "Subverting Ideology of Coherence," 66.

26. Martha's process here inclines toward some recent therapeutic methods in which the patient reprograms old psychic material by "editing" replays of past emotional scenes as a current observer. See Richard Bandler, *Using Your Brain—For a Change* (Moab, Utah: Real People Press, 1985), for a discussion of Neurolinguistic Programming (NLP) techniques, and Francine Shapiro, *Eye Movement Desensitization and Reprocessing: Basic Principles, Protocols, and Procedures* (New York: Guilford Press, 1995), for a discussion of the semihypnotic method of EMDR.

27. Barnouw claims Anna Wulf never does consciously seek her process, whereas in *FGC* "The concept of knowledge of the self as a process is consistently supported by narrative means." "Disorderly Company," 120.

28. Rubenstein, *Novelistic Vision*.

29. Sprague, *Rereading Doris Lessing*.

30. Whitaker, *Doris Lessing*.

31. Lessing emphasizes cultivating the cool, unemotional observer, which, according to Sufi teaching, is carefully disciplined to make fine distinctions that would be obscured by hot excitation, as she explains in "Learning How to Learn," *Asia* (July/August 1982): 12–15.

32. Rachel Blau-DuPlessis, *Writing Beyond the Ending: Narrative Strategies of Twentieth Century Women Writers* (Bloomington: Indiana University Press, 1985); Kaplan and Rose, *Alchemy of Survival*, introduction.

33. Lessing has commented on her own unsuitability for marriage, yet defends what women do as wives and mothers against attacks by feminists. Dietz and Galván, "Entrevista."

34. Holmquist, *Society to Nature*, 51.

35. Sprague would agree that Martha can never attain the goal of self-seeker in that "displacement, not arrival[,] is at the center of [Lessing's] imagination." *Rereading Doris Lessing*, 184.

36. Hannah Arendt, *Between Past and Future: Six Exercises in Political Thought* (New York: Viking, 1961).

37. Sage claims the whole novel is driven by that future, but I see it as the meeting-ground of both past and future, although Martha is not necessarily focused on the present and needs to be reminded of "here." *Doris Lessing.* Nicole Ward Jouve claims that Lessing is driven by past and future, unlike (e.g., French) feminists, who write from the present. "Doris Lessing: A 'Female Voice'—Past, Present or Future?," in Kaplan and Rose, *Alchemy of Survival,* 127–33.

38. Lessing seems to acknowledge that there is no inevitable evolution in her later novel *The Fifth Child,* in which an atavistic freak of nature, a monster of stupidity, amoral violence, and crude appetite, is loosed upon the world. Not only is he symbolic of our age, but of the element of chaos that can destroy even the most harmoniously inclined collective (like the loving family he is born into).

39. Lessing herself does have a sense of humor, which emerges better in her whimsical book, *In Pursuit of the English,* an autobiographical sketch about her early impressions of living among the eccentric English. And in the preface to the 1964 edition of her story collection, *This Was the Old Chief's Country,* she even supports "making comedy out of oppression." *Doris Lessing's Collected African Stories* (London: Michael Joseph, 1951), 1:7–8.

CHAPTER 5. THE CONCEPT OF SELF IN MARGARET ATWOOD'S LIFE AND WORK

1. Quoted in Sherill E. Grace, *Violent Duality: A Study of Margaret Atwood* (Montreal: Vehicule Press, 1980), 76, from a cassette recording by Hugh Barnett, Toronto, 1973, in which Atwood makes some remarks preliminary to a reading.

2. Valerie Miner, "Atwood in Metamorphosis: An Authentic Canadian Fairy Tale," in *Her Own Woman: Profiles of Ten Canadian Women.,* ed. Myrna Kostash et al. (Toronto: Macmillan, 1975), 192.

3. Atwood explains her rationale for a Canadian identity in an interview: "I think the reason for wanting to have a Canada is that you do not agree with some of the political choices that have been made by America and that you want to do it a different way. One that's fairer to the environment, a more cooperative view of how the economy should be run" (*C,* 90).

4. See e.g., Barbara Hill Rigney, *Margaret Atwood* (Totowa, N.J.: Barnes and Noble, 1987); Jerome H. Rosenberg, *Margaret Atwood* (Boston: Twayne, 1984); Shannon Hengen, *Margaret Atwood's Power: Mirrors, Reflections and Images in Select Fiction and Poetry* (Toronto: Second Story, 1993); and Grace, *Violent Duality.*

5. Grace, *Violent Duality.*

6. Hengen, *Margaret Atwood's Power.*

7. Atwood remarks, "[I]f . . . I felt I were being boxed in by Canadian Nationalism, I'd probably take another tack. The writer, as you know, is always on the side of the underdog" (*C,* 90).

8. Atwood reinforces this impression of her orientation explicitly: "I'm very suspicious of anything beginning with a capital letter like Man. Or Woman. Or the Novel. I seem to think from the ground up, rather than from the top down" (*C,* 201).

9. Miner, "Atwood in Metamorphosis," 178–79.

10. The details of Atwood's biography have been gleaned from various interviews in

Conversations; some of her pieces in *Second Words;* the first chapter of Jerome H. Rosenberg, *Margaret Atwood;* and the portrait sketch of her by Miner, "Atwood in Metamorphosis."

11. It is interesting that all three authors had unconventional educations. Atwood did not attend school full time until the eighth grade, having been taught school subjects by her mother, and by her father and brother informally, the part of the year they went North, which is a double-edged benefit in that she had ample time to develop the inner freedom and adaptability to take in stride the special problems of social adjustment that her isolation had imposed upon her.

12. Miner, "Atwood in Metamorphosis," 190.

13. Atwood is living with Canadian novelist Graeme Gibson and their daughter Jess.

14. "Self-Reliance," in *Selections from Ralph Waldo Emerson,* ed. Stephen E. Whicher (Boston: Houghton Mifflin, 1960), 152.

15. Atwood claims to have felt more gender bias as a writer in the United States than in Canada, where solidarity among writers for their Canadianness meant more than gender difference.

16. For an extensively detailed analysis of Atwood's work in terms of folktales and fairy tales, see Sharon Rose Wilson, *Margaret Atwood's Fairy-Tale Sexual Politics* (Jackson: University of Mississippi Press, 1993).

17. Miner, "Atwood in Metamorphosis."

18. Atwood reviews herself as a reviewer in her article, "Margarets Atwood" in *Critical Essays on Margaret Atwood,* ed. Judith McCombs (Boston: G. K. Hall, 1988).

19. Miner, "Atwood in Metamorphosis," 173, 173–74, 187.

20. Ibid., 192. Miner mentions Atwood's single encounter with psychoanalysis when her marriage in her late twenties broke up. Atwood recollects how she spent the session on her practical problems, since she had no self-torment to speak of.

21. Atwood claims that tragedy is for idealists such as Americans disillusioned with the American Dream. Canadians do not expect the glory of freedom and the pursuit of happiness from their government—just peace and order, modest goals (*C,* 57).

22. Two such volumes are *Murder in the Dark* (1983) and *Good Bones* (1992).

23. These novels of Atwood in chronological order are: *The Edible Woman* (1969); *Surfacing* (1973); *Lady Oracle* (1976); *Bodily Harm* (1982); *Cat's Eye* (1989).

24. T. D. MacLulich, "Atwood's Adult Fairy Tale: Lévi-Strauss, Bettelheim, and *The Edible Woman,*" in McCombs, ed., *Critical Essays on Margaret Atwood.* MacLulich may not have known that Atwood considers her own totem animal to be the red fox (Miner, "Atwood in Metamorphosis").

25. MacLulich, "Atwood's Adult Fairy Tale," 287.

26. Atwood calls for a poetic reformulation of our language along the lines of certain American Indian languages, such as one that has no nouns at all, but rather gerundlike verbals suggesting actions going on in a field of perception. She gives the example of "not a flower sitting on a table," but "the table flowering as it were . . . behaving like a flower in that area of space" (*C,* 92). Or perhaps tabling and flowering together, not to prioritize one over the other. The self, then, might be conceivable as a continuous stream of happenings marbleizing with the currents of other selves, Woolfian fashion.

27. Indeed, one of Atwood's personas not mentioned by Miner is that of graphic artist—including cartoonist under a pseudonym (for a Canadian magazine), illustrator for some of her writings, and occasional cake decorator. She does artwork only for her own amusement (*C,* 75, 80).

28. Quoted in Hengen, *Margaret Atwood's Power,* 11.

29. Atwood cites certain Eskimo rites of passage of fasting in the wilderness that parallel the biblical Jacob's struggle with the angel, in which one gains adult selfhood by assimilating an adversarial spirit rather than being overcome by it (C, 98).

30. Quoted in Hengen, *Margaret Atwood's Power*, 16. Part of Hengen's thesis is that Atwood's work revises the meaning of power, but Hengen does not define that new meaning in terms of the interplay of the love-power duality, although that might be inferred from her term "creative narcissism." Hengen's terms, "creative narcissism" and "regressive narcissism" are similar to distinctions Judy Little makes between more or less acceptable forms of individualism, i.e., between cooperative individuals ("creative" for Hengen) and isolated, competitive types ("regressive" for Hengen). Little, *Experimental Self*, 21.

CHAPTER 6. *LADY ORACLE*

1. Francis Mansbridge, "Search for Self in the Novels of Margaret Atwood," *Journal of Canadian Fiction* 22 (1978): 115. Atwood is also working out of the classic tradition of the maze to represent a testing—and questing—experience, e.g., the maze Aeneas goes through seeking his father's spirit in the underworld, and of course, the Greek labyrinth of the Minotaur.

2. Sandra Djwa, "The Where of Here: Margaret Atwood and a Canadian Tradition," in *The Art of Margaret Atwood: Essays in Criticism*, ed. Arnold E. Davidson and Cathy N. Davidson (Toronto: Anansi, 1981). Djwa puts Atwood's definition of the self within a Canadian tradition of identity in terms of *place*.

3. A term used by Clara Thomas, *"Lady Oracle*: The Narrative of a Fool-Heroine," in *The Art of Margaret Atwood: Essays in Criticism*, ed. Arnold E. Davidson and Cathy N. Davidson (Toronto: Anansi, 1981).

4. Thomas, *"Lady Oracle,"* 160.

5. Susan Maclean, *"Lady Oracle:* The Art of Reality and the Reality of Art," *Journal of Canadian Literature* 28/29 (1980): 180. Maclean's description of Atwood's fiction-writing personality (as distinct from her poet's personality) comes close to Atwood's own: "a curious, bemused, disheartened observer of society" (C, 214).

6. Maclean, "Art of Reality," 182.

7. Molly Hite, "Other Side, Other Woman: *Lady Oracle*," in *The Other Side of the Story: Structures and Strategies of Contemporary Feminist Narratives* (Ithaca: Cornell University Press, 1989), 127–67.

8. Thomas, in "Fool Heroine," finds that her female students respond sympathetically to Joan, laughing *with* rather than *at* her. How her male students respond is unclear, perhaps because they are more inclined to find Joan a ridiculous "other" figure from the traditional privileged perspective of male chauvinism, and thus are not as receptive to the thesis of Joan's "essential kindness."

9. Hite, "Other Side," 155.

10. Hengen, *Margaret Atwood's Power*.

11. Ibid., 68–69.

12. Roberta Rubenstein agrees that in this scene Joan is capitulating to her mother's power, not reclaiming it. *Boundaries of the Self*.

13. Maclean, "Art of Reality," 188.

14. Robert Lecker, "Janus Through the Looking Glass: Atwood's First Three Novels," in Davidson and Davidson, eds., *Art of Margaret Atwood*, 178; Sherill Grace, "Margaret Atwood and the Poetics of Duplicity," also in Davidson and Davidson, eds., *Art of Margaret Atwood*, 56.

15. Bauer attests to the human *tragedy* of masks in analyzing works in which heroines do end up suicidally or otherwise tragically precisely because their communities cannot cope with these women's unmasking the multiplicity beneath the fixed masks of their cultural norms. *Feminist Dialogics.*

16. Hite, "Other Side"; Annis Pratt, "*Surfacing* and the Rebirth Journey," in Davidson and Davidson, eds., *Art of Margaret Atwood*, 139–57; Hengen, *Margaret Atwood's Power.*

17. Pratt, "*Surfacing* and Rebirth."

18. Lecker, "Janus," 178.

CONCLUSION

1. The Social Ecology Program of Goddard College in Vermont, for example, promotes the idea of interrelated environmental, economic, personal, political, and cultural sustainability, which is more holistic than the strictly environmental kind.

2. See for example, Schwab, who advocates interdisciplinary approaches, for an interesting discussion of the holistic "ecology of the subject" using systems theories of physics to underpin cultural and intrapsychic communication theories, of which poetics is a subset. She credits both Freud and Bakhtin among others for recognizing the mutually enhancing interplay between Eros/Order/Centripetal forces on one hand, and the countertendency of Thanatos/Entropy/Centrifugal forces on the other. Schwab holds that the dialogic space between "chaos" and "order" surpasses either one by changing each into the other, which creates a sustainable complementarity instead of a destructive polarity. *Subjects without Selves,* esp. chap. 9.

3. Bauer, *Feminist Dialogics,* 5.

4. Jeffrey T. Nealon, "The Ethics of Dialogue: Bakhtin and Levinas, " *College English* 59 (February 1997): 129–48. Nealon cites Emmanuel Levinas, *Otherwise than Being, or Beyond Essence,* trans. Alphonso Lingis (The Hague: Martinus Nijhoff, 1981).

5. Norman N. Holland, in *The Critical I* (New York: Columbia University Press, 1992), relies on schema theory to support his reader-response view, which seems to both support Nealon and contradict him. Clearly the reader is responding to a text according to schemata implanted by the world (i.e., others in the same linguistic community); yet Holland gives the reader priority in the process, promoting the "I" and demoting the text (the "other") to something assimilated by the unique makeup of the reader. His view focuses on the active (cannibalistic?) subjectivity of the reader rather than that of the author. Neither Holland nor Nealon recognizes the equal subjectivity of the "other" sufficiently.

6. Nealon, "Ethics of Dialogue," 145.

7. While the Taoist philosophy celebrates a feminized ego-emptiness, it is more like Atwood's blank page or Woolf's night self in its capacity for infinite responses. Indeed, its passivity is paradoxical, because an active principle resides in it as a state of "mindfulness" (the same as the Buddhist term), which is respectful of the integrity of others, including the object self as "other" to the mindful observer. Thus, Taoism entails responsibility and deference to others as well as to the object self, without occupying either pole totally. See Greg Johanson and Ron Kurtz, *Grace Unfolding: Psychotherapy in the Spirit of Tao-te Ching* (New York: Bell Tower, 1991).

8. Little, in *Experimental Self,* differs from the emphasis here by deliberately excluding the semiotic uses of dialogism in her focus on textually constructed literary selves. Of course,

literary texts have poetic (semiotic) elements, but her primary concern is with how her authors "feminize" thetic discourses in ways besides the poetical.

9. Those cults who reject the world as evil and prefer to abandon it by suicide for the promise of a better one threaten only themselves and other monologic thinkers who need "the truth" expounded by a guru or single higher authority. A much greater threat is posed by cults like the one in Japan that was bent on destroying everyone else in the world with sarin gas and saving themselves alone. Such cults illustrate the deadly mix between monologic thinking and technology that threatens the planet.

10. Bauer, *Feminist Dialogics*.

11. Pamela L. Caughie, in her article "Let It Pass: Changing the Subject Once Again," *PMLA* 112 (January 1997): 26–39, advocates "a performative concept of the I" (28) that firms up the slipperiness of postmodern subjectivity by endowing it with at least the *responsibility* of acknowledging the uncertainty of identity. That is, she advocates showing students how we are always "passing," i.e., becoming other, in our representations of ourselves and others, rather than "passing as" a stable subject or representing others as stable. Two other articles dealing with the same problem of how teacher-scholars represent themselves and the authors they teach appeared around the same time: Ruth Spack, "The (In)Visibility of the Personal in Academe," *College English* 59 (January 1997): 9–31 and Phyllis van Slyck, "Repositioning Ourselves in the Contact Zone," *College English* 59 (February 1997): 149–70. In addition, Gesa E. Kirsch wrestles with the problem of authorial responsibility in new multivoiced textual forms in "Opinion: Multi-Vocal Texts and Interpretive Responsibility," *College English* 59 (February 1997): 191–201. All are concerned with prying out hidden assumptions of neutrality in texts and interpreters of texts and negotiating problematics in open, responsible ways.

Works Cited

Althusser, Louis. "Ideology and State Apparatus." In *Lenin and Philosophy.* New York: Monthly Review Press, 1971.

Arendt, Hannah. *Between Past and Future: Six Exercises in Political Thought.* New York: Viking, 1961.

Atack, Margaret. "Towards a Narrative Analysis of *A Man and Two Women.*" In *Notebooks/ Memoirs/Archives: Reading and Rereading Doris Lessing,* edited by Jenny Taylor, 135–63. Boston: Routledge, 1982.

Atwood, Margaret. *Bodily Harm.* New York: Simon and Schuster, 1982.

———. *Cat's Eye.* New York: Bantam, 1989.

———. *Margaret Atwood: Conversations.* Edited by Earl G. Ingersoll. Princeton, N.J.: Ontario Review Press, 1990.

———. *The Edible Woman.* New York: Warner, 1969.

———. *Good Bones.* Toronto: Coach House, 1992.

———. *The Handmaid's Tale.* New York: Fawcett Crest, 1986.

———. *Lady Oracle.* New York: Simon and Schuster, 1976.

———. *Life Before Man.* New York: Simon and Schuster, 1979.

———. *Murder in the Dark: Short Fictions and Prose Poems.* Toronto: Coach House, 1983.

———. "Margarets Atwood: A Review of *Second Words.*" In *Critical Essays on Margaret Atwood,* edited by Judith McCombs, 251–53. Boston: G. K. Hall, 1988.

———. *The Robber Bride.* New York: Nan A. Talese/Doubleday, 1993.

———. *Second Words: Selected Critical Prose.* Toronto: Anansi, 1982.

———. *Surfacing.* New York: Simon and Schuster, 1973.

———. *Survival: A Thematic Guide to Canadian Literature.* Toronto: Anansi, 1972.

———. *Wilderness Tips.* New York: Doubleday, 1989.

Bakhtin, Mikhail. *The Dialogic Imagination: Four Essays.* Edited by Michael Holquist. Translated by Caryl Emerson and Michael Holquist. Slavic Series, no. 1. Austin: University of Texas Press, 1981.

———. *Problems of Dostoevsky's Poetics.* Edited and translated by Caryl Emerson. Theory and History of Literature, vol. 8. Minneapolis: University of Minnesota Press, 1984.

Bandler, Richard. *Using Your Brain—For a Change.* Moab, Utah: Real People Press, 1985.

Barnouw, Dagmar. "Disorderly Company: From *The Golden Notebook* to *The Four-Gated City.*" In *Doris Lessing: Critical Studies,* edited by Annis Pratt and L. S. Dembo, 74–97. Madison: University of Wisconsin Press, 1974.

Bauer, Dale M. *Feminist Dialogics: A Theory of Failed Community.* Albany: State University of New York Press, 1988.

Bauer, Dale M., and Susan Jaret McKinstry, eds. *Feminism, Bakhtin and the Dialogic.* Feminist Criticism and Theory Series. Albany: State University of New York Press, 1991.

Bazin, Nancy Topping. *Virginia Woolf and the Androgynous Vision.* New Brunswick, N.J.: Rutgers University Press, 1973.

Beauvoir, Simone de. *The Second Sex.* Translated and edited by H. M. Parshley. New York: Bantam, 1961.

Bell, Quentin. *Virginia Woolf: A Biography.* London: Hogarth, 1972.

Bertelsen, Eve. "Who is It Who Says 'I'?: The Persona of a Doris Lessing Interview." In *Doris Lessing: The Alchemy of Survival,* edited by Carey Kaplan and Ellen Cronan Rose, 169–82. Athens: Ohio University Press, 1988.

Blau DuPlessis, Rachel. *Writing Beyond the Ending: Narrative Strategies of Twentieth-Century Women Writers.* Bloomington: Indiana University Press, 1985.

Bradshaw, John. *Homecoming: Reclaiming and Championing Your Inner Child.* New York: Bantam, 1990.

Butler, Judith. *Gender Trouble: Feminism and the Subversion of Identity.* New York: Routledge, 1990.

Caramagno, Thomas. *The Flight of the Mind: Virginia Woolf's Art and Manic-Depressive Illness.* Berkeley: University of California Press, 1992.

Carse, James P. *Finite and Infinite Games.* New York: Macmillan, 1986.

Caughie, Pamela L. "Let It Pass: Changing the Subject Once Again." *PMLA* 112.1 (January 1997): 26–39.

Cederstrom, Lorelei. *Fine-Tuning the Feminine Psyche: Jungian Patterns in the Novels of Doris Lessing.* English Language and Literature, vol. 99. American University Studies, Series 4. New York: Peter Lang, 1990.

Chekhov, Anton. "The Darling." In *The Tales of Chekhov: The Darling and Other Stories,* translated by Constance Garnett, 3–22. New York: Macmillan, 1928.

Chodorow, Nancy. *The Reproduction of Mothering: Psychoanalysis and the Sociology of Gender.* Berkeley: University of California Press, 1978.

Davidson, Arnold E., and Cathy N. Davidson, eds. *The Art of Margaret Atwood: Essays in Criticism.* Toronto: Anansi, 1981.

Derrida, Jacques. *Dissemination.* Translated by Barbara Johnson. Chicago: University of Chicago Press, 1981.

Di Battista, Maria. *Virginia Woolf's Major Novels: The Fables of Anon.* New Haven: Yale University Press, 1980.

Didion, Joan. Review of *Briefing for a Descent into Hell,* by Doris Lessing. In *Critical Essays on Doris Lessing,* edited by Claire Sprague and Virginia Tiger, 192–96. Boston: G. K. Hall, 1986.

Dietz, Bernd, and Fernando Galvan. "Entrevista: A Conversation with Doris Lessing." *Doris Lessing Newsletter* 9.1 (spring 1985): 5–6, 13.

Djwa, Sandra. "The Where of Here: Margaret Atwood and a Canadian Tradition." In *The

Art of Margaret Atwood: Essays in Criticism, edited by Arnold E. Davidson and Cathy N. Davidson, 15–34. Toronto: Anansi, 1981.

Emerson, Ralph Waldo. *Selections from Ralph Waldo Emerson.* Edited by Stephen E. Whicher. Boston: Houghton Mifflin, 1960.

Felski, Rita. *Beyond Feminist Aesthetics.* Cambridge: Harvard University Press, 1989.

Ferguson, Kathy E. " Genealogy and Gender." A seminar at the International Summer Institute for Semiotic and Structural Studies. University of Hawaii, June 1991.

Fishburn, Katherine. "Teaching Doris Lessing as a Subversive Activity: A Response to the Preface to *The Golden Notebook.*" In *Doris Lessing: The Alchemy of Survival,* edited by Carey Kaplan and Ellen Cronan Rose, 81–92. Athens: Ohio University Press, 1988.

Foucault, Michel. *The History of Sexuality.* Translated by Robert Hurley. 3 vols. New York: Pantheon, 1978.

———. *Technologies of the Self: A Seminar with Michel Foucault.* Edited by Luther H. Hartin et al. Amherst: University of Massachusetts Press, 1988.

Freud, Sigmund. *The Basic Writings of Sigmund Freud.* Translated by A. A. Brill. New York: Modern Library, 1938.

Furst, Lillian R. *Fictions of Romantic Irony.* Cambridge: Harvard University Press, 1984.

Fuss, Diana. *Essentially Speaking: Feminism, Nature and Difference.* New York: Routledge, 1989.

Gergen, Kenneth. *The Saturated Self: Dilemmas of Identity in Contemporary Life.* New York: Basic Books, 1991.

Gilligan, Carol. "In a Different Voice: Women's Conceptions of Self and Morality." In *The Future of Difference,* edited by Hester Eisenstein and Alice Jardine, 274–317. Barnard College Women's Center. Boston: G. K. Hall, 1980.

Goodman, Ellen. "The Doris Lessing Hoax." *Doris Lessing Newsletter* 9.1 (spring 1985): 3. Originally published in the *Washington Post* , 27 September 1984.

Gouwens, David J. *Kierkegaard as Religious Thinker.* New York: Cambridge University Press, 1996.

———. *Kierkegaard's Dialectic of the Imagination.* Vol. 71 of Philosophy. American University Studies Series, no. 5. New York: Peter Lang, 1989.

Grace, Sherill E. "Margaret Atwood and the Poetics of Duplicity." In *The Art of Margaret Atwood: Essays in Criticism,* edited by Arnold E. Davidson and Cathy N. Davidson, 55–68. Toronto: Anansi, 1981.

———. *Violent Duality: A Study of Margaret Atwood.* Montreal: Vehicule Press, 1980.

Greene, Gayle. *Doris Lessing: The Poetics of Change.* Ann Arbor: University of Michigan Press, 1994.

Hardin, Nancy Shields. "Doris Lessing and the Sufi Way." In *Doris Lessing: Critical Studies,* edited by Annis Pratt and L. S. Dembo, 148–64. Madison: University of Wisconsin Press, 1974.

———. "The Sufi Teaching Story and Doris Lessing." *Twentieth Century Literature* 23 (October 1977): 314–25.

Hayles, N. Katherine, ed. *Chaos and Order: Complex Dynamics in Literature and Science.* Chicago: University of Chicago Press, 1991.

Heilbrun, Carolyn. *Toward a Recognition of Androgyny.* New York: Knopf, 1973.

Henderson, Mae Gwendolyn. "Speaking in Tongues: Dialogics, Dialectics, and the Black

Woman Writers' Literary Tradition." In *Feminists Theorize the Political*, edited by Judith Butler and Joan W. Scott. New York: Routledge, 1992.

Hengen, Shannon. *Margaret Atwood's Power: Mirrors, Reflections and Images in Select Fiction and Poetry.* Toronto: Second Story, 1993.

Herndl, Diane Price. "The Dilemmas of a Feminine Dialogic." In *Feminism, Bakhtin and the Dialogic*, edited by Dale M. Bauer and Susan Jaret McKinstry, 7–24. Feminist Criticism and Theory Series. Albany: State University of New York Press, 1991.

Herrmann, Anne. *The Dialogic and Difference: "An/Other Woman" in Virginia Woolf and Christa Wolf.* New York: Columbia University Press, 1989.

Hite, Molly. "Other Side, Other Woman: *Lady Oracle*." In *The Other Side of the Story: Structures and Strategies of Contemporary Feminist Narratives*, 127–67. Ithaca: Cornell University Press, 1989.

———. "Subverting the Ideology of Coherence: *The Golden Notebook* and *The Four-Gated City.*" In *Doris Lessing: The Alchemy of Survival*, edited by Carey Kaplan and Ellen Cronan Rose, 61–69. Athens: Ohio University Press, 1988.

Holland, Norman N. *The Critical I.* New York: Columbia University Press, 1992.

Hollway, Wendy. *Subjectivity and Method in Psychology: Gender, Meaning and Science.* London: Sage, 1989.

Holmquist, Ingrid. *From Society to Nature: A Study of Doris Lessing's "Children of Violence."* Gothenburg Studies in English, no. 47. Göteborg, Sweden: Acta Universitatus Gothoburgensis, 1980.

Howe, Florence. "A Conversation with Doris Lessing (1966)." In *Doris Lessing: Critical Studies*, edited by Annis Pratt and L. S. Dembo, 1–19. Madison: University of Wisconsin Press, 1974.

Jacques, Francis. *Difference and Subjectivity: Dialogue and Personal Identity.* Translated by Andrew Rothwell. New Haven: Yale University Press, 1991.

Johanson, Greg, and Ron Kurtz. *Grace Unfolding: Psychotherapy in the Spirit of Tao-te Ching.* New York: Bell Tower, 1991.

Jouve, Nicole Ward. "Doris Lessing: A 'Female Voice'—Past, Present or Future?" In *Doris Lessing: The Alchemy of Survival*, edited by Carey Kaplan and Ellen Cronan Rose, 127–33. Athens: Ohio University Press, 1988.

———. "Of Mud and Other Matter—*The Children of Violence.*" In *Notebooks/Memoirs/Archives: Reading and Rereading Doris Lessing*, edited by Jenny Taylor, 75–134. Boston: Routledge, 1982.

Joyner, Nancy. "The Underside of the Butterfly: Lessing's Debt to Woolf." *Journal of Narrative Technique* 5 (1974): 204–5.

Jung, Carl G. *The Portable Jung.* Edited by Joseph Campbell. New York: Viking, 1971.

Kaplan, Carey. Review of *The Diaries of Jane Somers, Diary of a Good Neighbor* and *If the Old Could . . .*, by Jane Somers [Doris Lessing]. *Doris Lessing Newsletter* 9.1 (spring 1985): 4.

Kaplan, Carey, and Ellen Cronan Rose, eds. *Doris Lessing: The Alchemy of Survival.* Athens: Ohio University Press, 1988.

Kasulis, Thomas P. *Zen Action/Zen Person.* Honolulu: University Press of Hawaii, 1981.

Keats, John. "To George and Thomas Keats." In *Critical Theory Since Plato*, edited by Hazard Adams, 474. San Diego: Harcourt Brace Jovanovich, 1971.

Kirsch, Gesa E. "Opinion: Multi-Vocal Texts and Interpretive Responsibility." *College English* 59.2 (February 1997): 191–201.

Knapp, Mona. *Doris Lessing*. New York: Ungar, 1984.

Kristeva, Julia. *The Kristeva Reader*. Edited by Toril Moi. New York: Columbia University Press, 1987.

Lacan, Jacques. *Ecrits: A Selection*. Translated by A. Sheridan. New York: Norton, 1977.

Laing, R. D. *The Politics of Experience* and *The Bird of Paradise*. Harmondsworth, U.K.: Penguin, 1967.

Lakoff, Robin Tolmach. *Language and Woman's Place*. New York: Harper, 1975.

Lasch, Christopher. *The Culture of Narcissism*. New York: Warner, 1979.

Lecker, Robert. "Janus Through the Looking Glass: Atwood's First Three Novels." In *The Art of Margaret Atwood: Essays in Criticism*, edited by Arnold E. Davidson and Cathy N. Davidson, 177–203. Toronto: Anansi, 1981.

Lessing, Doris. *Briefing for a Descent into Hell*. New York: Knopf, 1971.

———. *The Fifth Child*. New York: Knopf, 1988.

———. *The Four-Gated City*. Vol. 5 of *Children of Violence*. New York: Bantam, 1970.

———. *Going Home*. New York: Popular Library, 1957.

———. *The Golden Notebook*. New York: Bantam, 1962.

———. *The Grass is Singing*. 1950. Reprint, New York: Plume, 1978.

———. *In Pursuit of the English*. New York: Simon and Schuster, 1961.

———. *Landlocked*. Vol. 4 of *Children of Violence*. New York: Plume, 1958.

———. "Learning How to Learn." *Asia* (July/August 1982): 12–15.

———. *Martha Quest*. Vol. 1 of *Children of Violence*. New York: Plume, 1952.

———. *The Memoirs of a Survivor*. 1975. Reprint, New York: Bantam, 1976.

———. *Prisons We Chose to Live Inside*. London: Cape, 1987.

———. *A Proper Marriage*. Vol. 2 of *Children of Violence*. New York: Plume, 1952.

———. *The Ripple Before the Storm*. Vol. 3 of *Children of Violence*. New York: Plume, 1958.

———. *A Small Personal Voice: Essays, Reviews, Interviews*. Edited by Paul Schlueter. New York: Knopf, 1974.

———. "The Story of Two Dogs." In *The Sun Between Their Feet*. Vol. 2 of *Doris Lessing's Collected African Stories*, 158–79. London: Michael Joseph, 1954.

———. *This Was the Old Chief's Country*. Vol. 1 of *Doris Lessing's Collected African Stories*. London: Michael Joseph, 1951.

———. *Under My Skin*. Vol. 1, *My Autobiography to 1949*. New York: Harper Collins, 1994.

Little, Judy. *The Experimental Self: Dialogic Subjectivity in Woolf, Pym and Brooke-Rose*. Carbondale: Southern Illinois University Press, 1996.

Love, Jean O. *Worlds in Consciousness: Mythopoetic Thought in the Novels of Virginia Woolf*. Berkeley: University of California Press, 1970.

MacIntyre, Alasdair. *After Virtue*. 2d ed. Notre Dame, Ind.: University of Notre Dame Press, 1984.

Maclean, Susan. "*Lady Oracle:* The Art of Reality and the Reality of Art." *Journal of Canadian Literature* 28/29 (1980): 179–97.

MacLulich, T. D. "Atwood's Adult Fairy Tale: Lévi-Strauss, Bettelheim, and *The Edible*

Woman." In *Critical Essays on Margaret Atwood,* edited by Judith McCombs, 179–97. Boston: G. K. Hall, 1988.

Mansbridge, Francis. "Search for Self in the Novels of Margaret Atwood." *Journal of Canadian Fiction* 22 (1978): 106–17.

Marder, Herbert. *Feminism and Art: A Study of Virginia Woolf.* Chicago: University of Chicago Press, 1968.

McCombs, Judith, ed. *Critical Essays on Margaret Atwood.* Boston: G. K. Hall, 1988.

Mellor, Anne K. *English Romantic Irony.* Cambridge: Harvard University Press, 1980.

Middleton, Victoria. "Doris Lessing's 'Debt' to Olive Schreiner." In *Doris Lessing: The Alchemy of Survival,* edited by Carey Kaplan and Ellen Cronan Rose, 135–47. Athens: Ohio University Press, 1988.

Miller, Alice. *The Drama of the Gifted Child: The Search for the True Self.* New York: Basic Books, 1994.

Mindell, Arnold. *Working with the Dreaming Body.* Boston: Routledge & Kegan Paul, 1985.

Miner, Valerie. "Atwood in Metamorphosis: An Authentic Canadian Fairy Tale." In *Her Own Woman: Profiles of Ten Canadian Women,* edited by Myrna Kostash et al., 173–94. Toronto: Macmillan, 1975.

Minow-Pinkney, Makiko. *Virginia Woolf and the Problem of the Subject.* Brighton, U.K.: Harvester Press, 1987.

Moi, Toril. *Sexual/Textual Politics: Feminist Literary Theory.* New York: Methuen, 1985.

Moore, Thomas. *Care of the Soul.* New York: Harper, 1992.

Naremore, James. *The World Without a Self.* New Haven: Yale University Press, 1973.

Nealon, Jeffrey T. "The Ethics of Dialogue: Bakhtin and Levinas." *College English* 59.2 (February 1997): 129–48.

Nietzsche, Friedrich. *Basic Writings of Nietzsche.* Translated and edited by Walter Kaufmann. New York: Modern Library, 1968.

Pfuetze, Paul E. *The Social Self.* New York: Bookman, 1954.

Phillips, Kathy J. *Virginia Woolf Against Empire.* Knoxville: University of Tennessee Press, 1994.

Pickering, Jean. "Martha Quest and 'The Anguish of Feminine Fragmentation.'" In *Critical Essays on Doris Lessing,* edited by Claire Sprague and Virginia Tiger, 94–100. Boston: G. K. Hall, 1986.

———. *Understanding Doris Lessing.* Columbia: University of South Carolina Press, 1990.

Poole, Roger. *The Unknown Virginia Woolf.* Cambridge: Cambridge University Press, 1978.

Porritt, Ruth. "Surpassing Derrida's Deconstructed Self: Virginia Woolf's Poetic Disarticulation of the Self." *Women's Studies* 2.3 (1992): 323–38.

Pratt, Annis. "*Surfacing* and the Rebirth Journey." In *The Art of Margaret Atwood: Essays in Criticism,* edited by Arnold E. Davidson and Cathy N. Davidson, 139–57. Toronto: Anansi, 1981.

Pratt, Annis, and L. S. Dembo, eds. *Doris Lessing: Critical Studies.* Madison: University of Wisconsin Press, 1974.

Raskin, Jonah. "Doris Lessing at Stony Brook: An Interview." *New American Review* 8 (1970): 170.

Restuccia, Frances. "'Untying the Mother Tongue': Female Difference in Virginia Woolf's *A Room of One's Own.*" *Tulsa Studies in Women's Literature* 4.2 (fall 1985): 253–364.

Rigney, Barbara Hill. *Margaret Atwood.* Totowa, N.J.: Barnes and Noble, 1987.

Robinson, Sally. *Engendering the Subject: Gender and Self-Representation.* Feminist Criticism and Theory Series. Albany: State University of New York Press, 1991.

Rorty, Amélie O. "A Literary Postscript: Characters, Persons, Selves, Individuals." In *The Identities of Persons,* edited by Amélie Oksenberg Rorty. Berkeley: University of California Press, 1976.

Rosenberg, Jerome H. *Margaret Atwood.* Boston: Twayne, 1984.

Rubenstein, Roberta. *Boundaries of the Self: Gender, Culture, Fiction.* Urbana: University of Illinois Press, 1987.

———. *The Novelistic Vision of Doris Lessing: Breaking the Forms of Consciousness.* Urbana: University of Illinois Press, 1979.

Sage, Lorna. *Doris Lessing.* London: Methuen, 1983.

Schlee, Eileen. "The Subject is Dead, Long Live the Female Subject!" *Feminist Issues* 13, no. 2 (fall 1993): 70–79.

Schwab, Gabriele. *Subjects without Selves: Transitional Texts in Modern Fiction.* Cambridge: Harvard University Press, 1994.

Scott, Ann. "The More Recent Writings: Sufism, Mysticism and Politics." In *Notebooks/Memoirs/Archives: Reading and Rereading Doris Lessing,* edited by Jenny Taylor, 164–90. Boston: Routledge, 1982.

Seligman, Claudia Dee. "The Autobiographical Novels of Doris Lessing." Ph.D. dissertation, Tufts University, 1976. Abstract in *Dissertation Abstracts International* 37 (1976): 1544A.

Shapiro, Francine. *Eye Movement Desensitization and Reprocessing: Basic Principles, Protocols, and Procedures.* New York: Guilford Press, 1995.

Showalter, Elaine. *A Literature of Their Own: British Women Novelists from Brontë to Lessing.* Princeton: Princeton University Press, 1977.

Singleton, Mary Ann. *The City and the Veld: The Fiction of Doris Lessing.* Lewisburg, Pa.: Bucknell University Press, 1977.

Smith, Barbara Herrnstein. *Contingencies of Value: Alternative Perspectives for Critical Theory.* Cambridge: Harvard University Press, 1988.

Smith, Paul. *Discerning the Subject.* Theory and History of Literature, vol. 55. Minneapolis: University of Minnesota Press, 1988.

Spack, Ruth. "The (In)Visibility of the Person(al) in Academe." *College English* 59.1 (January 1997): 9–31.

Spiegel, Rotraut. *Doris Lessing: The Problem of Alienation and the Form of the Novel.* Frankfort: Peter Lang, 1980.

Spivak, Gayatari Chakravorty. *The Post-Colonial Critic: Interviews, Strategies, Dialogues.* Edited by Sarah Harasym. New York: Routledge, 1990.

Sprague, Claire. *Rereading Doris Lessing. Narrative Patterns of Doubling and Repetition.* Chapel Hill: University of North Carolina Press, 1987.

Sprague, Claire, and Virginia Tiger, eds. *Critical Essays on Doris Lessing.* Boston: G. K. Hall, 1986.

Stern, Frederick C. "Doris Lessing: The Politics of Radical Humanism." In *Doris Lessing: The Alchemy of Survival,* edited by Carey Kaplan and Ellen Cronan Rose, 43–60. Athens: Ohio University Press, 1988.

Sukenick, Lynn. "Feeling and Reason in Doris Lessing's Fiction." *Contemporary Literature* 14 (1973): 515–35.

Tannen, Deborah. *You Just Don't Understand: Women and Men in Conversation.* New York: Morrow, 1990.

Taylor, Charles. *Sources of the Self: The Making of the Modern Identity.* Cambridge: Harvard University Press, 1989.

Taylor, Jenny, ed. *Notebooks/Memoirs/Archives: Reading and Rereading Doris Lessing.* Boston: Routledge, 1982.

Thomas, Clara. "*Lady Oracle:* The Narrative of a Fool-Heroine." In *The Art of Margaret Atwood: Essays in Criticism,* edited by Arnold E. Davidson and Cathy N. Davidson, 159–75. Toronto: Anansi, 1981.

Tolstoy, Leo. "Tolstoy's Criticism on 'The Darling'" In *The Tales of Chekhov: The Darling and Other Stories,* by Anton Chekhov, translated by Constance Garnett, 23–28. New York: Macmillan, 1928.

Tu, Wei-Ming. *Confucian Thought: Selfhood and Creative Transformation.* Albany: State University of New York Press, 1985.

Van Slyck, Phyllis. "Repositioning Ourselves in the Contact Zone." *College English* 59.2 (February 1997): 149–70.

Walker, Jeanne Murray. "Memory and Culture within the Individual: The Breakdown of Social Exchange in *Memoirs of a Survivor.*" In *Doris Lessing: The Alchemy of Survival,* edited by Carey Kaplan and Ellen Cronan Rose, 93–114. Athens: Ohio University Press, 1988.

Whitaker, Ruth. *Doris Lessing.* Modern Novelists Series. New York: St. Martin's, 1988.

Wilson, Sharon Rose. *Margaret Atwood's Fairy-Tale Sexual Politics.* Jackson: University of Mississippi Press, 1993.

Woolf, Virginia. *Between the Acts.* New York: Harcourt Brace & Co., 1941.

———. *Collected Essays.* 2 Vols. London: Hogarth, 1966.

———. *The Essays of Virginia Woolf.* Vol. 3, *1919–1924.* Edited by Andrew McNeillie. London: Hogarth, 1988.

———. *Granite and Rainbow.* London: Hogarth, 1958.

———. "*Jacob's Room*" and "*The Waves.*" 1923, 1931. Reprint, New York: Harcourt, Brace & World, 1959.

———. "The Mark on the Wall." In *The Complete Shorter Fiction of Virginia Woolf,* edited by Susan Dick, 77–83. New York: Harcourt Brace Jovanovich, 1985.

———. *The Moment and Other Essays.* New York: Harcourt, Brace & Co., 1948.

———. *Moments of Being: Unpublished Autobiographical Writings.* Edited by Jeanne Schulkind. London: Chatto and Windus for Sussex University Press, 1976.

———. *Mrs. Dalloway.* 1925. Reprint, New York: Harcourt Brace Jovanovich, 1953.

———. *Night and Day.* 1920. Reprint, New York: Harcourt Brace Jovanovich, 1973.

———. *A Room of One's Own.* 1929. Reprint, New York: Harcourt Brace Jovanovich, 1957.

———. *To the Lighthouse.* 1927. Reprint, New York: Harcourt Brace Jovanovich, 1955.

———. *The Voyage Out.* 1915. Reprint, New York: Penguin, 1992.

———. *A Writer's Diary: Being Extracts from the Diary of Virginia Woolf.* Edited by Leonard Woolf. London: Hogarth, 1953.

———. *The Years.* New York: Harcourt, Brace & Co., 1937.

Index

agency, human, 24, 30, 34, 201–2. *See also* authority; power

alienation: in Atwood's work, 160, 177, 185, 191; in Lessing's work, 108–9, 110–11; in *The Waves*, 64, 76, 87

Althusser, Louis, 30, 63

androgyny. *See under* Woolf

archetypes. *See* Jung, Carl G.

Arendt, Hannah, 147

Atack, Margaret, 217n. 8, 218n. 24

Atwood, Margaret: biography, 156–63, 165, 166, 169, 170–71, 219–20n. 10, 220nn. 11, 13, 15, 20, 24, and 27; concept of self, 37, 153–176, 200–203 passim, 220n. 26, 221nn. 29, 2, and 5; writing method, 156–57, 159, 161–67, 168, 170, 172–73, 174, 175, 180, 181, 196, 221n. 1. Works: *Bodily Harm*, 168; *Cat's Eye*, 168, 170–71, 172, 173, 175, 176, 179; *The Edible Woman*, 168–69; *The Handmaid's Tale*, 157; *Lady Oracle*, 149, 168, 176, 177–98 passim, 200; *Life Before Man*, 162, 165, 171; "The Page," 165–68; *The Robber Bride*, 171–76, 200, 201; *Surfacing*, 168, 169–70, 172, 193, 194; *Survival, A Thematic Guide to Canadian Literature*, 154–55, 160, 161, 204

authority: 20, 21, 69, 117–18, 121, 189, 200; as controlling author, 102–9, 162, 200–202; resistance to, 15–18, 23, 30, 49, 156, 188, 200, 203. *See also* agency; patriarchy; politics; power; superiority

Bakhtin, Mikhail: dialogic theory of, 18, 24, 26, 29, 33, 50, 53, 222n. 2; critique of dialogic theory of, 199–203. *See also* dialogic theory

Barnouw, Dagmar, 119, 217n. 9, 218n. 27

Bauer, Dale M., 200, 204, 207n. 21, 210 n. 11, 222n. 15

Bazin, Nancy Topping, 210n. 6, 211n. 18, 213n. 17

Beauvoir, Simone de, 18

Bell, Quentin, 44, 210n. 8, 212n. 8

Bertelsen, Eve, 106–7, 162

Between the Acts (Woolf), 56, 59

binary oppositions, 23, 31, 34, 37, 43, 47, 87. *See also* polarization

Bloomsbury, 61, 133, 212n. 9

Bodily Harm (Atwood), 168

body: attitudes toward, 56, 88, 97, 98, 158, 179; genetic code of, 36–37; versus mind, 37, 46, 113–14, 121–22, 128. *See also* sexuality; semiotic(s)

Briefing for a Descent into Hell (Lessing), 216 n. 22

brother(s), relation to: Atwood's, 158; Lessing's, 108, 158; Woolf's, 46, 67, 68–69, 70, 212nn. 9 and 13, 213n. 15

Butler, Judith, 36, 43, 44, 210n. 4, 214 nn. 22 and 24

capitalism, 16, 18, 30, 121, 155, 156. *See also* Communism

Caramagno, Thomas, 44, 47, 57, 77–78, 210n. 8, 212n. 6

232

p159
self expression